THE BUTTES

A NOVEL

JANE BUCHAN

ALSO BY JANE BUCHAN

Once Upon a Body
The Kinder Sadist
Transformation in Canada's Deep South
Under the Moon

THE BUTTES

A NOVEL

JANE BUCHAN

Dance Slow Farm
Essex County, Ontario, Canada

Copyright © 2024 by Jane Buchan

Author's Note

No part of this publication may be reproduced, stored in a retrieval system, or transmitted in any form or by any means, electronic, mechanical, photocopying, recording, scanning, or otherwise, without the written permission of the author.

This is a work of fiction. Any similarity to persons alive or dead or to corporate entities extant or defunct is purely coincidental.

ISBN 978-1-896760-01-8

Cover Photo by Theresa Bergeron, Founder, Thermohair Inc.

Lines from "Ulysses" from *Poems of Tennyson* by Alfred Tennyson, 1917, Oxford Edition.

Cover Design and Interior Typesetting by
FOGLIO | CUSTOM BOOK SPECIALISTS
Body set in *Bembo Std Regular* 12 pt
Titles set in *Fenwick Light* 32 pt

FOGLIOPRINT.COM

For my sister Anne and our Mermaid Days

Butte /ˈbjuːt/ U.S. [a. F. *butte* a hillock or rising ground]

In Western U.S.: An isolated hill or peak rising abruptly.

THE BUTTES

FRIDAY

1

Lila Butte ran in a trance. The scents of roadside scrub and the rhythms her feet created with the sandy gravel, both her usual early morning companions, in this moment were lost to her. Even the low, menacing growl of a slowing pickup truck meant nothing until her hypervigilance signaled its proximity. A jolt of fear released her from the dawn's grey-blue, opening eye. In that moment of startled awareness, she brought up her right arm so swiftly the driver couldn't swerve to avoid the length of chain she whipped against the truck's flawless cobalt-blue paint.

The driver, a man possession-proud and more than a little in love with Lila, knew the paint job could be repaired. But factory paint was factory paint. There would be no proper restoration. Thwarted in what he considered innocent plans for conversation, Hal Demos slammed his truck into reverse and made a dust scattering U-turn before Lila could complete a second swing.

When the unfamiliar truck's tail lights were no more than distant red smudges, Lila's heart resumed its steady rhythms. She returned to the day's opening eye, waited for the first blinding glimpse of sun. When it came, she closed her eyes, smiled at its bloody afterimage. With her eyes still closed, she rewound the cargo chain at her waist, then looped its tail end around her shoulders. The chain in place, she opened her eyes to the growing light greening the nearby fields. Stepping from foot to foot to test the chain's balance, she made several small adjustments before beginning a leisurely jog home.

2

"If this garden were a woman…" Georgia Butte said. She smiled when the goat at her side bumped her hip. "I know, Willy." She bent to kiss his snout. "It's hard to believe the calendar insists it's still Spring." She frowned remembering a fragment of recent conversation. "I was feeling as fecund as this garden until the phone range this morning." The goat nipped her hand, jealous of her preoccupations.

Earlier that morning, before Hal Demos's call, Georgia and Willy followed Ulysses Butte to the woods behind the barn. No one at the Butte farm allowed animals to remain on the road after they'd been killed. These days, with Georgia constantly planting or picking or weeding, it was Uly who moved their broken bodies from the asphalt to the rutted shoulder for the crows and turkey vultures, intending his offerings to the local cleanup crews as lunch or appeasement, depending upon the day's requirements. When the dead appeared as deceptively whole as this morning's rabbit, it was his habit to deliver the body to the woods, to warn of the insatiable appetite of cars.

During that early morning walk, Georgia studied the slope of Uly's shoulders and his easy gait as she might a stranger's. I have shared a life with you, she thought. I know every inch of your body, the wounds of your heart, the deep hungers of your soul. How do you remain such a mystery to me? She blushed when he turned to look at her, as if he, like Willy, could read her mind.

As she stood remembering in the warming light, Willy took the hem of Georgia's dress between his teeth and shook it. She rubbed his long, silky ears. "You have to share me, Willy. I don't belong to you alone. I should think you'd have learned that by now. You are a very old goat. I expect you to be wise." Willy shivered his pleasure as they walked, her hand a love-note on his neck.

After only a few steps Georgia stopped again. An exhalation of breath and the feel of velvet flesh beneath her free hand made her call out. "Lady Jane?" Both her hands fluttered to her heart.

In the distance, standing behind a tangle of lilac branches, the long-dead horse's afterlife dipped and raised her fine white head. "Come here, Beauty. Where have you been? I've missed you." The apparition vanished.

Georgia's eyes filled. "Every time, *every* time," she said, struck by the wonder of what she saw and heard – the Lady Janes of some parallel universe breaking into the material world considered reality by almost everyone she knew. For a moment, she wallowed in self-pity, indulging the grudge she held against her birth family for belittling her otherworldly gifts.

"A scandal," she said with fake fury, as if her mother stood before her now, fists on hips, insisting on the virtues of normalcy. Willy pushed closer. "Mother still thinks I'm a scandal." She shared a smirk with the goat. "And you, well," she said bending to kiss first one of Willy's ears and then the other, "you'd have been dinner a long, long time ago, if Father had had his way." Willy farted a loud protest.

In the throes of deep contentment, Georgia forgave his pungent odor, turning to bless her spiral beds with an approving gaze. "Just look how everything is coming early, Willy. The broccoli and cauliflower are coming on, and the few rows of corn we planted in mid-May already brush my shins."

She drank in this fertility as she would a tonic, her defense against ominous forces she sensed now and again darkening her otherwise sunny days. She'd long ago grown used to what others called ghosts or apparitions, but these days, darker, more confusing fragments of things to come exploded like mortar fire around her, leaving her heart racing and her muscles tensed for battle. Hearing footsteps on the shoulder beyond the front hedge row and exasperated by Georgia's preoccupations, Willy lowered his head and inclined toward the road.

"No!" Georgia attempted to catch Willy before he blustered through the greenery but the nimble goat escaped. "Alice Maude? Mae!" she cried. "Watch out. Willy is on his way." When no one answered, Georgia whispered a prayer to the resident protectors of the farm. "Whoever you are, I hope you have a good big stick," she called. "Willy, you must keep your snout out of people's crotches."

The unmistakable thwack of heavy-duty chain hitting the ground prompted Georgia to rush after Willy. "Lila!" she called, aware of this daughter's penchant for landing blows hard enough to dent metal. "Remember. You are too old to be fighting. There is a wedding in a week's time. I want neither you nor Willy bruised." She crossed the foot bridge leading to the county road that linked the Butte farm to the outer world, on her way passing through a gate more suggestive of Middle Earth than a contemporary farm in Essex County, Ontario, Canada. Beyond the cedar hedge, Lila and Willy maneuvered for battle positions, Lila swinging the end of her cargo chain, Willy, head down, dancing forward and backward.

"How about a truce in honour of Lola's wedding?" Georgia said, despising the wheedle in her voice. She smiled at Lila. "I thought I heard you with the chain saw out back. When did you leave for your run? It must have been well before dawn."

Lila flung the end of the chain over her shoulder as she would a silk scarf. "Nice try, Ma," she said, her eyes fixed on Willy. "You're always protecting him with your little segues into ordinary life, but he's a menace. And he stinks." Willy pranced a circle around

Lila, making her cry out, indignant as a child. "See? He's trying to intimidate me. I don't know why you can't see it."

"I see it all right. But you have to see something, too. You're the grownup. He's the goat."

"Goat, my ass." Lila smacked her chain on the ground so suddenly both Willy and Georgia leapt back in alarm. Willy trumpeted staccato snorts, pawed the gritty shoulder, then darted in to nip at Lila's bare knees. Lila kicked at him, narrowly missing his chest.

A clicking sound interrupted this skirmish. Willy raised his head, took aim at Lila with a contemptuous snort, then trotted toward the Vaughan farm across the road. From a safe distance, he turned to fix his enemy with a stare that promised future mischief. Lila cursed him with both her middle fingers then added an Amazonian Warrior's whoop promising more battles in which she would prove victorious.

Exasperated, Georgia squinted up the road. "Is someone walking on the shoulder? I hope its Mae. Unlike certain members of this family who torment him, Mae is kind to Willy."

Lila erupted. "He likes Mae because of the candy she's always feeding him. If you're wondering why he gets the trots, she's got the answer in her sticky pockets."

Her good humour restored by the myriad shades of green adorning their county road Georgia slid her arm around her daughter's waist. "What's up, Beauty? You're in a fine mood."

Quietly, with a strange mix of defiance and contrition, Lila said, "I smacked another truck this morning. I think it might have been Hal's new one."

Georgia fingered the chain before raising her hand to her daughter's head. As soon as she touched Lila's dark bristle, blurred images of delicate hospital procedures and police questions flooded her senses. Georgia looked away, squeezing her eyes shut to stop the familiar rush of horrors. Her efforts on this bright, benign morning came to nothing. The past knocked her off centre with images of eleven-year-old Lila's brutal rape by four drunk college boys, the nearby wood where Uly found her barely breathing, the compulsive sawing off of her long dark hair weeks later, the clippers her eldest sister sent to make what became a weekly ritual easier, these sights and sounds engulfing Georgia in grief and impotence.

Lila turned on her mother. "I know what you're thinking. I am not wearing that ridiculous yellow hat Lola's chosen. Or that lame yellow dress." Relieved Lila did not sense Georgia's present experience of her daughter's past traumas, her mother pushed through the gate. "I'm not kidding, Ma. I'm not wearing that crap. If Lola wants me to be her Maid of Honour at her crazy wedding, she'll have to take me like this."

"You know Lola wants you," Georgia snapped. "And you can wear what you like. Haven't you always?" She cringed at her own cruelty. She of all people knew Lila did not wear what she liked, had not for a very long time. She stopped, muttered, "You bring out the very worst in me when you're so obstinate, Lila." As they resumed their walk Georgia did her best to make amends. "You know it doesn't matter what you wear, Beauty. Lola wants you to be part of her wedding. She's like the rest of the brides of the world, wondering if she's doing the right thing. The details are window dressing – these getups and flowers – they're all just distractions for couples, so they don't think too much about the momentous decision they've made to spend a lifetime with someone they can't hope to know except through years of personal experience."

"You think Lola's unsure about the wedding? That would be a first."

Georgia left the sermon on her youngest daughter's humanity undelivered. Glancing toward the lilacs, she searched for another glimpse of Lady Jane but found only heat dancing in the fields beyond the wild bramble of heart-shaped leaves. "How could she not have doubts?" Georgia mused. "Marriage is such a huge step. And Lola's lived alone for years. She likes things her way."

"That's an understatement."

Georgia did her best to cast her youngest daughter's need for control in a kinder light. "Lola's developed routines. Inviting another person to share her space must feel like moving from high ground onto a flood plain." Lila followed Georgia into the dark, cool kitchen. "Your father ate the last of the opened jam," Georgia said, anticipating Lila's search and retrieving a new jar.

She marveled at this daughter's physical grace despite the forty pounds of metal draped around her torso. "One thing I'd ask," she said, hit by an ambush of middle-class concerns. "Could you get rid of the chain, at least during the ceremony?"

Her mouth full, Lila shook her head. After several more spoonsful, she said, "Mae's got this gorgeous red silk. She's making a shawl for me, with bells I think, or maybe a fringe. No one will notice the chain."

Georgia could imagine her daughter, not in demure maid-of-honour yellow sundress with matching hat on her finely shaped, shaved head, but in red-silk, the chain she insisted on wearing everywhere lewdly winking out at their new, very devout, relatives. "I think Juan's people are Lutherans." Once again, the mother of the bride felt entirely ineffectual. "Don't Lutherans disapprove of red?"

Lila smirked her scorn. "I don't know anything about Lutherans, but Juan's into Liberation Theology. Catholics love red. All their Cardinals wear it."

Resentful of having to think about appropriate wedding attire, Georgia made a feeble attempt to exorcise residual prejudices. "I'm sure the red cape will be fine. What are you wearing underneath it?" She laughed at herself. Despite decades spent casting off propriety, here she was nursing a lingering hope for it. She wanted Lila to say Mae was creating something to match the red shawl. Pants and a shirt would be better than Lila's Lycra workout gear, its variations on full view every day, no matter the season.

Lila placed the jam jar on the counter with a precision that telegraphed trouble. Georgia picked up a dishcloth in defense. "Mother, if my baby sister chooses to participate in this wedding charade, I can live with it. Although she'd deny it, we both know Lola displays a conventionality that doesn't align with anything she learned at home. But when my very unconventional, radically weird mother wants to dress me for the event, it's just too much." Lila snatched the dishcloth from Georgia, wiped her fingers and mouth, and, with a little bow, returned it before slamming out the screen door.

"Oh, well, there's a solution. Just tell me off and leave. That always solves our problems."

"I have no problems," Lila called over her shoulder. She'd be gone for the rest of the day, looking for logs to scavenge and men to terrorize. Georgia stared after Lila, the familiar pains and joys of mothering her four daughters plumping around her like a great, broody hen.

3

"Yoo Hoo!" Mae Simpson called from the front gate. "Are you ready for the dance tonight?" Georgia left the kitchen to bow her answer. In her deep bend to Earth, concerns about her daughters, especially Lola and her wedding, evaporated with the last of the morning dew. When she stood, Mae was before her, arms open wide.

Georgia loved Mae, her deep brown skin as voluptuous now as when Georgia first saw her in a vision, the dream-Mae's eyes closed beneath arched eyebrows studded with silver, her dream-mouth offering a supernatural version of the smile Mae now wore. Decades earlier, when Georgia told Mae she'd come to her in a vision before they physically met, she explained how she'd first confused Mae with the Black Madonna finding Her way into women's dreams, a Goddess not to be literally taken as a woman of colour but symbolizing the sacredness of the earthy and the dark in a culture mad for light.

Mae had listened, her ordinary, unstudded eyebrows rising and falling until she had to set Georgia straight about her Baptist heritage. Once Mae delivered her "Truth," Georgia never again referred to her friend's mysterious connection to the Virgin Mary's Alter Ego. Still, after all their years of deepening friendship, Georgia continued to feel the reality of the Black Madonna whenever she stood in Mae's presence.

Mae stepped back from their hug. For her part, she adored Georgia as the sister she never had. Not like the white women for whom she edited and even censored her views on racism and stupidity in their small, pale town, Georgia had long ago accepted all of Mae, including her rants on the vile prejudices held by privileged whites.

Mae studied Georgia for a moment. Tall, lean, her abundant auburn hair fading to a soft salmon made lighter by streaks of silver, Mae thought of Georgia as an ancient, tanned Botticelli Venus. She kissed her friend on each cheek. "Isn't this a day? I hope it's like this next Thursday. Every bride deserves a pretty day for her wedding." Mae looked around Georgia's garden with an appreciative glance. "Even Miss Snooty-Pants Lola."

Georgia laughed, linking arms and steering Mae toward the house. "She's getting the first day of summer, pretty or not," she said, indulging her urge to complain about the pummeling Lola's exacting wedding expectations delivered. "A Summer Solstice wedding," Georgia parroted, for the tenth or hundredth time, "with a new moon for good measure. And, as Lola is quick to tell anyone with patience to listen, it's all happening on a Thursday, Thor's day, the Norse God blessing and protecting humankind with fertility, home, and hearth. The Butte elders call him Zeus. Oh, yes. And Jupiter."

"Stop that heathen talk, Georgia Butte," Mae said. "I walked all the way down here to fit the mother of the bride in her finery. I don't want any blasphemy uttered to make me swallow pins."

Georgia held the kitchen door for Mae. "Being a heathen's a good thing, Mae, a dweller on the heath, like us. We call them hay fields." She grew thoughtful. "And, if the stars align, in the not-too-distant future, hemp fields."

Mae's eyes widened with mock shock. Secretly, Mae admired Georgia's plan to apply for a license to grow hemp, but her daughter, a news anchor for CTV in Windsor, vetoed any possibility that might negatively impact her ambitions to make the leap across the border to the big time in Detroit on an American network. When Mae mentioned following Georgia's lead, Darlene Simpson made very sure her mother understood it was a reckless thing to be doing given the sensitivity of the news business in 2001. Her mother would weaken her already precarious position if she grew pot in the county.

"Hemp fields!" Mae feigned disapproval. "Are you still thinking of applying for a license to grow the demon weed?"

Georgia laughed. "You know perfectly well the hemp is commercial grade. For building. For fabric. For oil and food." She felt an internal shift and shudder as Hal's earlier phone call bubbled up through a volatile fusion of past, present, and future. "Hal Demos called this morning. He says when we're licensed, our first crop could find its way north to a family that's making hemp ice-cream."

Mae tisked disapproval. "And why do we need hemp pretending to be ice cream, I'd like to know? Ice cream is good. It even says so in the Bible. 'And you will know them by their eloquence when they put cool honey on their tongues'."

"Look up that reference for me. We'll read it for all the dairy farmers feeling out of place at Lola's vegan reception." In one swift, elegant motion, Georgia shrugged off her long cotton dress to stand naked in the dim, cool kitchen.

Mae looked away, her Baptist beliefs about the virtues of modesty front and centre in matters of nudity. "Honestly, Georgia."

Georgia took her mother-of-the-bride dress from the back of the bathroom door and slipped it over her head. A Humbug tumbled onto the floor when Mae extracted a small box of pins from her smock pocket. Georgia eyed the brownish-green lump of horehound. "Did you have a good visit with Willy on your way here? I wondered if he'd gallop to meet you before heading to Alice Maude's." Mae picked up the candy, blew on it, then popped it in Georgia's mouth.

"The three of us had a word or two before Willy and Alice Maude headed out to her back field. She said they were going to the sugar bush, to inspect her sap lines. In case they need repair."

"Did Alice Maude seem okay?"

"What's okay after you reveal your naked rump to complete strangers in broad daylight on a busy highway? All I can say is the woman had her clothes on." Mae arranged Georgia's arms the better to examine the dress's neckline. "Are you wearing your hair up or down for the wedding?"

"Up, I think. Isn't it expected of a seventy-year-old woman to wear her hair in a demure twist for her youngest daughter's wedding?"

It was Mae's turn to laugh. "Since when do you care what people expect? You'll be sitting there without underwear in this gorgeous blue vision, just itching to throw it off and dive naked into that scummy pond as soon as you can. Why get all uptight about your hair?"

Georgia laughed again. "I may be a rebel, but I like to pass for obedient." Mae frowned. "Oh, all right," Georgia conceded. "At least for normal then."

"The day you pass for anything but trouble will be the day I drop dead, Georgia Butte. Where's Uly? I want to sort out his jacket. He's going to look pretty good in this Nehru thing we worked out."

Georgia looked away. "Nehru and the Wild Woman. That's us." She chewed the Humbug to bits before complaining. "Big surprise. After we delivered a dead rabbit to its family early this morning, he went to town. Again." Immediately, Georgia regretted this public airing of her private grief. "It's for a good cause," she added, hoping to undo her mean-spiritedness. "The men at all three plants are having an informal meeting about when to walk off the job. All week it's been hovering around thirty-five degrees Celsius in the plants." Seeing Mae's eyes fill, she stopped.

"I'm all right. Go on, Georgia Butte. I want to know how they're doing."

Regretting her blunder into this sensitive territory, Georgia told what she knew of the current automotive factory challenges. "You know what it's like in the plants when the weather gets hot and humid." She stroked Mae's arms. "Several men have collapsed already. Despite the risks, the union's been waffling about supporting workers who walk off the job without official permission." She bowed her head, wishing she hadn't mentioned Uly's trip to town. "Uly says there's still such poor ventilation. He says the current workers want him to give a history of labour disputes since the fifties."

Assessing and readjusting Georgia's dress, it took Mae a minute to regain her composure. "He'll give them a history all right. He'll tell them about my Tony, how they worked him in that terrible heat 'til he went crazy and accidently killed a man who'd been a good friend to him." Mae sobbed. "Over nothing," she said, brushing away tears. "Heavenly Angels! I moved out here to get away from city wickedness, but some days it just won't let me be. Memories find their way out here and light on my shoulder like some evil crow."

"It's not the crows that are evil." Feeling Mae's pain, Georgia swallowed tears.

"No. I won't blame crows when it's human beings who cause our troubles. Greed in the corporations, predators on back roads, insanity in the universities, and…"

"What?" Georgia asked, catching Mae's alarm.

"Some kind of craziness is sniffing around out here. I can't put my finger on it yet, but it's as real as you and me."

"You too?" Georgia pulled Mae into a fierce embrace.

After a minute, Mae returned to the comforting rituals of dress making. "You know I love crows, Georgia, even if they do go after my corn." She shook her head. "No matter how often I say my prayers, I still can't forgive what they did to Tony. They killed my son as surely as the gun that took his life. A gun he held in his own hand. I wish Jesus would help me forgive those places for taking my son. They made my beautiful boy crazy. They crushed his spirit. That's why he lost his way and…"

The women embraced again. "If I let myself think about injustices in this world for more minutes than one…" Georgia stepped back to dab at her eyes. "Let's talk about something happy. What are you wearing to the dance tonight? Have you whipped up something wonderful? You looked spectacular in that orange number you danced in last week, as if you'd conjured the marigolds and calendula out of your garden."

"I don't know what I'd do without our dances. All of us back there in the woods makes me feel so close to Tony and so far away from every bad thing that's ever happened in this world." She created two tucks in the back of Georgia's dress before turning her around to examine the front. "Not bad, Sister."

"Not bad!" Georgia cried, relishing their return to present joys. "A Montreal designer couldn't do better. I don't know why you're so generous with your time and talent out here in the sticks making wedding clothes for your impoverished neighbours."

Mae released a small explosion of pleasure and with it the last of this day's grief over her dead son. "You, impoverished? You're the richest person I know, Georgia Butte. More everything than Croesus. More everything than anybody in the whole wide world."

"I wonder if the bank will think so."

"My goodness!" Mae said. "Surely you aren't going to get involved with banks at this stage of life?"

For the first time, Georgia put her plan into words. "Hal called this morning. Webster's kids are pressuring him to sell the farm. I think he tried to tell Lila when he met her on her run this morning, but he startled her and she belted his new truck."

"Oh, my."

"He's sweet on her, so I doubt he'll make a formal complaint. Or an insurance claim." For a moment, Georgia worried over Lila's violent chain habits. "He knew I'd want to know about Web's plans. I'm going to find out how much the bank will loan us so we can buy his farm." There it was. Out in the open for her to walk around and poke at with her longest, sharpest stick. "With bank loans, I can plant half his acreage with hemp along with our back fields, you know, out by Lila's studio. If the hemp market takes off the way I think it will, I'll be able to pay off the mortgage in ten years. If hemp really catches on and the market for it builds, maybe even in five."

Mae shook her head. "Why go to the bank and stress yourself with their sneaky ways? Why not ask your mother to buy Webster out? You'd think she'd want to hold onto that farm for sentimental reasons. She was born there, wasn't she? Didn't she live next door until your Granddaddy got himself elected and moved the family to the big house in Walkerville?"

"Mother told me a long time ago I would pay dearly for the choices I've made. She's made it very clear that Scratch money will flow in directions other than mine. Besides," she said, feeling pleasantly self-righteous, "Money from liquor is no better than money from child labour. It's only fitting that the Scratch liquor business fund alcohol rehab programs and the other worthy recipients she's chosen as her beneficiaries."

In the midst of making this declaration, Georgia remembered something she had forgotten until this moment of dressmaking with Mae. Her Grandmother Jones left a sizable estate to her nephew, Frank, and her daughter, Marguerite – Georgia's mother. Frank, Webster's father, kept the farm as his share of the Jones estate. Georgia's mother received the farm's equivalent value in cash and stocks. Remembering this, Mae's suggestion that her mother buy Webster out became a possibility. Georgia had no doubt she could persuade her mother to keep the farm in the family for her granddaughters. Best of all, she could pay for the farm with Grandmother Jones's untainted money.

"What about talking to Webster yourself?" Mae said, interrupting Georgia's plotting. "You're family. Isn't Webster going to be at Lola's wedding? Maybe even his too-good-for-the-county Toronto kids will come. Lola would like them present, I'm sure, to help cancel out us hicks." Rambling on, Mae tucked in facing then smoothed the bodice of Georgia's periwinkle blue, mother-of-the-bride dress. "Don't you and Webster share the same great-grandfather? That makes you second cousins. What do they say? Kissing cousins?"

Georgia looked away, her cheeks flaming.

4

Webster Jones began walking his farm at dawn, the meeting his son set up with the TriChem team worrying him as badly as the ache in his fingers when temperatures dropped. Frostbite, he learned as a boy, never goes away. Although his fingers felt fine on this late spring day, an inner frostbite took hold as he mulled the pros and cons of selling his farm, his home.

His son explained that TriChem was on track to extend the growing season by a month, maybe more, in northern California. Investing in a farm in the Great Lakes Basin that sat at the same latitude as northern California was worth the $20,000-per-acre price tag young Frank's lawyer advised Webster to set. An astonishing per-acre price, it was one unheard of for small-to-medium farms in their part of the world. Webster could hardly believe what his son assured him he'd get if he sold out to TriChem.

As he walked the Jones and Butte shared boundary, Webster reviewed his kids' needs. College tuition for his three grandchildren – an arm and a leg, even with their scholarships to ivy league schools in the states – as well as mortgages paid off, something as rare as hen's teeth in Toronto in the new century. And a whole new way of being in the world for him, something his children pressed him to consider now his diabetes had been officially confirmed and health crises loomed.

They made good arguments. Still, the thought of leaving the farm where he'd been born activated that inner frostbite. He stopped, put his hands to his eyes, remembering. "We lost our virginity here, Gee."

Webster Jones and Georgia Scratch had celebrated their sixteenth birthdays together the spring before what Georgia called a 'mutually beneficial sexual experiment.' The entire family had gathered at the farm after a day of swimming at Point Pelee for Labour Day celebrations, this gathering called since they wouldn't share their customary farm Thanksgiving in October.

His mother had roasted two huge turkeys. Aunt Marguerite had her Cordon Bleu chef make more Potatoes au Gratin than anyone had ever seen. Grandma Jones, in charge of corn, had steamed at least five dozen ears. "Sweet corn. Our own sweet corn.

I'm pretty sure I ate a dozen ears myself," Webster said aloud, delighting in this memory of family ease and solidarity.

"Georgia was on her way to Normal School in Toronto," he reminded the trees. "But my God, there was nothing normal about her." He blushed recalling how she'd led him to the Jones bunkie, stripped him of his pants and shirt, then taken off her shorts and halter top. When she retrieved a rubber in a foil package from the pages of the dog-eared copy of *Rebecca* on the night table, he realized she'd been planning their rendezvous for some time.

"There's no time to play coy," young Georgia said. "I have to know what sex is like before I leave for school, in case I want to try it with someone there. I trust you, Webby. I won't catch anything and neither will you. It'll be like a science experiment." But when she kissed him, mouth open, tongue to tongue, any thoughts of science were eclipsed by his very healthy erection. "Is that supposed to happen?" she'd asked, drawing back to get a good look at his penis.

He thought of their afternoon together as a Revelation, an Act of God. He knew as she kissed and touched him that he had always loved her, that the whole of him had been swimming into her, that finally, when they climaxed, they were fused together forever. At least that was what he felt at the time. He realized over the next couple of years it had been very different for her. She'd never written to him about any of her college adventures, and when she'd come home for the summer after each college year, she had no time for him. With effort, he'd shaken off his hurt, reminding himself they'd made no promises. And when she and Ulysses married, he'd found Moira and started his own family. Since then, his dealings with the Buttes had been cordial, his coolness he felt sure, a mystery to Uly.

Looking through the trees to the Butte farm, what he saw was so much a part of him that it seemed an extension of his very self. He peered down the bank to the stream, half expecting Georgia to be standing in the centre of it, her pant legs rolled up, her lovely rump expressing everything worthwhile in life as she bent over, her hands cupped, to drink. They loved this land, together, separately. "We are as much grown by these farms as you," he told the trees, laughing when he heard their answering 'yessssss.' A slight rustling off to his left made him turn to see a doe and her fawn pick their way along the stream the farms shared.

"Hello, Beauty," he said, hearing not his own voice, but Georgia's.

5

Alice Maude collected birch leaves from her back wood with Willy Butte in mind. She clicked her tongue as she walked to the barn, knowing he would hear her. He always heard her, always came when she called. "Willy," she crooned. "Come out, come out, wherever you are." She listened for his answering call.

The goat cantered over the small rise that made the roadway and the Butte farm disappear when Alice Maude stood in the hollow to the east of her ramshackle barn. Essex County's flatness made some visitors feel as vulnerable as a prairie mouse circled by hawks, but Alice Maude Vaughan loved the wide, broad-sky openness as much as she loved Willy Butte.

"Come, my Darling," she sang. Willy stopped, pretending to nibble at a cluster of dry and dusty colt's foot leaves. He enjoyed teasing her. The second time she called, the timbre of her voice acted like a switch. He maaed in petulant protest but closed the space between them. "Don't be like that, Willy. I want to tell you something very important." She paused to swallow the happy tears threatening to flood this moment. "Tess is coming home. Isn't it wonderful?" Willy bumped her hip.

That call from Germany delighted Alice Maude even more than her husband's death a little more than a year earlier. "I'm flying home, Mom," Tess shouted, defying their sketchy connection. "Lola invited me to her wedding. I have time off. I'm flying in to Detroit on Tuesday." Alice Maude printed every word of their conversation on the memo pad she kept by her phone so she could read any news to Georgia. She'd been telling Georgia everything since the younger woman moved to the farm across from the Buttes in the spring of 1960. Had they been friends that long? Alice Maude began to count decades on her fingers until she remembered the note she'd written after talking to Tess. The moment she retrieved it from her pocket, Willy snatched it from her hand and ate it.

Startled, Alice Maude grabbed his horns. "You'll have to remember now, Willy. Tess is coming on Tuesday. Tess is coming home. Don't forget." Willy pranced away.

6

Her dress making duties over for the day, Mae walked with Georgia through the whimsical gate Uly created to ward off the horrors of the world. The women stood in companionable silence watching Alice Maude for a moment, her slight figure bent over Willy's burly body, the pair absorbed in private conversation. Georgia kissed Mae, told her to be sure to return by five for their potluck, pre-dance supper, waved at Willy and Alice Maude, and, at the sound of the phone, headed back to her kitchen.

She answered the phone on the ninth ring. Lela, her second daughter, sounded as if she were down the road and not half a continent away. As soon as she heard Lela's voice, a song flooded her heart. Lala's song, the first she'd heard, was a la-la-la soprano that tuned her first pregnancy in nineteen-fifty-five, five years after she and Uly took over the farm. Lela's song came in nineteen sixty, adding alto harmonies. Lila's song came in sixty-five, the descant, and Lola's, in sixty-seven, another clear soprano.

"Hi Mom." Lela's voice was full of Vermont sunshine. "Fiona and I are coming to Lola's wedding after all." Despite her disapproval of Lola's plans to marry a person she'd privately described to Georgia as 'a virtual stranger and mere child,' Lela's heart had apparently softened toward her youngest sister. "We hired new apprentices for the Permaculture team, so we're good to leave here for a week, maybe two."

"I'm so glad, Le." Relief flooded Georgia's heart. "You know it wouldn't be the same without you." She hesitated a moment. "Lola would miss you. And Lila always misses you. And your father…" Lela's sharp intake of breath spoke volumes about her relationship with her father. "Besides, you and Fiona are the only family capable of organizing the reception to Lola's satisfaction." She paused, added, "You know it's true."

"Yeah, yeah," Lela said. "I'll be there to organize."

7

Returning to the farm's subtle harmonies and opulent generosity usually exorcised Windsor labour troubles, but on this fine, fair Friday, Ulysses Butte's distress over union tensions lingered after he left the busy highway for tranquil county roads.

And there was this other thing, so big he couldn't quite comprehend its shape and size. He needed to work out his thoughts before he spoke to Georgia. Parking on the dirt shoulder at the farm's northern property line, he considered the best way to tell her what he planned.

At this same moment, Georgia kneeled before infant cabbages and kale, daikon and tomatoes, coaxing out the miniscule weeds that were always popping up, nudging straw mulch over uncovered patches of soil. Beneath the straw, the moist dirt providing this bounty yielded to her fingertips. So far, despite early spring waves of furnace heat, she hadn't needed to water. She sent a prayer of gratitude to her full rain barrels, ready for any dry spells that might come.

"We're close to drought-proof." She spoke to this green, growing world as she would to Mae. "What with mulching and the late afternoon barn shade. If we get three-quarters of last year's rainfall, we'll make it." She firmed up the trenches around her plants, Lilliputian reservoirs ensuring moisture would feed delicate roots long after any rainfall ended. Moving to the interior beds, she passed her hands through carrot ferns, a blessing from their Goddess. Cicadas, celebrating the heat and humidity, penetrated her revery with deafening screams. Farther away, red-winged blackbirds chuckled invitations from the cattails surrounding the pond.

With aching body and burning eyes, Georgia assessed her late morning efforts. The garden was perfect, at least for now. Gritty and lustrous with sweat, she made her way through the orchard, anticipating a swim, a reward for her work. Boughs laden with miniscule apples and pears brushed her arms as she passed among the old trees. A Great Spreadwing Dragonfly circled her twice before settling on her hair, taking off again after a brief walkabout.

The meadow – permanent home to grouse, mice, snakes, voles, countless insects, and the favourite resting place of wild turkeys and any deer surviving hunting season – shimmered before her. Over the past winter, it had also become refuge for a skulk of foxes regularly trotting between field and wood while pretending to be elsewhere. As she walked through this teeming world, Georgia noticed the path Uly mowed from the barn to the meadow, perhaps that morning, perhaps the day before. She smiled with the sudden memory of his first push mower, a relic belonging to Nana Fields, passed on to him when he and Georgia moved to the farm soon after they married. In the years before this passing on of implements, Uly's mother mowed this same path, and when the grass was too long for mowing, scythed it, a job she took on when she was not much more than six or seven. Spring Persephone Fields his mother had been then, the farm she treasured, the Fields Farm.

Uly's attention to the path softened a little of her hardness toward him for the amount of time he continued to spend in town. They'd hashed out his reasons many times, never quite naming his sense of guilt over what had happened on his watch twenty years before. The men saw him as their champion. Georgia saw him as an ordinary man traumatized into taking on responsibilities that weren't his. The mown path beneath her feet proved the farm remained important to him. It prompted her to admit her jealousy, an ugly emotion she did her best to deny.

As Georgia approached the pond, Uly ended his truck ruminations, tamping down his excitement as he walked the old logging road barely visible beneath tenacious Switchgrass, his knowledgeable feet guiding him along invisible ruts to the farm's hidden heart. In his parents' time, the sign at the mouth of the logging road warned, "Danger, Hidden Driveway. Drive Slowly. Farm

Wagons Turning." Now, many of the letters had been weathered into graceful hieroglyphics. He stared at these strange markings with a wonder more felt than understood, sure they'd somehow reconfigured, so the weathered letters took on the grace of Friday night dancers. Before he could move in for a closer look, he heard rustling near the pond. Seeing Georgia, he called to her. Looking up from her own ruminations, Georgia waved.

When they met, she greeted him with a grateful kiss. "Thanks for mowing the path to the pond." He didn't seem to hear her. The community garden squatting at the far reaches of the meadow had long been a symbol of her husband's on-going preference for city life. She misinterpreted his focus on this garden now. His mowing forgotten, her resentment against his city passions flared.

"I suppose the men will be out tonight." His wife's voice carried an edgy coolness all too familiar to Uly. Preoccupied with how to best express his plans, he said nothing. In the silence that followed, Georgia reminded herself to accept the fact that the mostly wordless city men and near men were not going to disappear from her husband's life any time soon. "I thought I'd worked through my feelings about your city friends. Goodness knows they're nice enough to me." Uly put an arm around her waist, seizing on a possible segue into his news. "Now you're trying to shame me," she said, laughing. He stalled for more time by kissing her neck and tipping her into a tango dip.

She righted herself. "I know the men you worked with need you, especially your gentleness, if they're ever to find the courage to nurture their own." Uly continued silent. She found his silence odd, then considered where he'd been. The bravest and loneliest of these men came to dance on Friday evenings, sometimes leaving small objects – stones, pinecones, feathers – in the centre of the circle, tokens of gratitude for time lived outside the brutal exactions of industrial life, but they didn't say much. In a moment of fleeting honesty, she admitted that even these offerings had failed to soften her heart toward them. Her husband had never quarreled with her resentment toward his factory mates. Instead, Uly spoke of invisible threads of peace spreading out from the farm – to Kingsville and Harrow, to Essex and Maidstone, to Windsor and beyond – through the men that visited the farm. The first time he casually mentioned the farm's effect on his city friends, she asked the garden to swallow her whole. The land, far wiser than she, left her above ground to ponder her shortcomings.

Wanting to feel connected to him, she pressed her body against his. "I'm glad you don't know how bad I am," she said. Still pondering what he might say to her, he remained mute. As he held her, the Spreadwing revisited her hair, danced a little, and then lifted off to skim the surface of the pond in lilting circles. He decided he would begin with their mutual love of the farm, but before he could speak, she broke away from him and threw off her dress. Her eyes on the dragon fly, she slid otter-like into the cold water, breast-stroked to the pond's centre, hungry for soothing buoyancy. When the Spreadwing flew off, she rolled onto her back and stared into the wide blue sky.

Seeing her stare, Uly took his moment. "Remember our honeymoon, when you told me the Georgia you were named for was a painter, not a place?"

Georgia did remember although the event he referred to happened more than half century before. Because of his dyslexia, Uly had confused the 'Georgia' paintings his soon-to-be-wife had seen on a visit to the Stieglitz Gallery, a New York City trip her mother arranged in hopes of ending their romance, with the State of Georgia, a concept far less esoteric, a place he could find on a map. Surprising her with a trip to Georgia after their civil marriage ceremony, she heard the whole tangled mess he'd been carrying in his head following her mother's unsuccessful attempts to change her mind about 'that farm boy' with closeups of Georgia O'Keeffe blue skies. Her mother didn't stand a chance in a battle with Georgia's passion for Ulysses Butte. On their honeymoon in the State of Georgia, Uly observed she might be named for Georgia O'Keeffe, but her hair was the colour of State-of-Georgia dirt.

Uly's dyslexia confusion tickled Georgia. She loved, far more than he, the havoc his challenges brought to the simplest communications. She believed it strengthened their bond, especially when her forays into other dimensions left her feeling disoriented and isolated. In some peculiar way she could not explain but did not doubt, his exclusion from the world of print and her inclusion in unseen realms made them a perfect match.

Oblivious to Uly's current inner tumult, Georgia sculled around the edge of the pond until the cicadas drove her to seek silence beneath its surface. Try as it would, the sun couldn't penetrate this nether world, illuminating only the merest suggestion of the pond's teeming green and brown universe. "Hello, Beauty," she burbled to the inhabitants floating around her before she kicked her strong legs, resurfaced, gulped air.

"The cattails are glad you're back," Uly said, ready to begin his arguments. Georgia focused on the cattails. Chic in tight brown velour and a full season from the bursting seams and flagrant seeding to come, Georgia felt the reeds study her slow sure strokes to the dock. Seeing their fall bounty in her mind's eye, she hove herself up, stretched against the hot, weathered boards, and saw how, come fall, the reeds would send out progeny in all directions.

"Making another summer possible," she whispered. "For me, for you. For those who know to stop and look."

Uly studied her as she dried off, squelched impatience at her slow dressing. Still, when the time came for him to reveal his plan, his courage failed him. "The guys in town have heard rumours, Georgia. They say Web's getting ready to sell."

Avoiding any talk of her plan to ask her mother to buy the Jones farm, she said, "I heard. Hal let me know this morning."

He could tell she hadn't heard the worst, sensed his advantage. Muting his enthusiasm for the project he and his former co-workers had spent the better part of the morning developing, he said only, "Web's being courted by an outfit called TriChem."

"TriChem?" The name sucked air from Georgia's lungs. A howl built in her gut and moved to her chest. Webster's selling was one thing, but selling to a chemical giant felt like her cousin had declared war on everyone and everything she cherished.

8

In the middle of the farmhouse lawn a copper beech hosted chickadees, sparrows, and nuthatches curious about the humans gathering beneath the old tree's shade. It usually pleased Georgia to see this tree fill with birds anticipating their Friday evening potluck. On this late-spring afternoon she ignored them in her rush to the house.

In her kitchen, panic overwhelmed her. Without thinking, she opened the French doors to the summer kitchen at the moment when a sudden breeze shifted shadows cast by the cut-leaf maple standing sentry behind their home. This room returned Georgia to her senses. As she took in its commonplace beauty, a glancing, gilding sunshine drew the room's ordinary appurtenances toward some higher purpose. Taking in its familiar loveliness, she released the breath she didn't know she held.

"Yes, everything is as it should be. The cistern..." She'd studded the indoor reservoir's curved sides with odd ceramic tiles she'd found during yard-sale excursions in her early days on the farm. Now these old friends blinked in the shifting sunshine, and the cistern's water-lilied breath filled her nostrils. On sunny days in winter, this room warmed the entire lower floor of the farm house, ceiling fans circulating its moist breath throughout the downstairs rooms where the Buttes lived their indoor lives. It was one of the many embellishments Uly added when they first took responsibility for the farm.

Georgia blinked back tears. TriChem's interest in the Jones farm threatened the small harmonies they'd created, harmonies she'd long taken for granted. In the shadow of this threat, she felt the farm's startling fragility. When Mae arrived carrying Lila's red shawl, Georgia went numb. "Lila's not here."

Bewilderment settled on Mae's face. "What is it, Georgia?"

Telling Mae, speaking the name of the evil threatening their peace, made it too real. "It certainly is red," she said, glancing at the shawl before busying herself with nasturtium blossoms she picked earlier that afternoon when she'd been blissfully ignorant of the approaching TriChem menace. She took a little comfort from her contribution to their potluck, a smooth sloped, ancient butter bowl filled with fresh picked, young salad greens. With Mae close enough to hear her staccato heartbeat, she pretended the dropping of nasturtium petals onto this green abundance the most important task in the world. Mae waited, wanting to understand. But Georgia could not speak, could only focus on the nasturtium's brilliant elfin faces.

To keep hysteria at bay, she conjured the memory of starting the first of this year's flowers in January. The miracle of their dark journey from hard white seed to this peppery, jewel-coloured extravagance usually comforted her. But in this moment of amorphous threat outdoor cold frames, the thrill of winter plantings, of seeds sprouting in frigid temperatures against all odds, could not comfort her.

Not knowing what else to do, Mae headed for the stairs. "I'll take this upstairs and corner Lila before we head out to eat."

Georgia released a little of her anxiety. "Don't put it in Lila's old room. Or the bathroom. Hide it in my closet or Willy will eat it." Climbing the stairs, Mae tisked loud enough for Georgia to hear. "You don't know him like I do," Georgia muttered. Her fear made her mean. "Willy will eat whatever he thinks is Lila's, even if you do feed him Humbugs."

As if on cue, Lila made her entrance, banging the screen door behind her. "Are you talking to yourself?" She peered into the summer kitchen. "You *are* talking to yourself. What's the matter, Ma?"

Georgia focused on Lila's grimy clothes and swampy stench to avoid speaking of TriChem. "What have you been doing? People are starting to arrive for the dance."

Lila took refuge in the bathroom, leaving the door open as she stripped for her shower. "Uncle Web's got a tamarack down. You know how rare they are around here. I was on my way over to the Beam place to check out a fallen cedar when he told me about the tam. We had to wade through that wetland patch to get to it." She disappeared behind the shower curtain.

Georgia did her best to tamp down her fear with ordinary worries. "Don't come out without a towel around you. Do you need anything? Are there shorts in there? Remember to rinse that chain." In minutes, Lila reappeared in ratty but clean overalls and t-shirt, her father's clothes. "I see you're determined to make an impression."

Lila put her arms around Georgia, kissed her forehead, then held her at arm's length. "I promise, I'll change into my clean bike shorts and jersey before dance. Why the bad mood?" Georgia was about to tell Lila when Mae dropped something upstairs. "Is that Mae?" Georgia nodded, pulling away and rummaging through the silverware drawer to hide her filling eyes. "I bet she's got my cape." She dried her chain and headed for the stairs.

Georgia resumed her salad preparations. "You know," she confided to the nasturtium blossoms. "If she were anyone else's daughter, I wouldn't care. But this one's ours, for now at least. And we've got a proper wedding in a few days." She peered through the screen door at the gathering crowd. Ben, one of the older men from Windsor's Ford plant and a faithful visitor on Friday nights, welcomed guests as they arrived. Seeing him carry a potluck offering to their outdoor table, Georgia snarled, "Why don't you offer them sun tea and a tour? Why don't you invite them all to stay the night?"

A few minutes later, she placed her own potluck offering on the crowded table, a frozen smile on her usually friendly face. Squinting into the late afternoon sky, she made her excuses. "Willy is at Alice Maude's," she said to no one in particular. "I'll bring them both back for supper." She reached the garden gate, her pleasure in its bird handle lost to dread.

Crossing the road, gooseflesh rose on her arms. Through some trick of time, four drunk, predatory boys found Lila, not decades earlier, but now. "No," she whispered. "Not this, too." Frantic, she scanned the horizon for comfort, her eyes coming to rest on the Vaughan house.

In the period of celebration following her husband's sudden death the year before, Alice Maude asked Uly to build the screened porch she'd been wanting for decades. Uly began the porch the week after the recently widowed Alice Maude fell into a delirious manic state marked by walks on back roads, sometimes all day, often with scandalous consequences. Twice her bare bottom, though not her face, had appeared in the local paper. Out of respect for Professor Vaughan, his widow's name had been omitted from both reports. Still, locals knew the identity of the woman troubling visitors intending nothing more exciting than visits to Jack Miner's Bird Sanctuary and Point Pelee National Park.

During porch construction, Uly hadn't minded Alice Maude's craziness. As long as she kept her clothes on when he was around, he was happy to build her porch. When he was finished, it ran the entire width of the white frame Victorian and was deep enough to contain all the furniture Alice Maude had a mind to stuff into it.

After Uly finished the work, he told her it would make a good sleeping porch, at least until the weather changed. Taking Uly's comment to heart, Alice Maude slept on the new porch until late fall when rain and wind drove her indoors.

On this June afternoon, with Alice Maude's front garden in full bloom, the porch suggested to Georgia an ample bosom plumped within a floral bustier. She laughed at this image. Feeling more herself on this side of the road, she rapped on the wooden screen door Uly created from Vaughan farm maple.

"Alice Maude? I've come to walk you and Willy to dinner. I've made a salad. Cornbread, too, with sweet peppers, just the way you like it." Hearing Willy's snorts, Georgia followed the sound. The goat stood at the end of the weedy drive, statue still, wool draped around his nubby horns.

9

Winding yarn into a lopsided ball, Alice Maude offered Georgia a contented smile. Willy preened. "I've come to fetch you for supper." The fear she first felt when she heard of TriChem's interest in the Jones farm resurfaced. Of course, she thought, they would want this farm, and Mae's, and the Butte farm. The size of the government's research centre in Harrow equaled a little less than the Jones and Buttes farms together. TriChem, a private company, had resources to develop a much bigger enterprise.

Alice Maude's calmness centred Georgia. Without her usual darting, terrified eye movements, it seemed as if Ordinary were her very best friend and not the passing acquaintance it had become over the past few decades. "I found this wool in the sewing room," she said holding up the nubby, loopy ball to the sun. "Willy and I are getting to be quite a team." She looked at Georgia with a look that telegraphed the importance of her next revelations. "Tess called from Germany. She's flying in Tuesday. Lola invited us to her wedding." Georgia stared. Alice Maude gentled Willy's bobbing head. "I didn't know Lola could be so kind."

For a moment, Georgia all but forgot her TriChem anxieties. "They were great pals as kids. Remember the fort they built in the grape arbour? We thought they'd never get over that case of the blue runs." Alice Maude laughed. "What about dinner, Alice Maude? It's dance night."

Her neighbour tucked the ball of yarn into the basket at her feet, fussily arranging the few remaining loops she removed from Willy's horns over the basket handle. When she'd finished this task, Alice Maude embraced Georgia. In mid hug she asked, "Do you think Uly will drive me to the airport on Tuesday?" Her reedy voice lifted tendrils of Georgia's hair. "I want to meet Tess. She'll be so tired after that long flight. I don't want her to have to take the bus."

Georgia kept the airport limo service to herself. "I'm sure he will."

Alice Maude looked across the road to the flowers and herbs set out on Georgia's farm stand. "This is your busy time. I don't want to take Uly away from the garden."

"No worries about that, Maudey. The neighbourhood kids are home from university. A few are always looking for work. It's easy to be on top of things. And if we get a special order, Lila will pitch in." Alice Maude stiffened, dipped her head, then reared back as if struck. Georgia immediately regretted her blunder. Lila in the past, eating grapes and getting the runs evoked joy. Present-day Lila, chained and staving off nightmares, did not.

"Come on, Willy," Georgia coaxed. "It's time for supper." In answer, Willy bumped Alice Maude's hip before following Georgia down the drive. At its mouth, Georgia stroked Willy's warm neck. Seeing visitors across the way, Willy shook off her hand and dashed home for food and attention. With TriChem terrors nibbling at the edge of her awareness, Georgia stared after him. A car banking the curve to the north caught her eye. What at first glance appeared to be a cough drop hurtling toward her turned out to be a small red car. Surprised when the driver turned into Alice Maude's driveway, Georgia bent to the window. Erie Woodburn turned her pale, tragic face to her.

"Hello, Georgia."

"Erie? Is that you? Have you come for the dance?" Erie nodded. "Do you think you can coax Alice Maude to come for supper?"

"I'll do my best." As if it were the most natural request in the world, she asked, "Would you let Lila know I'm here?"

Erie inched her car up Alice Maude's drive. Georgia stared after her. She knew Erie Woodburn had returned to Windsor after almost two decades in Toronto. She closed her eyes, waited. When she opened them, she still did not know why Erie wanted to see Lila.

10

In her own garden, Georgia suppressed speculations about Erie and Lila to greet visitors who'd come for their potluck and dance. With a calm that surprised her, she called out welcomes on her way to the house. In the kitchen, she found Lila crumbling goat cheese into a bright red bowl. Beside her, Mae unpacked her homemade maple fudge, a Black Madonna frown playing on her cherry-red lips. "Did you two get the red number sorted out?" Although she was not yet ready to share her TriChem fears, Georgia longed to reconnect with Mae. Her good intentions vanished when she opened the fridge and found a large piece of cornbread missing from the pan. "Lila! This was for supper."

"I won't eat any tonight, Ma. I promise I'll only have a little water and gruel."

"I don't ask much," Georgia began, cutting short her martyr's lament when she remembered Erie's request. "The most peculiar thing just happened. Erie Woodburn is visiting Alice Maude. She asked me to tell you she's here." Lila handed the cheese to Mae and rushed from the house.

Without a word, Mae resumed cheese crumbling. "What do you suppose that's all about?" Georgia asked. Mae continued silent. "We'll have to cut up this cornbread and put it on a platter, thanks to Lila." Georgia looked sideways at Mae, hoping for forgiveness.

Mae focused on the cheese until she said with a casualness intended to irritate, "I was all set to tell you about Erie earlier but you were in a mood. What's got you worried?" She fixed Georgia with a potent stare.

Georgia shook her head to clear it of TriChem terrors. "Not now, Mae. It's... Not now, but soon." She kissed Mae's cheek. "Forgive me. Tell me about Erie. I need to empathize with other people's joys and sorrows for a while."

Mae raised her unstudded eyebrows. She opened her mouth, then thought better of whatever she was going to say. "About Erie," she repeated. "She's arranged to stay with Alice Maude from time-to-time this summer." Mae spoke as if it weren't remarkable for a person mysteriously absent from their lives for close to twenty years to suddenly start visiting rural neighbours.

"What?"

"Darlene's worried about Erie."

"No wonder, after all that's happened."

Mae set the cheese wrapper on the counter. Georgia picked it up, glad to have something to worry. "We haven't got much time," Mae said, nodding toward the garden. "It's almost six."

"There's more?"

Mae turned Georgia to the garden. There, Erie and Lila stood in the foreground of a thicket of visitors, their arms around each other's waists, their heads almost touching, talking together. Georgia gaped. One of the worst after-effects of Lila's rape was the physical distance she put between herself and most people.

Mae took hold of Georgia's shoulders to prevent her from bolting. "I can't tell you much because we're about to walk out into the garden and be our social selves, but I'll give you a hint of what's to come. Darlene called this afternoon. She said to expect Erie, that she's been calling Alice Maude since she got back. Because of dreams she's been having. About Persephone. And George.

Darlene's worried Erie's going off the deep end."

Georgia put her hands on the doorframe for support. "Dreams about Persephone and George? She talks about these dreams with Alice Maude?" Mae turned Georgia from the unfolding garden scene. "What else?"

"When Erie got back in March, she told Darlene about Alice Maude hearing George..." Mae dabbed at her eyes. "I'm never surprised by what we mothers are capable of when someone hurts our children. You told me how you were crazed with grief about Lila. About wanting to go to court to whack off the manhood of those hoodlums. You told me it was Uly who held you here, day in and day out, so you didn't make things worse by maiming them."

Colour drained from Georgia's face. If Uly hadn't kept her on the farm, she'd have gone to court with her pruning shears and done her best to castrate the first one of the brutal, drunken rapists she could catch. "I had no idea I could hate like that."

Mae tucked an unruly wisp of hair behind Georgia's ear. "We know what we've got in us when they hurt our children. Dar doesn't know about this because she's chosen to be childless, so she thinks Erie is crazy. But Erie's no different from us. She was alone is all. George getting himself killed before their child was even born. And her without a partner ever since." Mae took a tragic breath. "Darlene says Erie's convinced everything would have been different if she'd made a normal life for Persephone. You know, if she hadn't been brooding over George, if she'd married some nice man and given the girl a father. She's convinced herself that if she'd done those things, Persephone would be grown now, with children of her own." Mae's voice dropped to a whisper. "I remember how I blamed myself when Tony..."

A nebulous form stirred in Georgia's imagination. "Did I ever tell you Uly and I heard the crash that killed George?"

"You did." Mae squeezed Georgia's shoulders, willing their shared present eclipse past horrors. "It was such a terrible thing."

The women stood in silence before gathering up food and stepping into the tranquil early evening. Georgia fixed her eyes on the cornbread she carried, willing the Woodburn tragedy find resolution and the TriChem threat dissolve into nothingness. On the way, the birds in the copper beech caught her eye at last, twenty or so witnesses to their escape from the world's madness. Seeing them, she almost wept with relief.

11

People who couldn't make it to the potluck arrived in ones and twos, silently joining the post-supper procession making its way through the woods to what the Buttes called their Dance Temple. Chatter stopped among these seekers after peace, their everyday selves left in the garden with the packed-up food. Most carried candles and smudge sticks to keep the mosquitoes at bay. Spring is dying, Georgia thought, aware of the reverence all around her, and in this same moment, Summer is being born. While she did her best to remain present, the TriChem interest in her cousin's farm worried at her heart. As she walked through the welcoming woods, her earlier thoughts about her mother buying the farm became a life raft. Her mother was on her worst days a formidable opponent, but Georgia was sure she could persuade her to save them from TriChem. Convinced Marguerite Jones Scratch would want to rescue her birthplace, Georgia anticipated the dance, whispered prayers of gratitude for the beautiful evening.

Mae walked a little ahead of the group, her votive candle held high, an offering to the descending dusk. After supper, Essex County's personal Black Madonna shared her cache of sequined scarves, belts, skirts, and harem pants, their sparkles symbols of the sacred radiating out from their time together. Trip trapping back and forth among the dancers, Willy accepted treats, bobbed his head from side to side when he farted, and pranced his own unstoppable four-step. Lila sent mortified looks in her mother's direction, but Georgia only smiled. Sibling rivalry would not ruin the dance for her this evening. Nothing would.

Earlier that afternoon, after he returned from his Windsor duties, Uly swept the floor of their woodsy healing space, cut borage and day lilies for their centrepiece, and set out fresh candles to mark the four directions. During the potluck, Lila slipped away from the gathering to change her clothes, light the Dance Temple candles, and turn on the twinkle lights circling the twelve-sided ceremonial space she'd built with her father, her Uncle Webster, and Maxwell Love two decades before. Now these tiny lights winked out through the trees' dense shadows to welcome this evening's human visitors.

Georgia retrieved the stereo's remote from inside the screen door. In silence, dancers placed their votives in the centre and took hands. Tracing simple steps so new folks could dance with the regulars, Mae demonstrated three slow steps forward and a lilting backward dip. When the music soared, the circle slipped into the ever-present but hidden world of sacred connection that, in the Butte dance space at least, seemed always to be waiting for them beneath the chaos so many mistook for real life.

1

Georgia burrowed into the quilt she reached for when the temperature dropped in the small hours of the night. Her eyes still closed, she felt for Uly, ready to talk about TriChem. The previous evening's potluck and dance made it impossible, but now they could talk. Now she would face TriChem head on.

When she found his side of the bed empty, she opened her eyes, barely registering the delicate rose streaks of a dawn heralding rain. And then she remembered. It was Saturday, the day a group of friends repaired fences, inner and outer, meeting a little after five at Maxwell Love's place, the group's only bachelor and possessor of a kitchen where ten or more exuberant men might congregate at that hour without serious marital consequences. Georgia sensed Uly with Max now, sipping cold barley and lemon water from the jelly jar he carried everywhere, from time to time shouting into the bathroom so Max was sure to hear him over the shower. Perhaps at that very moment, they were talking about TriChem.

Fully awake now, Georgia reached for the scrap of paper peeking out from beneath her current stack of gardening books. Squinting, she studied the note. Lela and Fiona were taking the train from Montreal on the nineteenth. "Oh my," she muttered, assaulted by a crowded future that included the toxic TriChem threat. "When did Alice Maude say Tess was arriving?" Overwhelmed by thoughts of a trip to Toronto and a trip to Detroit on the same day, she read the note a second time, found there was no need for her to fret. Lela and Fiona were traveling from Montreal to Toronto on Tuesday, then connecting with the train to Windsor around noon.

They'd arrive at four or so. She sighed her voluptuous relief. No trip to Toronto. With luck and good timing, Uly would pick up Fiona and Lela on his return from Detroit with Alice Maude and Tess.

Willy tapped a staccato greeting along the hallway floor before nosing open her bedroom door. Georgia left her travel preoccupation to greet him. "Did you bring my tea?" she asked.

Chuckling deep in his throat, Willy trotted across the room to attack the bed with one foreleg then the other. His front half secure, he kicked off the hardwood and hopped his hindquarters onto the bed. Once settled, he nuzzled Georgia's hair. "Hello, Beauty. You are such a comfort." Willy chuffed contentment.

Willy loved Saturdays. Curiosity seekers stopped by for a look at the marvelous, a goat living among humans for close to three decades. Most goats didn't live beyond twenty if they were lucky enough to be breeding stock and avoid the county's stew pots and spits. At his great age, Willy Butte was almost as famous as their neighbour, Jack Miner, and the geese that flocked to the Miner bird sanctuary each spring and fall.

With maternal pride, Georgia twinned Willy's fame with Lila's, for a moment basking in the glory of her notorious third daughter. Despite her eccentricities and general prickliness, Lila continued to make a name for herself in the international art community. Calls for her work came from as far away as England and Italy. Privately, Georgia took comfort from Lila's association with more than gang rape, car and truck vandalism, and the other crazy woman living across from them on their county road.

The thought of Alice Maude prompted Georgia to sit up. "I wish I knew what's going on." Willy raised his head. "I mean with Erie Woodburn and your sister." Willy uttered a vicious snort. "You are not to bother Alice Maude with your squabbles, Willy.

Do you understand?" The goat closed his eyes and turned his head away. "Come on, Willy," Georgia coaxed. "You can be a great little brother when you put your mind to it. Just for a week, until this wedding is over. I want you to be good to Lila." She thought for a minute then showed him the paper she held. "Look. Le's coming." She counted on her fingers for him. "Not tomorrow, not the next day, but the next day. She and Fiona will stay in the barn. You can visit with them as often as you like. Le says Fiona can't wait to see you again." Willy remained unmoved.

Relieved to feel annoyed at Willy rather than anxious about the farm's future or Erie Woodburn's distress, Georgia threw back the covers and planted herself on a floor reflecting the pewter tones of an increasingly threatening sky. "A storm's coming," she said. "Won't the garden be glad?" At the mention of rain, Willy sprang from the bed. He stank appallingly when it rained. Georgia knew his stench troubled him.

Downstairs, she built a fire in the wood stove, then set the kettle to boil. From the kitchen threshold, she squinted into the south, sensed low dark clouds over Lake Erie in her agitated, charcoal-tinted persona. She rubbed her arms to ward off chill. Subtle footsteps sounded. She looked up to see Lady Jane wander into the garden from the meadow. She left the house to greet her.

"Hello, Beauty. Where have you been?" Unlike Friday's visit, this morning Lady Jane kept a steady pace, her body translucent in the muted light. The mare halted. Georgia reached out to stroke her neck. Lady Jane nudged her shoulder.

As fate would have it, Georgia and her mother-in-law were together the first time the ghostly Lady Jane revealed herself to Georgia. The women were on a walk along the stream bed close to the house, foraging for the season's first fiddleheads, Georgia only a few days from birthing Lala. When she took a wrong step, she reached out for Spring, small, wiry, always reliable. Recovering her balance, she looked up, startled by the horse standing in the stream a few feet away. "Where do you suppose she came from?"

Spring saw nothing. Georgia described the white mare. With brimming eyes, Spring told Georgia that her beloved Lady Jane often cooled in the very spot where they stood. That same day, as Spring wept her joy, Georgia saw her young self with Webster and the Butte children on the hunt for tadpoles.

Present-day Georgia kissed Lady Jane's nose. Long after Spring and Jason left the farm to perform Greek classics as members of the Hilberry Classic Theater touring troupe, Lady Jane continued to visit, often bringing with her Georgia's childhood adventures. These past adventures reminded Georgia that whenever she'd visited the Jones farm next door, she escaped to the Buttes. They were the reason she could endure the drive from the city with her overbearing mother. The Buttes were the family she most wanted to join. And now, both farms were… She couldn't bear to think of their destruction. Lady Jane nudged Georgia again. "Spring says you are part of the farm's Great Mystery now." The horse swung her head, worried by flies. And then she was gone.

Georgia returned to the kitchen to feed the fire before finding her rain coat and heading to the garden. Messy, labour intensive, tactile, weeding and planting had the power to comfort her. With her hands in the soil, she felt alive to the beauty of growth and the balancing beauty of decay. On her knees in the garden, she'd come to trust cycles, to let go of the spent, to watch how one season's debris supported the next season's sprouting wonders. When the rain began, she turned her face to the sky, relished the first great stinging spatters. Rain never troubled her on the weekends. No matter the weather, people were out and about doing their weekly shopping, many stopping for herbs or vegetables, many more for a glimpse of Willy Butte.

Georgia left off weeding to pick a few herbs, red and green lettuce leaves, sorrel, and arugula, creating this salad mix for the connoisseurs of the county. As she worked, she made a mental note to harvest small bunches of herbs to set out separately. That task, she decided, would wait until after a warming ritual of tea and toast.

In the kitchen, she set the basket of greens on her work table in the summer kitchen before adding small birch branches to the fire. Her tea steeping, she washed and dried her salad mix. This task complete, she returned to the garden. On her way to her farmstand and its morning wipe down, a prickle on the back of her neck prompted her to look across the road. A pale arm beckoned. Erie Woodburn's small red car remained parked among the weeds in Alice Maude's driveway. Georgia felt a twinge of curiosity then more motherly emotions. She decided to invite Alice Maude and Erie for lunch. A little later, comforted by the fire in the wood stove, Georgia sipped tea, rocked a little, and whispered her gratitude for the life she loved and felt privileged to live. As she nibbled at her toast, she began to form arguments she could use with her mother that would persuade her to buy the Jones farm and save them from TriChem.

Before she could formulate any reasons, vivid fragments of Erie Woodburn's life took over her inner sight. She rocked, waited, hummed. The process's speed sometimes shocked her, like a lightning strike out of a clear sky. This morning's revelations came slowly but with bright and distinct images. These pictures, because of her own experiences with Lila, she knew signaled deep, unhealed trauma.

2

Georgia relaxed, opened to the vivid images and the story they told. A week after Erie Woodburn's secret wedding to George Three Feather Abernathy, her young husband was dead. Georgia had known Horace Abernathy, George's adoptive father, since childhood, knew too that the boy's death almost proved fatal for the old man. Rocking slowly, Georgia experienced again the stir Dr. Abernathy caused when he legally adopted the orphaned baby he'd accompanied to Toronto's Sick Kids for emergency medical treatment, flying the infant in from the wilds of Temagami in 1945.

Georgia had been serving petit fours to her mother's bridge club when one of the women said that Dr. Abernathy had 'gone native' while doctoring in the north. A few weeks later, she learned from the doctor himself that he had volunteered for the Northern Ontario Medical Service after his wife and infant daughter died of tuberculosis. When Georgia married and settled on the Butte farm in 1950, she often met Dr. Abernathy and young George at the bird sanctuary, the three of them summoned by the magic of migration patterns and returning geese.

Sitting before the fire, Georgia saw her newly married self walking with the doctor while young George communed with the peafowl kept as curiosities across the road from the geese feeding fields. On one of their walks, she remembered a cacophony of peacock screams, and how, as if answering those mournful cries, Doctor Abernathy shared his guilt about taking the Temagami First Nation child away from his extended family and his culture. Remembering his torment, Georgia's stomach churned. She didn't want to believe the doctor's love and good intentions precipitated the fiery crash that ended young George's life.

Unsettled, Georgia rocked, sipped tea, stoked the fire, until a shower of sparks summoned more visions. After young George passed his driver's test, she frequently met him on his own at the sanctuary. On one occasion, she found him communing with a caged eagle, the wisdom of the day recommending captivity as the best cure for a broken wing. Although the boy did his best to sound cheerful, Georgia glimpsed a dark pool of sadness around him.

The eagle had been reunited with its convocation nesting in the elms along the banks of Cedar Creek two years before George died. At the time of the bird's release, Georgia longed to believe the eagle to be George's Spirit Animal, so foreshadowing the time when George himself would fly free, returning to his northern home after his medical studies. But George's freedom had come at a terrible price and in an altogether different form. No one, not even Georgia, knew if the boy accidently or intentionally smashed into a wagon hauling gasoline to a storage shed.

At the moment of the crash, Georgia had been standing in the garden with Uly in a scorching, starry darkness. They'd left the house hoping for a cool breeze. Almost immediately, a sudden flash illuminated the night sky. Her intuition working, Georgia asked that the unknown Spirit rise on the pillar of gasoline-fed fire to find peace among the thousands of stars overhead. The next day, she learned it was George for whom she'd prayed.

Her motherly curiosity about George's visits to the sanctuary had been at least partially satisfied the year before the young man died. She'd been out walking off garden aches and pains, glad to leave the tedium of picking rainbow-hued slugs from cabbage leaves to her helpers for a time. It was late August. She left Lala and Lela reading in the gazebo after playing in the pond, and Uly working nearby on a bookcase for the bunkie. Alone and at peace, Georgia walked in a trance, happy to find herself approaching the Miner sanctuary when she finally came to her earthly senses. Before her, parked on the shoulder of the road bisecting the Miner homestead and feeding fields, the Abernathy Imperial sat in a pool of sunshine.

On the lookout for the young man, Georgia scanned the landscape beyond the old red-brick farmhouse where George Three Feather often meditated. Squinting into the light, her peripheral vision caught sight of something in the cornfield across the road. She turned, shielding her eyes against the bright afternoon sun, doubting what she saw. "Mrs. Butte," he called. "It's George." As a requirement of Western Ontario's undergrad degree, Horace Abernathy's adopted son had exchanged his renegade sixties shag for the conformist crew cut of the day.

"I wouldn't have known you, George, you look so grown up," Georgia heard her long-ago, dreamy self say. Present-day Georgia would have spoken a different truth. "I didn't see you at all. You made yourself invisible to me." He was still in his teens, but he radiated huge power that swirled around Georgia in a friendly, 'I know you,' kind of way.

Georgia had been good friends with Erie's mother and grandmother from the time they first bought Georgia's organic fruits and vegetables for their catering business. Lillie Woodburn, Erie's mother, had already confided her daughter's plans to marry George before he began his studies at the University of Western Ontario. Mothers together, the women fretted over the couple's youth before admitting they'd been equally impetuous when passion infused them with know-it-all, adolescent conviction.

Georgia watched as her young self asked George if he looked forward to the studious life waiting for him in London. She felt his inner turmoil, and because she knew of his plans to marry Erie, asked if it was hard for him to leave. "It's the next step," he said. Georgia found his voice strangely flat and noticed another oddity. A very crisp light surrounded him, a bright, pulsing circle of brilliance she'd never seen around anyone before. "You can see me," he said.

"Yes," she answered, putting to rest a brief internal struggle regarding what it might be safe to reveal. "I see you. And you see me."

He nodded. "I thought it was a Native thing."

"It is," she said, answering as one grown and claimed by the land on which she stood. "There are different kinds of native, yes?" He took her arm, walked her to the road. Long afterward, she contemplated the knowledge powering his sudden materialization in the corn field. One day, it came to her. Whatever energy he'd accumulated, he nourished with his frequent visits to the sanctuary and its geese. On the day of seeing the light around him she asked, "How did you discover you belong to this place?"

He'd gestured to the feeding field. "It's like Point Pelee. And the bridge. What lingers talks to me."

Again, Georgia felt the excitement of discovering she shared with this young man the land's exhalations, its sighs of present grief and past loss. She wondered if George understood how he'd brought her comfort in those days of isolating discovery and expansion into unseen worlds. "The bridge?" she'd repeated. "Which bridge?"

"The Ambassador. I go down there at night sometimes. They dance there, the old ones who lived before the traders made a business out of living. They tell me stories about giving the land away, for liquor, for promises. I'm finding my way back."

Rocking by the comforting fire, Georgia heard her young self ask, "Back where? To the north?"

"I guess." It was only after his death that she understood how naïve her question had been.

Soon after George's earthly life ended in a geyser of gasoline sparks exploding into the sultry summer night, Georgia learned of Erie's pregnancy. Persephone, named for Uly's mother, Spring Persephone Fields, and that other Spring Maiden, made her appearance fittingly, in March of nineteen sixty-five. Mae's Tony was born in June, Alice Maude's Tess, in August, and Lila, in September. Tragedy had taken each of them out of ordinary life.

In the years following the crash that killed George Three Feather, Georgia visited with Erie and Persephone on their trips to pick up catering orders. Persephone, lively and interested in everything, Erie, tragic and remote, offered a study in contrasts. As she grew older, Persephone came to the farm with her grandmothers, once insisting Georgia tell her how she'd chosen her daughters' names. As she sat before her fire, Georgia blushed over the seeming absurdity of what the county called her 'four-Ls and goat son.'

"When they were inside me, you know, growing," she watched herself telling the child, "I heard them sing, each of them a different song. First La la la sang, then Le le le, then Li li li, then Lo lo lo."

"What happened to Lu lu lu?" Persephone, proud to know her vowels, asked. Georgia said, laughing, that Willy must have butted the last song right out of her. On another occasion, Persephone, a tiny eleven-year-old at the time, asked if she might have a ride in Willy's cart. Georgia deferred to Willy, a husky yearling at the time.

To her astonishment, Willy dragged his small cart from the barn to the garden, then brought his halter to Georgia. With the feel of the buckles in her present-day fingers, she watched Willy balk at

Lila's attempts to ride in his wagon. Yet on that day, to Persephone, Willy deferred. His harness in place, Persephone climbed into the wagon and asked him to take her to the orchard. Willy set off on a stately walk up the garden path. Well into the orchard, Persephone asked Willy to stop. When he did, she plucked an apple and fed it to him. Unlike other occasions when he'd nipped people holding food for him, Willy ate his prize in dainty little bites.

3

"Hey," Lila said, the door banging behind her. Georgia's visions scattered. "Sorry, Ma. I didn't mean to startle you. The rain's letting up. Want to come for a run?"

Georgia laughed. "I was just recalling the time Willy took Persephone for a ride into the orchard."

"No way," Lila said.

"You were watching from your bedroom window and hornet mad because he fought like crazy whenever you tried to harness him."

Lila pulled the hood from her mother's head, the better to gauge her seriousness. "You're making it up. I don't remember that at all."

"Are you sure? Persephone came out to the farm a lot with her mother and grandmothers when she was young," Georgia said, keeping the association with Lila's rape to herself.

"Erie talked about Persephone last night," Lila said. "I forgot that we were the same age. Almost. She was born in March."

"You, and Tess, and Persephone, and Mae's Tony. All of you born in sixty-five." Briefly, she wondered why trouble stalked these sixties children. "Tony was born in June."

"Why didn't I meet him?" Lila asked.

"He was eighteen when Mae moved out here. He chose to stay with his dad in the city. He had a life there. He was working at GM by then." She added another birch branch to the fire, then patted the chair beside her. Lila sat. "Tess was born during the last days of the worst August drought we'd had at that point. Alice Maude came over to our place dripping sweat and needing a ride to Leamington General because her waters had broken and her contractions were regular. I was already big as a house with you," she said, smiling at Lila. "You were such an easy birth."

"Where was the *professor*?" In Lila's mouth Chauncey Vaughan's title became profane.

"At school, most likely."

"Most likely at the Dominion House, hitting on first-year students," Lila muttered, her tone pure acid, "or their little sisters."

Georgia swallowed building sorrows. There were many things she wished her daughters might never discover even as she understood the inevitability of such discoveries. TriChem hovered above and beneath these recollections. To avoid slipping into that fear, she focused on Lila. "What's Erie doing with Alice Maude?" She asked this as much to distract Lila from Chauncey Vaughan's criminal violence as to catch up on Erie Woodburn and postpone thinking about the farm's precariousness for a little longer. "Anything I can know? Or do these Rites of Spring exclude old post-menopausal women like me?"

"Alice Maude's only ten years younger than you are. And Erie's in her fifties. You're all post-menopausal. I can't wait until I am." Then she changed the subject, telling her mother that earlier in the week, Lola asked if she might have some of her carvings brought to the meadow for her wedding celebration. Lila agreed and now wanted help transporting them from the studio.

Glad of the distraction, Georgia agreed. "Once I've had my tea and stocked the vegetable stand, I'll start bringing the sculptures you've chosen for Lola to the meadow. What do you want me to load up first?"

Lila made toast and sat again with her mother. Toast in hand, she propped her feet on the fender. "To balance my younger sister's preoccupations with virginity – at least with this latest guy – we'll bring up my new phallic pieces. I've got thirteen Hermae ready."

"Is that what you'll use Webster's tamarack for?" Georgia eyed the toast Lila waved in the air. "Should you be eating that before you run?"

Lila stuffed the last of her toast in her mouth. "No, I prefer sycamore for the Hermae." She chewed and swallowed. "I found some gorgeous hickory taken down by the wind out near Copegaron. Hickory works well, too." She sucked jam from her fingers. "I'll cure the tam and wait to see who she is. And Mother," Lila added, her narrowing eyes telegraphing trouble, "given everything I do, I should be eating all the time."

Georgia perked up. "Some gorgeous hickory?" Lila held up three fingers. "How did you get them all home?"

Lila turned away to hide a telltale blush. "You know perfectly well I asked Max. You and dad were busy choosing wedding food with Lola."

Georgia feigned indifference about Lila's secret relationship with Maxwell Love. "Well, look at us, the day is already hard at work, but we are not." She stood, took Lila into her arms and offered silent thanks that her daughter was not post-menopausal. Of her four children, she felt sure it was Lila whose evolution would most benefit from the blessings and challenges of motherhood. She cupped her daughter's face before touching her forehead to Lila's.

"Just like in Tibet," she whispered.

Lila hugged her mother. "You're a kook, Georgia Butte, a big, goofy kook."

4

The farm's largest wooden garden cart leaned against the barn, its blonde wood darkened by what had become a teasing, on-again-off-again rain. "Willy," Georgia called. "We've got work to do." She waited, knowing he would take his sweet time, revenge for her earlier rain snipe. Stinking and unhappy, she had no doubt he would dance in the compost and track his mess through the house to get even. He was an exacting goat when it came to revenge. Georgia had discovered his bloody mindedness early, embracing it as another lesson she'd been called upon to learn in her life as a clairvoyant on a farm populated by beings of this world and that other.

She tightened the hood of her rain coat before positioning the wagon behind her. Willy or no, Lila's sculptures waited. She was grateful for this physical work. It would help her plot how best to approach her mother about TriChem.

Grasping both pole handles, she began her walk on the familiar, uneven path. As she passed the gazebo where she read to Uly by lantern on sultry, buggy nights, Georgia saw, not her negotiations with her mother, but the day Lillie Woodburn asked if she would accept her granddaughter in the Saturday School. Erie's Max Factor training placed her in television's glamour vanguard. Given Erie's degree of sophistication, Georgia wondered at Lillie's request. In the end, the worldly, punk-rock Persephone declined the invitation to rove over the countryside with the less worldly county children. Instead, Georgia learned from Lillie, Persephone took over as lead vocalist in a Windsor rock band, got the required piercings and tattoos, and reinvented herself as the archetypal Bad Girl. This metamorphosis felt inevitable given the tragedy burdening the girl and her mother.

Shaking off her ruminations, Georgia crested the farm's most unequivocal hill with tingling thighs. Her respite from the past didn't last. In the early days of their acquaintance, she recalled how much the girl resembled her father, her hair dark and straight, braided most days, as Lila's had been before the rape. Georgia hadn't seen much of Persephone that last year. She'd have been fourteen, no, fifteen, too old to travel with mother or grandmothers to a boring farm to buy vegetables. Involved with teenage things, Georgia knew, and desperate to understand the madness of adults before whatever it was that afflicted them made her crazy, too.

Georgia's first glimpse of Lila's sculptures ended her Persephone musings. Set out on tarps, some looked to be at least six feet tall. Each trunk, dominated by a large phallus protruding at a right angle from its midpoint, appeared ready for battle. "Oh, dear," Georgia whispered. "I wonder if Lola has seen these." She inched down the slope, the wagon's weight making her brace against the inevitable meeting with Lila's newest artwork. She left the wagon on level ground before grabbing hold of the closest phallus.

Too thick for her to close her hand around, she guessed its length to be at least a foot and a half. "An eagle's perch," she said, patting it. Painstakingly detailed, from the folds of foreskin to the excavated opening of the urethra, Georgia felt how much time and energy Lila had been giving to the study of this particular male organ. She gave it another pat. "Uncircumcised," she observed, wondering if Lila's training in the University of Windsor's BFA program had provided circumcised and uncircumcised models.

"This is a phase bound to generate interest beyond the art

world," she said, exploring other sculptures, some shorter, so that the centre penis aimed squarely at her crotch, some in pairs, as if poised for phallic duels. One she was tall enough to look down on had a face carved at its apex. She tipped several toward her and discovered all had faces staring skyward. These images – little girls' big-eyed stares, beautiful youth in the classical style, ogres from fairy tales, one exquisite Moon Goddess in her gibbous phase – made the pieces seem to search for meaning, for spiritual connection.

"I'd love to hear what your therapist has to say about these," Georgia muttered. Turning at the sound of footsteps, she discovered Uly descending the slope from the woods. "Hi," she said, glad to return to human concerns. "I thought you and Max were off fixing the world."

"Rain date," Uly said before glancing a kiss off her cheek. "I got here just in time. That one was about to come at you." He laughed at his own joke.

"What do you make of them?"

Uly wandered among the sculptures, studying them as he studied all Lila's work. "If she weren't our girl, if we didn't know a thing about her, we'd say she's a genius."

"But she is our girl."

"I think she might be a genius anyway." Uly turned to Georgia, a secret hope radiating from his soft, moist eyes. He did not speak of this hope but of Lila and her healing process. "Maybe this is her way of finally having power over what happened. She had to evolve from all those emerging demons and grasping hands, Gee. I'm glad to see these peckers. At least they're out where she can see them and chop them off if she's inclined."

"She can see them, but so can everybody else."

Uly grinned. "My very own contradiction, refusing to be a

lady but worrying about what ladies might be saying about you and your nonconforming children."

"I don't worry about ladies," Georgia snapped, annoyed because both of them knew she did. She sensed an unnerving energy around him. "What are we going to do about these?" Her question helped her stall for time. "Should we discourage Lola from having them at the wedding?"

Uly upended a large log from Lila's wood pile, steadied it, then climbed up to check out the tallest sculpture's sky staring image. "She's carved Juan up here."

"No!"

Her gullibility pleased him. "I'm wrong. It is I, the paterfamilias."

"Better you than Juan. He's Catholic, you know. Or Lutheran. I forget which. I'm sure neither are penis friendly."

Uly lifted one of the shorter carvings into the wagon. "We'll tie them together, so they don't fall over and break off their woodies."

Leaving him chuckling at his own adolescent joke, Georgia disappeared into Lila's studio in search of rope. The warm stove told her Lila spent the night in the studio and not with Erie and Alice Maude. Dirty dishes from more than one meal littered the old deal table, a relic from Grandmother Spring's childhood she'd stored in what had been the barn's hay loft until Lila announced her need for a studio. The table and the complete works of the Greek tragedians, her Grandfather Jason's gift, were Lila's very first homey touches.

The twin bed, bought for her first and only artist apprentice the summer before, remained in the corner of the room. Seeing it, Georgia wondered aloud. "Where are you now, our high-flight Wayne? Where on earth are you now?" A Somali boy sent to the farm by a Kitchener judge determined to keep him out of Hope Manner, a juvenile lock-up, the child had been christened Wayne by his school chums on his first day at middle school. Eleven going on forty, Georgia decided after listening to the boy raised in Kenyan refugee camps before being flung across the sky to an uncertain fate in Canada.

Lila's bed, a rumpled mess of quilts topped by an old parachute someone had brought for an outdoor day dance and left behind, stood on four sturdy posts at the far end of the room. Beneath this sleeping platform, a large window faced north. It was here Lila drew, painted, and quilted during hard-weather months. Any carving, no matter what the outdoors might be brewing and spewing, she did en plein air. In winter, Georgia often found Lila sitting beside a fire blazing in her outsized fire pit, her face ruddy with heat and wind, her raw hands wielding a large knife.

Georgia surveyed the space. "Your personal habits would bring on Grandmother's Scratch's vapours." She resisted the urge to wash dishes and pick up clothes, knowing from past experience that any acts of interference, however well intentioned, might catapult Lila into a rage. Georgia felt again the difficulties of having a thirty-five-year-old daughter living at home, one stuck in unimaginable trauma. "But perhaps not stuck for much longer," she said, seeing a replay of Maxwell Love's secret transport of downed hickory trees in her imagination.

Hearing Uly call to her, Georgia looked up from her reverie to grab a coil of rope from a peg by the door. "Didn't she do an astonishing job with the sycamore?" she said. "They grow more mottled in the rain." She touched the closest carving with reverent fingers, feeling Lila's special gift in what she left untouched and what she carved, no matter the subject.

Georgia and Uly loaded and bound several smaller carvings together, then pulled the wagon up the slope and into the woods. They walked in silence, Georgia more aware of the unfamiliar excitement in Uly. Each time she tried to speak of it, he stopped to rearrange the carvings. At the edge of the woods, she put her hand on his arm, determined to learn what agitated him. Before she could speak, he pointed toward the house. "Perfect timing. Lola's here."

"Oh dear," Georgia said. "More wedding madness."

Uly slid his arm around her waist. "Don't worry. Lila's sculptures will protect us. Hear them stirring for battle?"

She looked him in the eye. "Let's get together for a TriChem talk later. I can tell, Uly. You're nervous about telling me something." He left without answering her.

5

"I came for jam." Lola, shrouded in a purple rain slicker, called to her parents from her perch on the platform swing. "I've arranged for the marquee to be delivered Wednesday, Ulysses, and…" She interrupted herself to sip coffee.

No 'hellos,' Georgia thought. Only this crazed wedding business.

"The Marquis," Uly said, bowing. "Royalty at our little girl's wedding."

Unamused, Lola said, "As in garment architecture, not royalty, Ulysses. M-a-r-q-u-e-e: a large and elegant canvas structure reminiscent of the entertainment palaces of Arab Sheiks. Mine is a fresh white and yellow striped rental to be delivered and set up by a crew from Windsor Tent and Awning. It should be here early Wednesday afternoon and ready to go well before the rehearsal dinner at seven." She smiled stiffly before launching into a cross examination of her parents. "You remember Juan's family will be here Wednesday night? To eat? To socialize? To stay over?"

Georgia leaned forward to kiss her youngest daughter's cheek. "You look radiant, Lo. Just like a bride." Lola frowned, making clear her mother's compliments were irrelevant. "Yes, Dear, we remember. We've been sorting the food orders from Gordon's for weeks. And the barn is…"

"Good," said Lola. "I want to be sure the bread is fresh and all the dips…" her voice trailed off on her way to the garden.

"When did our youngest graduate from Military College?" Uly asked.

Georgia leaned against him. Together they studied their most puzzling offspring. Strawberry-blonde, Shirley-Temple curls enhanced by artificial highlights, wide brown eyes, skin as flawless as the day she was born, this daughter appeared to have journeyed from a different star to join the family. When Georgia first said this to Uly soon after puberty created Lola's voluptuous body, he decided this daughter had journeyed from the Kewpie Doll star.

Lola Butte might look like a doll, but her actions were of the Five-Star General variety. She had a low, melodious voice and a brain that never stopped its analysis of every moment of every day. Lola herself told anyone interested that she was the only student to graduate from Kingsville's public schools with honours for her entire elementary and high-school life, and without a single late or absence. While earning academic kudos, she'd also captained the synchronized swim team and starred in every drama staged during what Lila called her sister's Kingsville Reign. Georgia learned via the grapevine that the boys she'd gone to school with, now men working in town, called her Smart Food whenever her youngest flew through town in her beautifully restored, canary yellow, sixty-eight Mustang convertible. Given Lila's early tragedy, Georgia didn't find the lust of former school chums the least bit funny.

"Your spirals have such beautiful proportion, Georgia, like flowering sea shells. Nautili," Lola called. As her parents looked on, she bent to inhale the fragrance of the roses blooming amid budding cabbages and broccoli. Despite her military forcefulness, Lola remained Nature's child. All the time she spent in musty libraries and urine-scented schools couldn't change that.

Lila flung open the gate to find her parents unloading her sculptures. "You got them," she said, a little breathless from a scavenging run. "Princess Lola," she said with a bow. "How goes life in the palace? Has the groom added any more gargoyles?"

Lola fixed Lila with a Medusa stare. "Hi Sis. Still running the roads looking for balls to break, I see." Lila nodded to her carvings. "What do you think?"

"Oh, Li!" Lola's voice contained a mixture of admiration and surprise. "You've carved Hermae."

"How do you know about Hermae?" It annoyed Lila that her little sister often appeared to know as much about art as she did.

"Classical Civ 101. You and your arty friends should come slumming in the library sometime. Books can be just as informative as trips to the Greek Islands." This dig at her sister's special trips to Greece to support her healing, including several to the Greek Islands with her Aunt Clytemnestra, conveyed years of little-sister jealousy.

Uly unloaded the last carving and turned to Georgia and his daughters. "I'm going to the woods." His tone dismissed all possible arguments. "I have to do a little trimming around the Dance

Temple." He blew Lola a kiss. "What time's the tent coming?"

Lola smiled her most dazzling artificial smile. "I scheduled it for one sharp on Wednesday, to make sure everything's ready for the Rehearsal Dinner. I'll be out as soon after school as I can make it."

"They're making you teach the day before your wedding?"

"They're not making me do anything, Lila. It's the last week of school. There are lots of loose ends to tidy. OSRs. IEPs. IPRCs. Promotion meetings. Class lists for next year. Time tabling. I'm working Thursday, too."

Lila laughed. "Forgive me. I forget how indispensable you are to the Windsor Board of Education. Sometimes I confuse you with a workaholic Harpy whose fantasies prompt her to believe she is saving New Canadians from ignorance."

Lola sneered. "I don't have wings, Lila. I do my snatching on the ground." She turned to the carvings. "Really, these are wonderful, Li. How many do you have?"

"Why?"

"We could surround the marquee with them."

"Oh, my," said Georgia. "Isn't Juan's mother religious?"

Lola scoffed at her mother's concerns. "She's a woman, Georgia, just like you. She's had several children. I suspect she's seen one of these before." She patted the nearest phallus. As she did, Willy bumped his way through the front gate. To torture Lila further, Lola immediately made a fuss over the family goat. "Oooh, there you are, Will."

Willy sauntered to Lola, making a grand display of affection while smirking at Lila. "You smell a little raunchy," Lola said. "But don't worry. I'm going to bathe you on Wednesday, before the Rehearsal Dinner." Willy rolled his eyes in ecstasy.

Lila snorted disgust. "He only lets you give him a bath because you rub his penis with a loofah."

Lola looked into Willy's upturned face. "Well, someone has to, right Will?"

"For the life of me, Lola, I can't figure out why you'd bother going through with a wedding when you don't even believe in marriage." Exasperated by her daughter's contradictions and sexual inuendo involving the family pet, the words leapt from Georgia's mouth.

"This wedding is for Juan, Mother. He needs to wear a tux and be the centre of attention for at least one day in his life." She paused to kiss Willy's snout. "He lives a miserable existence, apprenticing for practically nothing at the antique shop, breathing in fumes and sawdust, every sound muffled by earphones and earplugs. He needs a party."

"But Lola, what do you need?"

Lola turned on her mother, excitement widening her intelligent eyes. "How many times must I tell you? I'm marrying on the Summer Solstice, under a New Moon, and on a Thursday – Thor's Day, Jove's Day, Zeus's Day. How often do you think such Heaven-and-Earth events align so auspiciously? This will be one of the few weddings in the sad history of human relations that has all the power of the Universe backing it." She took a folded paper from her bag. "This is for you and Ulysses to read at the wedding. It's an Epithalamium." Georgia stared at the paper.

Impatient, Lola explained. "It's a poem celebrating the wedding-day events of a mythical couple. You'll have to read it to Ulysses beforehand, so it looks as if he's reading. Or you can both memorize it and say it by heart."

Georgia stifled the furious response whizzing through her exhausted brain to focus on her tried-and-true mantra, 'Practice detachment practice detachment practice detachment.' But these words were muscled out by, 'Of all the nerve. What a brat. Who does she think she is? I can't stand another minute of this.' With an effort of will she returned to, 'practice detachment, practice detachment, practice detachment.'

"Georgia? Georgia!" Lola cried. "You're not having a stroke, are you? You're not allowed to be sick or silly until all of this is over. You said you'd do whatever you could to make my wedding beautiful. This is one of the things I want you to do. It's a tradition, a lovely, ancient tradition. No real wedding is complete without an Epithalamium."

After a potent silence, Georgia said, "You know I can't speak for your father."

"He'll do it for me. He'll do anything for me." For a moment, Lola radiated uncharacteristic softness. "Don't forget. Juan and I are coming out for supper tonight. We'll talk more then." She retrieved her jam and headed to her car.

Willy looked after Lola with undisguised lust. Georgia took him by the horns to let him know she meant business. "Get those wicked thoughts right out of your head, Willy. She's your sister." Indignant, Willy shook himself free then tore the Epithalamium from her hand. After a few vicious bites, he swallowed his prize.

Georgia patted his head. "Well, that solves that. We can't memorize what's been chewed and swallowed." In spite of the many worries circling her, Georgia laughed, kissed Willy between his yellow eyes. "Maybe you'd like to recite the poem for the guests next Thursday," she said. "I'm sure Lola will teach you all the big words in no time at all."

6

The earlier morning's rain forgotten, Lila stood with her mother beneath a wide blue sky and warming sunshine. Georgia tipped her face to the sun. "Do you think Lola was serious about having the Hermae around the tent?" She touched the skyward looking face of the Herma Lila brought to guard their roadside vegetable stand.

"I think she was." Lila shifted the carving into the stand's shade, then moved it to its original position. "It's so typical. She's gone from Virgin Princess to Miss Phallic Bride in a blink. Summer must be getting to her."

"Perhaps she and Juan no longer keep to their 'no pre-marital sex' rule?" Georgia opened the gate as she took in Lila peripherally, yearning to ask if summer might be getting to her as well. Her chain remained in place, but Georgia noted a new wistfulness and a hint of vulnerability in Lila's eyes. It was a look that made her wonder if they'd passed through some stargate precipitating the return of Lila's ability to trust. Sudden movement in Alice Maude's driveway ended Georgia's speculations.

Erie Woodburn backed out to the blacktop and pulled onto the shoulder in front of the Butte farm. "Is it new?" Erie asked, nodding at the Herma by the vegetable stand. "It's terrifying. And wonderful." She offered the Butte women a rare smile. "Thanks for asking me to the wedding, Lila. Are you sure it's okay with your sister?" Georgia stifled a worried moan.

"Lola wants Lillie and Gert to come, too. It's pretty informal. She didn't send out invitations. It's like dance night."

"Speaking of dancing, thank you for the beautiful night, Georgia."

"I hope you'll come again."

After waving Erie off, Lila and Georgia returned to the garden. "So much for my plans to invite Erie and Alice Maude for lunch," Georgia said. She turned to Lila. "You know there will be hell to pay for inviting them to the wedding."

Lila shrugged. "I asked Erie for my sake, Ma. What am I going to do with all Lola's teacher friends? Her child groom? His transplanted family?"

Georgia felt moved to begin the conversation she knew they had to have sooner or later, decided it would be sooner. "It's good to see Erie again. It's been far too long."

Lila squinted at the sky. "Help me put the carvings inside the gazebo until Wednesday afternoon. They shouldn't bake in the sun after that rain." Mother and daughter moved the sculptures, each aware of the wisps of untold story swirling around them.

When they finished, Lila led her mother to the swing. "I wasn't going to tell you this, but now it feels important that you know. Erie told me about moving to Toronto. She took a job there to be closer to the man convicted of the Windsor child murders. When she wasn't doing TV makeup for the CTV studio or character work for the Young Peoples' Theatre, she was at the penitentiary. She begged him to tell her if he'd killed more children, and if so, where he'd buried their bodies. The warden gave her access whenever she wanted it because of pressure from other families." Lila's eyes filled. "Last winter, someone got to him. Erie's sure it was a community effort, because inmates hate child killers and he wasn't interested in making friends. Erie found out that guards left him alone in the shower. After his murder, she thought she'd never find out what happened to Persephone. Then, out of the blue, Alice Maude called her."

Georgia could not remember her daughter crying since the day Uly brought her home, torn and bloody, after she'd been raped. Her tears hadn't lasted long. By the time police arrived at the hospital in Leamington, Lila appeared composed. Tears, she'd assured her mother years before this moment in the sun, were something she saved for her therapist visits.

Now, as she told Erie's story, Lila wept. For Erie. For Persephone. When she spoke again, she leaned into her mother. "That man dad worked with, David Daniel Lawson, he was arrested in nineteen-eighty-one, right?"

Georgia nodded. A sudden, blaring horn, brought her to her feet. "Stay here, Lila." Her mother's voice admitted no argument. Beyond the cedars, a Dodge with BC plates idled in front of their farm stand. Georgia pointed to their No Idling sign, relieved to have influence over at least one important thing. Her visitors commented on Lila's carving then asked for strawberries. She explained hers had come early and were finished. They chose a salad mix and wondered about her pulmonaria mix medicinal value for respiratory challenges. She told them what she knew. The exchange of information and sale took five minutes. By the time Georgia returned, Lila had dried her eyes and set her jaw.

As if they hadn't been interrupted, Lila continued. "When the police arrested Lawson in August of 1981, Persephone would have turned sixteen the March before. You remember, it was the year Tess and I had that joint birthday party in our barn. On Labour Day. Just before Tess took off for Toronto."

For no reason she could name, Georgia felt compelled to look at Webster's distant alfalfa field. As she stared, the field transformed into a mature hemp crop, its cannabis sativa leaves waving in victory. She thought of telling Lila she wanted to buy her Uncle Webster's farm to save it from a nightmare fate. She swallowed this impulse, said instead, "I remember the call from Gertrude. Persephone went missing on New Year's Eve, nineteen-eighty." Georgia blinked in sudden panic when Webster's alfalfa crop burst into flames. "Look," she whispered. "Look."

Lila followed her mother's gaze. "What? A heron? I missed it."

Georgia looked from Lila, to the burning field, then back to Lila. She turned to the field a third and fourth time, seeing only alfalfa. She shook off the field's fiery after image. "Yes," she said, anchoring herself in the here and now by pushing her spine into the swing's warming boards. "Erie saw her for the last time on New Year's Eve. At first, she thought Persephone had run away."

"She told me that's what everyone believed." Lila's voice dropped. "Erie said she and Persephone fought a lot before she disappeared."

Georgia bowed her head. "How stupid you must find us. How inept at keeping you safe."

Lila studied her mother's profile. "But Ma, Persey threatened to run away lots if times. To Toronto. To Temagami. How could Erie know that some crazy man was killing children? A crazy man who worked with Dad no less?" Lila paused, rubbed her eyes, added, almost as afterthought, "Before she disappeared, Persey told Tess that one of her dad's cousins came through Windsor every few weeks on his truck route. He made a point of looking in on her. On Erie, too. She said he wanted to take her north, to get her head straight. Last night Erie told me that when Persephone went missing after their New Year's Eve fight, Erie believed she'd gone north with this cousin. A couple of days later, Erie called the cousin's mother. When the woman said Persephone wasn't there, Erie called the local Mounties to check the story out. They confirmed she wasn't there."

Restless, Lila stood, shielded her eyes from the sun, searched for whatever it was her mother had seen, sat again. "Erie finally accepted that the woman couldn't put Persephone on the phone because she wasn't there, had never been there." Lila closed her eyes. "Erie said she and the aunt bonded during those calls. They've been talking, every week or so, since Persephone went missing." As Georgia listened, Webster's field, fiery again and belching black smoke, raged. She closed her eyes against this vision, heaved a great, internal 'No!'

Lila didn't notice her mother's distress. "After a while, Erie wondered if maybe Persephone had enough of gigs, of punk rockers, of band groupies. Wondered if she'd disappeared to reinvent herself. She remembered her own tormented adolescence, how she defied her mother, quit school at sixteen, to enroll in the Detroit Max Factor School of Makeup for Film and Television. She decided she had to trust Persephone's instincts. She said she believed she'd come home when she was ready."

The women sat in silence, Lila remembering the young girl she used to know, Georgia bracing against the next TriChem horror. She stared at Webster's field, waiting for the worst. Instead, she saw Lila, isolated and lonely after the rape. Her daughter couldn't speak the word aloud until the summer before her own sixteenth birthday. Before then, she refused to see friends or leave the farm. After she was able to describe what had happened to her to her therapist, she determined to visit the woodlot where her childhood ended. The day of that visit, her father watched her take the cargo chain from his workshop, thinking she was hauling a fallen tree from the woods beyond the meadow. The next time he saw her, she had wound the chain around her body, one end at her waist, the other dangling from the loops on her shoulders. She told her parents where she was going. When they said they'd come with her, she insisted on going alone.

Georgia remembered trying everything she knew that might support Lila's healing. More often than not, Lila asked to be left alone. To avoid going mad, Georgia walked every inch of their land, gathering the detritus of generations of farmers, hauling away all the brokenness she could find, willing these acts of sympathetic magic restore Lila's sense of self, her ability to trust.

Unaware of Georgia's memories, Lila said, "When they finally figured out that the disappearing kids had crossed paths with the same person, Persephone had been missing for months. Then Dad's co-worker confessed. That's when Erie's nightmare began." Lila took her mother's hands.

"Last night, Erie told me she regretted not being with it, you know, making her mother and grandmother responsible for Persephone while she took on more and more work. I told her you and Dad were always here for me, but that didn't stop those guys from running me down. That comforted her a little. I think that's why she's planning to spend time out here this summer. She thinks Alice Maude and I can help her feel closer to Persey, dead or alive, so she can make peace with whatever she learns."

Lila closed her eyes. "Erie told me she felt her mother and grandmother were taking Persephone's side in their fights, so she moved them into their own place. In less than three months, Persephone disappeared." She opened her eyes. "She wondered if we fought, too. I said we had a common enemy, so we didn't have to fight with each other. We fought with what happened to me. All of us. Are you okay, Ma?"

"No," Georgia said, leaking tears. "But I will be."

"I didn't get why Tess and Persey became close until Erie told me about Tess's dad. We'd play here, but whenever I suggested we play at her house, Tess always came up with some excuse – her mom was shearing sheep or weaving, or her dad was hosting seminars at home. I was oblivious to what he was doing to Tess, and she didn't tell me. I do remember hating the way he looked at me whenever we met. It's strange Tess and I never talked about him, especially after what happened to me."

As hard as it was to hear these details, Georgia offered up a silent prayer of gratitude for their conversation. Since her attack, it was unlike Lila to sit still for five minutes, let alone talk for any length of time about difficult things. For years, decades, Lila had been running and working compulsively, her defense against too much feeling. Now, here she was, talking about the worst that had happened to her and to her small circle of friends. Beside her, Lila shifted her chain then crossed and uncrossed her legs. A murder of crows erupted nearby.

"Those birds express our anguish," Georgia said. "I don't often feel it as strongly as I do today, but in this moment, I know with certainty that you, me, those crows, Tess, her dad, Persephone, everyone and everything, we're all connected."

In the space following the crows' sudden silence, Lila asked what she'd been afraid to ask since she'd been hunted and brought down as a child. "If we're connected, why did they hurt me? Why didn't those boys know?"

"I wish I knew," Georgia said. "Maybe they never learned to feel their connections to everyone and everything, Beauty. Or maybe because they were drunk, they forgot." As she whispered these words, Georgia felt Lila's Soul mending, mending.

7

Georgia found Uly on the living-room sofa, an empty bowl in his lap. In front of him on the coffee table sat a new stack of library books. "I'm weak with hunger," she said, feeling the same jangly excitement around him she felt earlier that day. Before she could ask him about it, he held up his hand to silence her.

"I ate while you and Lila were having your big talk out there. I fixed dance leftovers."

Georgia found her meal in the refrigerator. He'd slivered almonds onto salad leaves and made croutons from leftover cornbread. Taking up her bowl, she returned to the living room.

Before she could say a word, he said, "You two looked very serious out there. I wanted your thoughts on where to plant a couple of cedars I rescued from overcrowding in the back woods, but you were too hard at it for tree talk. I planted them near the borage, on either side of the path to the pond. They'll be slow growers, because of the waning moon, but that will be good for them. Give them time to put down deep roots. They'll need them out there. It gets so hot in summer. They'll have to dig for every drop."

Georgia said nothing. With obvious nervousness, he tossed her salad, tasted it, and with upraised fork pronounced it good. She pulled away from him. "Okay, Uly. Enough is enough. What's going on?" Loud knocking at the kitchen door startled her.

"Finish your lunch," he said, grinning with what she knew to be relief. "I'll see who it is."

It wasn't like customers to come into the yard, Georgia mused, watching Uly on his way to the kitchen door and drawing a blank regarding the possible reasons for his odd energy. She wondered if men from the city had come to enlist him in yet another cause and he was nervous to tell her he expected them.

"It's Alice Maude," he called from the kitchen. "I asked her in, but she's glued to the flagstones. She hasn't said in so many words, but I think she wants to see you."

Georgia set down her bowl, amazed her legs could carry her into what was sure to be more emotional turbulence. "We'll talk when I get back," she said, fixing Uly with an 'I mean it' stare. He laughed, lifted her dress with the toe of his boot. Meant to charm her, his antics had the reverse effect. She opened her mouth to ask him again about his energy, but thought better of it. She didn't want to keep this friend waiting.

8

Alice Maude, her eyes fixed on the flagstones aproning the Butte back doorstep, muttered secrets to the warm, moist air. Georgia touched her shoulder to call her back to their shared time and place. "What a lovely surprise, Maudey. What's up?"

Alice Maude looked at Georgia, her eyes wide, terrified. When she came to herself, she took Georgia's hand and led her to the front gate. Seconds later the women were rushing across the road and up her drive. At the back of the house, Georgia discovered Willy rubbing his horns on Alice Maude's back stoop.

"Here you are," Georgia said, scratching the goat's head. "I wondered where you were drying out, Willy. What have you two been doing?"

In answer, Willy trotted across the back garden. In the distance, the heat elongated the tall meadow grasses, making them appear as insubstantial as Georgia felt. She regretted not wearing her straw hat. Beyond the field, the sugar bush offered an inviting, shadowy coolness. With Alice Maude still tightly holding her hand, Georgia and her neighbour followed Willy toward the woods.

The meadow's stubble made it hard going despite Alice Maude's daily walks along the meandering path. As they grew close to the woods, the younger woman stopped. Fixing wild eyes on Georgia, she cried, "Can you hear him?"

Georgia listened, at once aware of two hawks gliding on thermals high above them. Although she heard nothing, in her mind's eye the land exhaled a taupe mantle flecked with black and white. Georgia thought of a coverlet rising and resettling over a giant's bed. She looked from this vision to the hawks circling in the cloudless blue sky.

Alice Maude steered her into the woods. Sap lines dangled from a few of the maples and branches brought down by high winds lay scattered throughout the understory. Georgia did her best to pull away from Alice Maude, but the small woman would not let her go. "Can you hear him?" Before Georgia could answer, Alice Maude yanked her to the right. Shadows gave way to brilliant sunshine infusing an open field with bright yellow light. Georgia blinked away sudden blindness. The Miner Sanctuary feeding field that shared a boundary with her friend's back woods blurred in her vision.

"Can you hear him?" Alice Maude asked again, this time in her normal voice. "I hear him all the time."

Georgia did hear the unmistakable sound of a racing engine. In an alternate universe, on the road bisecting the Miner properties George Three Feather Abernathy drove his father's dove-grey Imperial toward inevitable disaster. Somehow, Alice Maude had conjured for Georgia the moment just before the young Native died.

"Wait! Listen," Alice Maude said when Georgia turned back to the woods for comforting shade. "In a second you'll hear Walt Peterson gun the tractor to get the wagon off the road." Alice Maude smiled at Georgia, a mad woman's smile. "Can you hear him sing?" She looked at her feet then back to Georgia. "I hear him sing. Then everything explodes."

"George sings?"

"He used to dance out here, too. Before he died, he came out here all the time. I watched him learn about things." Georgia stared at Alice Maude.

"You're surprised," Alice Maude said. "You thought I was gone. I was, I still am, but I can come back when I want to." The small, delicate woman looked inward. "I started coming back after Tess escaped to Toronto and I knew she'd be safe with my sister Grace. A little bit here. A little bit there. Then I learned how to pretend to be gone. He left me alone when he thought I was gone. He wanted to make me suffer. He knew I never suffered when I was gone." Alice Maude's eyes leaked indignant tears. "He liked being the professor with the crazy wife. He gorged on the sympathy."

Like some ancient Hag at a Crossroads, the younger woman raised her arm, pointed into the distance. "The geese shared their secrets with George. I saw them together. Lots of times. When I heard on the news that Lawson had been murdered, I called Erie. I told her about George, about how he sings and dances here. Once that man was dead, she had no reason to stay there. She'll find out more here. She wants to hear George sing. She wants to see him dance. That's why she's coming. He's like the geese. He's loyal. He knows his way home, to her, to Persephone. I told Erie he sings and dances for her. And for their daughter."

Alice Maude stole a shy glance at Georgia. "It comforts me to hear him, Gee. It comforts me to think it will make her happy to find him again. Hearing him will comfort both of them." She turned, took Georgia's face in her hands. "Listen, Gee, listen. He sings for you, too."

9

Although five-feet-five, Juan Elias created the impression of a much taller man. Struck by his biceps straining the short sleeves of his t-shirt, Georgia caught a fleeting glimpse of the hours he spent at the gym, his antidote for out-of-place loneliness in his new country. His longing for home cast a purple oval around him. Lola chose to ignore his sadness.

"Georgia! Are you listening to me? Gertrude Bradshaw simply cannot come to our wedding. She's at least a hundred and ten."

"She is one hundred and one, Lola," her father corrected.

"Ulysses, please don't be obtuse. You know that however old she is, she's too old to be at anybody's outdoor wedding in a heat wave. Besides, it's supposed to be Juan's family, ours, and friends of my choosing. Lila is ruining everything. As usual. Please, Georgia. Be on my side. Just this once."

Georgia shook off her Juan trance. "I love Gertrude Bradshaw and all her one hundred and one years, but it is your party, Lo. Would you like me to call them and cancel?"

Lola swept a damp curl from her forehead. Juan's face expressed alarm when his bride-to-be answered with no small amount of venom. "And say what? 'You were invited to Lola Butte's wedding by her wonderfully sensitive sister Lila, but now the bitch bride disinvites you?' It's too late. How would it look if I said she couldn't come?"

Exhausted by the aftershocks of her intense morning with Lila and more intense afternoon with Alice Maude, Georgia let her irritableness have its way. "You're fussing over nothing, Lola. It is highly unlikely Gertrude and Lillie will come. If this afternoon is any indication, it will be, as you've pointed out, baking hot on Thursday. Add the heat to the drive out here in their ancient minivan, without air conditioning…"

"Mother," Lola said, her voice a few decibels higher. "Please don't play dumb. You know Lila invited Erie, too. She'll drive Lillie and Gertrude to the wedding, a reliable Erie, no doubt driving a reliable, air-conditioned vehicle."

Georgia grasped at irrelevancies. "Erie came to the dance last night."

"Well, bully for her. Lila can invite Erie and her ancients to her own wedding." She paused for dramatic effect. "Oh, dear. I forgot. She won't be having a wedding, just like my other sisters, not because she's a lesbian like Lela or a saint like Lala, but because she runs around in heavy armour looking for men to kill." Terror replaced alarm on Juan's handsome face.

"She's exaggerating, Juan," Georgia said, smiling, patting his hand.

"Tell that to the people who have chain dents on their vehicle hoods." Then, imitating one of Lila's victims, Lola said, "Really, Officer. I just stopped to ask for directions when this woman smashed my car with a chain she just happened to be wearing." She turned on her mother. "How many times have you and Uly had to talk people out of pressing charges? How many repair jobs at the Kingsville body shop have you paid for?"

Uly squared his shoulders. "Where's your compassion, Lola? Your sister is in therapy."

Lola's wail of frustration caught Uly off guard. "Oh, rush to her defense, Ulysses, like you always do." She turned away so he wouldn't see her full eyes.

Georgia felt how close they were to serious rupture and waded into this torrent of feeling with what she hoped was an appeal to Lola's reasonableness. "Lo, what is your intention here? Is this about solving a problem or attacking Lila? If it's about problem solving, I can very easily let Gertrude Bradshaw know Lila overstepped her bounds with her invitation. We're old friends. Just say the word and I'll call. If it's about attacking Lila, then admit it, at least to yourself. Find a therapist to sort through your feelings. And talk to Lila. She'll support you in caring for yourself at this high-pressure time." Lola opened her mouth to have the last word but sipped coffee instead. "I take it your silence means Gertrude and Lillie are welcome?"

Juan cleared his throat, prompting Georgia to wonder how much of the conversation's subtleties he'd understood. "It is good they come, Miss Lola," he said, his tone appeasing. "My grandmothers, they are no longer in…" He gestured to the air around them. "Signora Gertrude, she brings to us the old peoples, their blessings, and I am feeling so happy about this."

Lola offered him a small, tight smile. To her parents she said, "Thanks for dinner Georgia, Ulysses. It's been stimulating. We'll wash up."

"No," Georgia said. "I've had one of those days. My hands need warm soapy water, and my eyes need to stare at this gorgeous sky."

"Of course," Lola said, her tone prompting Mae to dub the Butte youngest daughter 'Miss Snooty-Pants.'

Georgia and Uly waved them off. "What do you make of that?" Georgia stared after Lola as she groped for Uly's hand.

Uly moved toward the gate. "I think Lola will go back to the city, on the way stopping for a large, caffeine-and-sugar concoction. As she sips, she'll forget all about Lila's interference, at least temporarily. If I were a betting man, I'd put money on a coffee stop in Kingsville." He met Georgia's eyes then. "Come Thursday, Lila should have more than her chain for protection when she walks down the aisle for her sister."

"I wish I could understand what's gotten into our youngest daughter. She's become so desperate about this marriage thing." She resisted adding 'and I could ask the same of you.'

"And you thought the worst would be over when she graduated from university."

"Wasn't I the optimist? Who would have thought a child of ours would develop such an appetite for institutional life."

10

On their way to the house, Uly caught Georgia off guard with a surprise embrace. She struggled to free herself. "Okay, Uly. What's up? And please, no more stalling. I can feel your anxiety about…" His earlier defense of Lila during Lola's tirade made her long to be kind. At the same time, she knew from past experience his avoidance meant more trouble up the road. Given the TriChem threat to the farms, his secrecy frightened her.

Without protest, she allowed him to lead her into the meadow. When they reached the pond, she saw that while she'd been tearing through Alice Maude's sugar bush, he'd been scything the grass around the cattails and hauling split wood to the pond fire pit. She softened toward him. Whatever his current city interests, they didn't keep him from caring for their home.

He gestured to one of the old blue Adirondack chairs squatting near the dock. Georgia sat, accepted with muted surprise the Mason jar of sun tea he retrieved from beneath her chair. "Oh, my," she said, doing her best to hide her worry. "I'm in for it if you've been strategizing." Seeing his blush, she knew she was right. She studied him as he lit the smoker, their defense against teeming gnats and mosquitoes at dusk. Soon, a lavender haze lazed up into what remained of the sun-painted sky.

To distract herself from worries about contributing to air pollution in a region already overburdened by industry emissions, Georgia listened for the pond's resident Banjo frog but could hear nothing over the million-insect choir at home in this wet spot. Peering through the reeds encircling the pond, she smiled at the familiar sight of water bugs skimming the surface oblivious to swooping, hungry swallows. She turned from the pond to the meadow fireflies, too many to count, flashing secret messages to the setting sun. Dreamily, she inhaled the lake's fishy breath. She startled when Uly cleared his throat.

After a moment's hesitation, he sat beside her, took her hand. With effort, she resisted the urge to pull it away. "Some of the men have been getting the money together to make an offer on your cousin's farm. We'll have to mortgage this place to come up with our share."

For a moment Georgia couldn't comprehend his meaning. In her mind, her mother had already purchased her cousin's farm – her family's farm. Her plan would cost them little. It would make them safe. She fretted that he didn't agree with her until she remembered. She hadn't told him of her plan to ask her mother to buy her old farm. For a time, she sat in confused silence. Insects buzzed around her. The setting felt ordinary. She sat by the fire as she so often did on late spring evenings, listening to the frogs, watching the swallows.

With effort she returned to this new reality. Her husband wanted to buy her family's farm, not with her, but with men from the city. She made silent arguments against his plan, the very arguments she anticipated he would make against her plans to have her mother buy the Jones farm. When it came to make these arguments, she couldn't speak.

Uly laid more cedar on the smoker. Watching him, his city life crashed over her, smothering the life they'd made together. Without knowing she was going to speak, she heard her voice, low, desperate. "Why would the bank loan us anything?" She already knew the answer. The bank would loan them a great deal. That was the trouble. Predatory lending policies leading to foreclosures had become all too common. She looked away from him. She had to think without hearing any more. When she spoke, it was more to herself than to him.

"For decades we've been giving whatever surplus money we made to your parents to make up for the loss they took when they transferred the farm to us." Uly focused on the smoker. "We've been homesteaders all this time, figuring out what we need as we go along." He straightened, squared his shoulders. She did her best to ignore his preparations for a fight.

"This place has helped all kinds of people, Uly. Troubled kids like Wayne. All the adults who let us know how important dance nights are. To say nothing of the folks who eat the food we grow. We can't risk losing the farm to…" She stopped herself from saying she refused to risk the farm's future with men who might visit now and again but who knew nothing of the life hidden in the subtle, layered folds of earth, in the creeping, racing vegetation, in the pallet-knife bark of trees, men who came to their home, she was sure, only because Ulysses Butte had some sort of messiah complex.

Uly stood over her. "I visited the co-op with Max this morning. Jake confirmed TriChem is looking for a place to experiment down here because so many of the old boys have made serious money with GMO'd corn and soybeans for livestock feed." He swigged tea, searched for words. "Whatever inputs they develop here will increase yields all across the northern states, Georgia. It'll make this company billions. The integrity of a little farm like ours won't matter a whit to them."

She looked to the pond. The tidal wave of grief rising in her chest made her hard. "Why would men from the plant – men who didn't know one end of a trowel from the other until you taught them – want to save a little farm from chemical marauders?"

"You know damn well why. They're doing it for themselves, Georgia, for their families." He stared at her, defiant. "They're doing it for me."

Her eyes didn't leave his. "Help me to understand. You're asking me…no, you're telling me you want to mortgage our farm so you can buy another one with a bunch of men with no farming experience? Good God, Uly. These know-nothing city boys will come out here and take over."

"Know-nothing city boys? Haven't I been one of them for half a century?"

Georgia sat forward so abruptly she knocked her tea to the grass. "And whose damn fault is that? Who made you go in there day after day after week after month, year in and year out, torturing your arms, your back, feeding those monster machines your life's blood, letting them chew up most of the cartilage in your hands, your elbows, your knees? Tell me that, will you? Who made you sell yourself for wages?"

She paused, searching for restraint. Finding none, she hissed, "You know you're still involved with those damn factories because you think you can prevent what happened back then from happening again. Because you're their great…saviour."

He hovered over her. "Don't stop now, Georgia."

Knowing whatever she said would be cruel, knowing she wanted to be cruel, Georgia swallowed her bile. What she really wanted was for him to say that the boundaries drawn up by fools who believed people could actually own the living, breathing loveliness that gave them life were ridiculous fictions. Then, only then, might she reclaim her ability to say something kind to him, something hopeful. At this moment of impasse, she couldn't trust herself. Their weapons were drawn and bloody. His throat was beneath her boot.

"I need to walk." She flung the words at him. "Don't wait up for me." When she was only a few yards from him, she stopped to look back, afraid she'd crushed something more than his desire to save the Jones farm. She fled to the woods.

1

Bedeviled by dreams, Georgia woke at first light. Her usual greeting of the new day forgotten, she got up quickly, stumbling into the old cedar chest Grandma Jones filled with linens for her new life in the county – embroidered wonders Georgia long ago stitched into the quilts she'd made for each of her daughters. It was already far too hot, for the day, for the season. She recalled the unusual chill of the previous morning. Fear clouded her mind.

With an effort of will, she ignored her distress, searched her dresser top for the knitting needle she used to fasten her hair. Fixing a loose chignon in place, she wrapped herself in a sarong from Lila's print-making period, on this bleak morning oblivious to the feel of fine silk against her bare skin. Winding the sarong around her torso, she asked its sky blues and lagoon turquoises to soothe her troubled spirit. Before leaving the room, she glanced at their bed. Uly's eyelids fluttered before dreamland – or cowardice – reclaimed him. Georgia wanted him to sleep. She needed more time, to reflect, to understand.

In the kitchen, she retrieved a small bowl from the dish rack and ventured out into the humming, muggy morning. She closed her eyes, breathed, wondered where her feet might be taking her. And then she knew. The pond. She would harvest their few remaining strawberries, on the way opening to a literal and figurative cleansing.

As she walked through the garden, one of several disturbing dreams replayed in her imagination. In this dream, she and Alice Maude stood together in the Miner corn field watching a young man dance and sing. Clouds gathered. Rain fell. Alice Maude vanished. The young man transformed into an even younger girl. Persephone Woodburn's eyes fixed on Georgia. The older woman did her best to shake off the anxiety creeping from her stomach to her chest, concentrating instead on the textures and warmth beneath her unshod feet.

Walking, walking, walking until she stood before the sprawling strawberry patch. Most of the berries had been harvested, but here and there she found just enough for her penitent's breakfast, the reason for her penance not yet named.

Her bowl half full, she took in the Sunday morning silence. Not a tractor, not a mower, not a single diesel engine could be heard in her version of paradise. Farmers, even those up and moving, ignored their machines until they paid their respects to their Lord. She raised her face to hers.

In the meadow, she found indentations in the long grass where deer bedded under the dazzle of stars that ended her struggles with outrage and suspicion the night before. After her quarrel with Uly, she felt bereft until she looked up. Now, sweating and anxious, she was glad to discover she'd shared that sky with a few of the wary deer roaming the dwindling forests of the county.

The pond, glass still, transformed into a deep, black, scrying bowl. Georgia unwound her sarong, let it fall to dew-slick boards. For a few minutes she sat on the platform's sticky edge, swinging her feet back and forth as she'd done as a child. Back then, the Fields' makeshift dock tilted dangerously close to the water, so that the farms' gaggle of children slid into the pond when they meant to and when they didn't. TriChem, she knew, would end future joys, erase past ones.

Georgia looked out over the pond's placid surface, humbled by the miracle of water in desertifying times. When she'd eaten the last strawberry, she slipped into the pond's stillness, undulating beneath the surface, her arms at her sides, her legs together, overcome by the utter wonder of life, now as woman, now as water snake. She dove deeper, deeper still, willing the future reveal itself until unseen, protective hands yanked her to the surface. She gulped fishy, humid air.

In a few strong strokes she reached the platform, pushed herself up, swung around to face the pond. Four young jays argued in the closest birch tree, the ordinariness of this scene crowding out the last of her unease. She squeezed the water from her hair, recoiled and speared a loose knot, then used the sarong as a towel before wrapping it around her torso. With a growing sense of direction, she left the pond for the woods, at the mouth of the narrow, well-traveled path, bowing her head.

TriChem. The name dizzied her mind and disoriented her body. Pushing against this brute energy, she took one step, another, and another, then dipped back. She danced this familiar pattern as the land's darker stories flooded her consciousness. From time to time, she stopped to speak aloud her prayers – for the farm, for all of its inhabitants, past, present, future – for those subtle beings nurturing every leaf, every bud, every mycelium and microbe. Her cheeks wet, she looked into the canopy overhead, felt how essential these guardian trees were to the balance of their region. One step, then another and another, then a dipping and rocking back.

Her own voice startled her when she began to chant, the first sounds taking her deep into her anxiety about everything that threatened the peace of their existence. The stupid decisions people had made, were making, her judgments about them, her own impotent fury. She stopped then, opened to the grace of the moment, to the stillness beneath her mental tumult. She walked on, her chant louder until it rose to a wail then fell back into somber grief. She closed her eyes, felt her way forward, the scents of the place guiding her. She opened her eyes when a young poplar brushed her hair. With its touch she entered a deeper mystery.

She arrived at the place of protective brambles and thorny, obscured paths. Her pitch shifted, her song swelling into leaves shielding her from building heat. She opened her eyes, startled by the luminous outlines of trees. She bowed her head, knowing she'd been brought to this place to listen.

Listen.

After moments or hours, the woods released her. She walked on, finally reaching the pair of elms standing a little apart from other trees, their existence a miracle after the blight of the sixties. Beyond the elms, in an open circle, the farm's largest stone beckoned her forward. As soon as she glimpsed this older-than-time friend, her inner eye flickered open. She stepped lightly, felt new visions spring from the mossy carpet beneath her feet. Passing a waist-high tamarack, she touched its soft new needles, welcoming this visitor brought by the wind from higher, colder ground.

Arriving at the place she recognized had been her destination all along, she put out her hands. Caressing the stone geologists named 'erratic boulder,' she felt the power of the glaciers passing through this part of the world, sculpting the Great Lakes then disappearing into their own mystery. Georgia laid her head against the great stone, felt her awareness shift from her small human worries to the timeless world of endless passage through heat and cold, birth and death, dance and stillness.

After a minute of wordless ecstasy, she lifted her head. Tenderly, she kissed the stone. With the reverence of the forgiven, she lay on the moss-covered earth.

2

Uly and Juan sat across from one another on the platform swing, carefully avoiding eye contact. The older man noticed the younger man's scratched hands, wondered if Juan had been in a recent fist fight. So many of the men he informally counseled had similar scratches, their down time in bars often ending in fights about nothing they could remember afterward. Juan noticed Uly's attention to his hands. He opened and closed them, proud of these signs of his growing carpentry skills. He thought of telling Lola's father about the arbour he'd made for his daughter. Just then, Georgia emerged from the orchard, calling out her good morning to him. Juan waved, relieved to be rescued from uncomfortable silence.

"It's lovely to see you again, Juan," Georgia said on the way to the house. "Good morning, Husband," she added, hoping she sounded conciliatory.

"You were swimming very early." His stiff smile telegraphed anger and hurt. With a lightness he didn't feel, he changed the subject. "Juan has come to talk with us. About the wedding."

Georgia blinked surprise. "I'll change and join you."

The men continued their vigil in silence, Juan searching for the words he needed for this wedding conversation, Uly rehearsing what he wanted to say, felt he had to say, to Georgia about the farm's future. Each man ruminated until Georgia took her place with Uly across from Lola's groom. When neither man spoke, Georgia took the lead. "It's always good to see you, Juan. No Lola?"

"I came by myself, Mrs. Georgia. I made this journey when Miss Lola is doing the exercising." To break the tension, Uly offered Juan breakfast. "No, no, Mr. Ulysses. I ate many of the pancakes at The Tunnel Bar-B-Q. They have the specials on Sunday morning, with the ribs, the pancakes, the maple syrup. These I eat with great gusto." He smiled as he patted his stomach, hard and flat beneath his dress shirt.

"Your visit is a wonderful surprise," Georgia said. "You're always welcome here." Juan continued smiling, nodding. Georgia smoothed the light fabric of her sundress where it covered her thighs.

"Is this about the marquee for the wedding?" Uly's impatience suggested he longed to be elsewhere.

"Oh no, no." Juan looked down at his hands. "I mean, it is about the wedding, yes, a small problem. But I have the fear to tell Miss Lola."

Georgia studied Juan's open face. She had all but given up hope for a display of good sense from either the bride or the groom, and yet here was a promising sign of that very thing. She looked down at her weathered hands, took in her ragged nails, her mosquito bites, her missing wedding ring. As she stared, her hands metamorphosed into large brown claws. She looked away from them, sensing everything. "You want to call off the wedding." She hadn't meant to say the words. They were his after all.

The groom's sudden tears prompted Uly and Georgia to glance at one another. Georgia leaned forward, placed a hand on Juan's shoulder. "It's all right, Juan. It's very important that you call off the wedding if you feel it's wrong to marry so quickly. We understand." Juan's shoulder trembled beneath her fingers. Then, reckless, she asked, "What can we do to help?" When he didn't reply, she asked, "Would you like us to speak with Lola?" Uly's eyebrows shot up in alarm.

Juan blinked his astonishment. "You can do this? You can talk to Miss Lola?" Uly sat forward, ready to contradict Georgia if she agreed to run interference for Juan. "Because I tell you the truth, Mrs. Georgia. I have the fear of your daughter." Stunned by the young man's fine instincts, Georgia did her best to hide her relief. As far as she knew, Lola Butte inspired fear in almost everyone.

Uly said, "We're the first to admit how intimidating Lola can be."

"Yes, the intimidation," Juan repeated, nodding. "Oh, yes."

Georgia attempted to clarify. "Are you afraid she won't live with you if there's no marriage ceremony?"

Juan shook his head. "Oh, no." He giggled, a small child's nervous giggle. "After many letters from home, from friends who are remaining in the country of my birth, I now make the decision. I must return to El Salvador. If the wedding must come, Miss Lola will travel to my home. To farm there. Like you here, at this farm." Juan looked to Georgia's lush green beds.

Holding back sarcasm, Uly imagined his youngest daughter's reaction to her groom's new plan. Before all else, Lola was a city girl, and an international city girl at that. He doubted this daughter would agree to El Salvador, married or not.

"Oh, Juan." Georgia struggled to find her gentlest voice. "You must talk with Lola." She grasped his hand. "You must tell her you want to return home."

"She will not the understanding give to me."

"No," Uly agreed. "She probably won't. But you must talk with Lola anyway." The older man shook his head. "How on earth did the pair of you let it get this far?"

"No, no, no, no, Mr. Ulysses. I am not the question as-ked." Juan searched for words. "I am not the consultation given about this wedding Miss Lola is saying will happen."

"She conscripted you?"

Georgia was about to explain what Uly meant when Juan said, "She writes to my mother. When I am making her house so beautiful because I the English classes enjoy and she says she is so sad without the husband and the children. I do not know about her letters. Soon she is showing me the answers from my little brothers. I learn how she is telling all of my family to come to Canada to celebrate with the wedding she says is happening. I see all the letters of reply. How happy my family would be to come to the Canada to live with the pretty schoolteacher. She will teach them English. They will be finding the good jobs at the car factories."

"Do you love Lola?" Before Juan answered Uly, the young man left the swing to pace.

"Oh, yes, we all have the love for the pretty teacher. My hands make her beauty from the wood. Flowers and vines and birds like back home, even the sun and the moon. She is thinking I am asking her to make the marriage with me when I carve this beauty for her, but I am only saying the thank you to her." Juan blushed. "And she is the pretty teacher. She kisses me so good. I like her smells and her making my boss give me holidays and this truck to do the driving. I like this and that. But the marriage, no."

"Let me get this straight," Georgia said. "Lola mistook your gratitude for a marriage proposal, but you couldn't tell her she was mistaken? You are willing to marry her, but only if she'll return to El Salvador to farm with you?"

A smile transformed Juan's face. "This may be so! But I am knowing now the beautiful Miss Lola will not want to come to my country. It is so different from here and I am thinking she will miss Mr. Ulysses and Mrs. Georgia and Mr. Willy, and she will miss all the other New Canadians the students who want the marriage to give to her."

Georgia struggled to take in this new information. "Are there many?"

Juan nodded. "But yes. In my class she had many of the proposals. I think twenty-three and the three girls also from El Salvador who love Miss Lola but do not want the marriage with her, only to do good writing for the assignments. Miss Lola reads our words to us. We listen, and then we all make the good grammar she makes us to use." He smiled a sheepish, child's grin. "We have fun in this class."

Uly made a mental count. "If Lola teaches six classes a year, with twenty men in each class, and only half of them ask to marry her, that's…"

"Surely some are already married?" Georgia asked.

"Yes, but they still make the proposal to this teacher."

"Even you?"

"Oh, yes," Juan said. "I learn how to write I want to marry the beautiful Miss Lola, but though my grammar is now so good, I must not stay here. I see no more places on her house to decorate." Juan shrugged his helplessness. "The place for sitting is made the best. The man who has the hammers and the saws, the man who says I can use the tools of power and drive the big new truck, this man he says I must do his hard working for many more years if I am to get the papers to do the work in this country. Where I live in the Windsor, the City of Roses, it is a sad place with many rooms of peoples who walk to the casino in the nights and in the days are talking to the spirits and crying. The sadness passes through the walls. I want to take all the peoples back to my country. We need the farmers. So many farmers the bad soldiers are killing. And the big companies cut down the trees and the coffee beans plant and the pineapples and spreads the poisons everywhere so the water is no good and the dirt flies away on the wind. If Miss Lola comes, she will teach the English and make the good fight with the good words to the big American companies. She is saying everyday she is liking the fighting of the oppressions. She is teaching us about this in our lessons to learn the good grammar."

Juan's fears and hopes conjured for Georgia the looming TriChem threat. She patted one of Juan's battle-scarred hands, swallowed tears. "You must tell Lola all of this. She's got a great streak of adventure, Juan. You could teach her Spanish." Uly's sudden cough ended her fantasy. She back peddled. "I can't speak to Lola for you, Juan. It was wrong of me to offer. You're the one who has to tell her about your decision to return home. If your relationship is strong, you'll work all this out. If not it's best to…"

Juan giggled again. "I am so big with the fears because Miss Lola may the yells give me and use the words I can't know, and… the ham-i-hi-late give to me."

Uly's colour rose. "If she tries to annihilate you, you'd be well rid of her." Juan shrank from Uly, perplexed.

"Humiliate, not annihilate," Georgia said, knowing she, not Lola, triggered Uly's outrage. "Has she humiliated you in the past?"

"No, no, no. Not to me she does this. But to the many others, yes, at the school. Miss Lola, she gets the big anger when we do not understand what she is trying to be the teacher of information to us."

Speaking to Uly as much as to Juan, Georgia said, "You must be brave enough to discover what you've got here." She searched for inspiration. "Brave and…"

"Forthright?" Uly's tone conveyed no small amount of irony.

"Yes," Georgia agreed, as if he'd spoken a simple truth. "Brave and forthright. No one should be made to marry." She muttered something neither man caught. "You mustn't marry a woman you're afraid of, Juan, here or in El Salvador." Out of the corner of her eye, she saw Uly turn away.

"I thank you so much," Juan said, reaching for Georgia's warm hands. "I will see Miss Lola is talked at."

Alarms went off in Georgia's head. "You'll talk to her?"

Juan blushed. "Yes, yes. Miss Lola will be the talked TO."

Georgia followed him down the path to the gate. "You do mean you'll talk to her, don't you?" She waited a second or two before saying, "All husbands and wives have to learn to talk through tough issues." She rattled on. Uly said nothing.

Juan opened the gate, walked backward to his employer's pickup. Uly and Georgia dogged the groom until, safe inside the loaner pickup, he took off without a backward glance.

Uly muttered something over squealing tires. Without waiting for the truck to round the distant bend, Georgia flung her arms around his neck. "Let's not fight anymore, Uly. This farm needs us." He did not return her embrace.

3

Uly looked to the horizon, moved away from her.

"What is it, Uly. What's troubling you?"

"About Lola's wedding?" She meant something very different and he knew it, felt something like shame when her eyes flashed hurt. They had been in this place before, one of them, obdurate, aggressive, the other, bewildered. He couldn't help his satisfaction that, in this moment, it was Georgia on the backward foot.

"Gracious." She turned from him. "Thursday is only a few days away. Lola is teaching and volunteering every minute until then, at the school and the community centre both. When will she and Juan talk?"

Without thinking, Uly placed his hand on the nape of her neck. "You've got pond skin."

With the touch of his warm hand, Georgia felt a little of her hurt drain away. "I have. I got up early. To reflect. To ask for guidance. I'm sorry if…"

He opened the gate. Before she could step through, he turned on her. "You know Gee, I'm just giving you a taste of your standard of togetherness. When problems come up here, you always go off and dream up solutions. Then you tell me what we're going to do." He wore an expression she couldn't read. She opened her mouth to argue but stopped when he held up his hand. "Let me finish. No matter what you think of the men I worked with, they want to help us. This TriChem thing is too big for any of us to face alone." Although she hadn't moved, he held his arm across the gate's opening as if to block her. "I've never been able to figure it out. What do you have against them? Why don't you like them?"

Georgia said nothing. What could she say? That she'd resented his attachment to these strangers? What was the point when he would match her, grievance for grievance. She floundered in grief until she admitted the truth. "I just… I don't know why anyone would choose Windsor factory work over this farm, especially after what happened to…"

Uly pounced. "Choose? You think we choose factory life over farming? Or office work? Or selling cars?" His anguished face hung over hers. His spittle stung her cheeks. "You live out here in this…cocoon, but in my world…the one you think I *choose* over this life with you, men get born into families who load everything on them as if they're little mini-christs born to save the world. Or at the very least fulfill all their parents' unlived hopes and dreams.

And then they're shipped off to schools that hate boy noise and boy smell and boy humour and make this hatred clear every minute we're made to spend unmoving, learning by rote, in pinching, miserable desks that hold at least a century of our confined, demented energy."

He gestured for her to pass through the gate, but she was too stunned to move. He pushed past her. "And if that's not enough to do us in," he said, turning on her, "we're rattled almost every minute by the promises of escape on every TV channel, unless of course we're white men with our white-collar legacy stories, unless we're driven by money to dominate in every soulless preoccupation dreamed up by the ad boys and girls. The rest of us make sleek beautiful cars to travel down all these roads leading nowhere, nowhere Georgia, because in this goddam world that hates men like me, that blames us for everything, there is nowhere to go. Except to factories. Oh, yes, and to war. To die a noble death for countries that really don't give a damn about us, the human fleshly feeling thinking loving creatures who yearn and dream and…"

Georgia stood frozen at the gate's threshold knowing his rage had been building over years, over decades. When he stepped toward her, she stepped back. "Don't you ever say we choose, Georgia Butte. Maybe we say yes when they shunt us into vocational and trade programs when we're young. But we say yes because we don't yet know how little they value our hands, our grace with making. Maybe we say yes on our application forms for the big three or the Japanese car companies because the money and the car discounts lessen the pain of our incarceration, but we're prisoners of that life, Georgia. Make no mistake about that. Prisoners."

He turned to go, then stepped toward her again. "And yes, I could have lived and worked on this farm, with you, entirely dependent, completely overwhelmed by your gifts. But I didn't want to be afraid of you. I wanted us to be equal partners. I had to find my own place."

He stepped nearer to her. When she stumbled backward, he made no move to steady her. His rage, decades in the making, at this moment blinded him to her fear. "The factories in town have been all mine. The men I work with, we stand together to face the inhumanity of our fate. But Georgia, if any of us could refashion the world, there'd be no factories in it. Not a one." He snorted phlegm. She thought of bulls, of vaulting, of ancient Minoan rites. Of bloody sacrifices. She moved toward him slowly, as if he were of Lady Jane's world and not her own. Before she could touch him, he fled.

4

In the emotional aftermath of their battle, Georgia looked for comfort in the garden. She breathed slowly as she weeded, aware of the relentless, rising temperature, the stinging sweat in her eyes, the screams of cicadas. If she lost herself in the work for a moment, Uly's image, raging, hovered before her, sucking her back into the muck of their battle. When a desultory breeze rattled the front gate, she heard guidance. "Walk," it said. "Take your confusion and your heartbreak to the clean line of the horizon." Obedient, she rose to her feet.

At the shoulder of the road, she felt gripped by a compulsion to visit the Miner corn field. "No doubt some unfinished business from yesterday," she said, fighting numbness. She headed for Alice Maude's driveway, but swerved to the right after only a few steps. Grim, she accepted the punishment of walking the long way around, a walk that would take her up their concession road, along the busy highway leading to and from town, and down the Miner concession road, this route radiating blistering asphalt heat.

Georgia hadn't been out on this part of the road for the better part of a week. While she usually enjoyed picking up trash and humming along with the drainage-ditch choirs, in her desolation she trudged along the dusty shoulder blind to the landscape. Her fight with Uly replayed again and again in her imagination. Each time her defensiveness against his accusation grew. Salty sweat dripped into her eyes, temporarily blinding her. With a vicious swipe, she used her dress to dry her forehead and blot her eyes. In a moment of unusual honesty, she admitted she had made several important decisions without him.

Almost immediately, her defensiveness kicked in. He was gone so much. He told her, countless times, whatever she decided was fine. She stopped, ambushed now by her own rage, convinced he'd set her up for this guilt, this bad-guy role.

Self-righteous, she made her counter-arguments. All the years since his retirement, Uly had chosen to return to those inhuman places when he might have stayed to work with her at the farm. What did he mean he felt overshadowed by her? Why couldn't he see that the reading didn't matter, that even with his dyslexia his intuition made them equals in every way? Her mind churned up all the times he left the farm for his city life, settling finally on his intention to buy Webster's farm with men from the plant. The possibility terrified her. She felt invaded.

Unnerved, she pushed Uly's alliance with the men into the depths of her heart, counting on this overburdened organ to contain her terror until she could decide what to do. In her anguish, she summoned Lola as replacement obsession, deciding she would call her youngest daughter that afternoon, never mind her resolve to leave sorting out the wedding tangles to the terrified groom. But her plans to meddle in Lola's business could not compete with the haunting specter of Uly's distorted face. She told herself she must not forget his raging unfairness, not for a single moment.

Feeling martyred, she decided she would do her part to prepare for Thursday's wedding, no matter what the bride and groom might do. People were converging on the farm from near and far for the event. With manic force, Georgia conjured people dancing and singing no matter what might happen between her youngest, head-strong daughter and her bolting groom.

When she reached Webster's driveway, the Jones farm claimed her attention. She turned to look at its familiar beauty full on. Before her an ordinary farm basked in violent sunshine. Beyond the frame of the picturesque, a somnolent, poisonous, giant stirred. TriChem. In the distance, the farmhouse front porch called to her. Two cottonwoods, old trees that had been planted decades before she'd been born, beckoned to her. She remembered how she, Uly, his sister, and Webster christened them the tire-swing cottonwoods to distinguish them from the cottonwood grove where they met for wilder adventures.

Her past, she suddenly realized, had been absorbed into these trees as nails had been absorbed, the rings growing around them, swallowing them whole. Until this moment, she'd lost the pleasures of the tire-swing cottonwoods to the busyness of her farmer's life. If Webster's children had their way, the old trees would be destroyed. The house where her grandmother and mother had been born would be bulldozed. No doubt TriChem would construct an efficient concrete box in which to concoct its poisons, its smoke stacks and exhaust fans spewing death in all directions. She saw this horror as she saw Lila's long-ago rape, again and again. Weeping impotent tears, a car's approach prompted her to turn her back to the road. When the car passed, she moved on.

At the southern edge of the Jones property the voluptuous hedgerow of lilac bushes offered her temporary relief from inner tortures taking on the shape of a fat green dragon, its dead blossoms frozen puffs of smoke. "Last year's rain made this year's flowers," Grandma Jones reminded her. The Jones lilacs were mostly deep purple although here and there, scattered among the French exotics, a few paler varieties could be counted on to perfume the early spring air. The lilacs were one of her Aunt Vi's numerous legacies. "If you were mine," she whispered, "I'd plant a few white ones for contrast. And columbine along the inside edge, to keep you company in spring." She blew a kiss to the abundant, green, heart-shaped leaves.

Resuming her walk, she became aware of her sundress straps chafing her shoulders. Looking down, she took in her dusty, flip-flopped feet. She plodded on, the cicadas echoing Uly's outrage. An impotent fury seized her. What was he doing, moaning about boys in school? Schools were appalling for everyone, most of them, anyway. And why was he telling her about them? Was it her fault he worked with men whose parents didn't fight the system? Could she be blamed for his dyslexia? Her mind raced on, distracted temporarily by a tree or the memory of a barking dog, then returning, always returning, to Uly's distorted, raging face.

At the corner gas station, Georgia resisted going in for a glass of water, feeling she deserved her terrible thirst. She was at least a kilometer from the Butte farm now, an easy walk on a good day. This was not a good day. For the life of her, she couldn't understand why she was on this hellish journey beneath an unforgiving sun. Guilt, she knew from long experience, could be indulged anywhere, and in comfort. As she turned onto the Miner concession road her heart lifted. In the distance, generous maples promised shade.

She quickened her pace, intermittently thinking of Thursday and ancient guests suffering heat stroke or worse, cardiac arrest, beneath the trendy yellow-and-white-striped marquee. She thought of Lola's many student proposals, puzzling again over her daughter's absurd wedding demands. Deer flies bit her bare, sweaty arms. She wished for a horse's tail. She wished for her bee-keeper's hat.

Uttering a great involuntary wail of frustration at her absurd situation, she stopped. She would return home. There was nothing preventing her from doing so. She told herself she need not be afraid of Uly. He was simply expressing feelings he'd been storing up for…

An inner prickling interrupted her mental chaos. She glanced around, aware of something she was called to see. She froze. A few feet ahead of her, at the lip of the drainage ditch to her left, a bare human foot pointed skyward.

She squinted against the sun. Yes. A foot. A human foot. A foot protruding at an odd angle from the ditch. Inching forward, she steeled herself against the grisly possibility of a hit and run. Upon closer inspection, she found the foot dusty but unbloody. It was a young foot, by her lights. For an instant, she gave in to the terror of what she might find detached from this small bit of human fragility.

She stepped closer. A sunburned leg attached the foot to a body, a leg in blue-jean cutoffs. A matching leg rested a little further down the ditch's slope, its foot sandal-shod, an empty sandal nearby.

Above the shorts, a t-shirted chest, above this, shoulders, arms attached and spread wide. Above the shoulders, a sunburned neck and, at last, an intact, human head. She peered into the face. He appeared to be quite young, she decided, far too young to be dead.

Moving swiftly, she picked up the closest arm, felt the wrist for a pulse. There it was, faint but steady. He was alive. She stood.

Guessing the closest house to be farther away than the gas station behind her, she turned. Walking quickly, she coaxed and pleaded with the faint heart beat to continue its rhythmic dance. Despite the heat, she broke into a bone-jangling trot.

5

The Ontario Provincial Police arrived first, confirming after much radio static-and-crackle and a search of the young man's pockets that Georgia had found a Windsor man who'd not been seen or heard from since the previous Thursday evening. The garrulous officer, oblivious to Georgia's overwhelm, continued to recite the facts of the case long after it was productive to do so. Georgia took in the basics. The lad had been out drinking with friends at the Kingsville Hotel for their usual Thursday night blow out. When he didn't check in by Saturday, one of his drinking buddies called his parents. Fearing the worst, they notified the Ontario Provincial Police. "Another hour in this sun," the OPP officer said for the fourth or fifth time, "would have done him in."

Georgia feared a similar fate. Mercifully, the ambulance's arrival distracted the officer and she was able to disappear into a loose knotting of neighbours and passersby. The officer left soon after she'd made her escape into the small crowd, called by more static-distorted cries announcing yet another crisis. Soon after, with screams and bloody flashes, the ambulance bolted toward the heat-shimmering horizon and Leamington General Hospital. Finally, the distant landscape swallowed what appeared to be a squat, red-eyed, white beast somewhere in the vicinity of the Graham Side Road.

Georgia threaded through a crowd animated by gossip about the woman who'd saved the young man's life. With surprising energy, she walked away from this small, chatty group toward the short-cut through Alice Maude's sugar bush. She stopped when she came to the hedgerow boundary marking the Miner bird-sanctuary acreage.

She blinked and blinked again. About fifty feet in front of her a taupe mantle flecked with black and white lifted, settled, lifted again. Once more, she thought of a giant smoothing the coverlet on an enormous bed. The scene, identical to the vision she'd seen with Alice Maude the day before, included geese, hundreds of them, moving as a single being, lifting, falling, lifting, drowsing down. Staring at this vision, a sound drew her attention, a high wail from the midst of the birds. She stood very still, feeling what she couldn't see. He was here, dancing a heart-beat step among the feeding birds. She set out across the field hoping to find him.

In only a few steps she entered a barely penetrable sea of grief, knowing well this feeling of indescribable loss. Sometimes the reasons for the land's pooling emotions would come unbidden and Georgia would know what it was she was passing through and do what she could to honour and release the sorrow. Other times, as now, she was given the raw suffering of a place without its cause. The first time she'd shared these experiences with Uly, he called her awareness of these sorrows a blessing, because "so few feel much of anything these days and all those denied feelings have to go somewhere."

Why not, Georgia mused, to wild places that healed? Why not to the protected Miner corn field and its geese? As this current wave of grief receded, she moved forward, no longer hearing the young man's song.

An unfamiliar energy took hold of her. She picked up her pace, moved swiftly toward the inviting coolness of Alice Maude's sugar bush. Desperate to be home, to sit in her cool kitchen and ponder this experience, she rushed forward.

6

When Georgia reached the edge of the Vaughan woods, crows and jays began to bicker. Across the road, a peacock screamed. Georgia's mouth went dry when Alice Maude emerged from the shadows, a splitting maul in her upraised hand. "Alice Maude!" Hearing Georgia's voice, the younger woman slid unfriendly eyes over her neighbour's face and body. "I was on a walk. I was taking the short-cut through your woods. It's too hot to take the long way home. I didn't think you'd mind."

Alice Maude spoke to Georgia as she would a stranger. "This place is contaminated. You can't come in here."

Georgia forced a smile. Behind her neighbour, Lady Jane appeared in the trees. "I've come for my horse," Georgia said, not taking her eyes from the maul. "She strayed into your back pasture."

Alice Maude relaxed. "All right. Walk her through."

Lady Jane stepped to Georgia's side. "Do you remember, Alice Maude? You brought me here yesterday. You wanted me to hear the young man sing. Erie's husband, George, he's like Lady Jane. He died a long time ago, in a car crash just down the road. You saw the fireball. Uly and I did, too."

With a glimmer of understanding in her eyes, Alice Maude turned back to the woods. Georgia and Lady Jane followed. "Tess is coming, Alice Maude," Georgia said, searching for a way to bring her old friend into their present time and place. "She's flying in from Germany on Tuesday. For Lola's wedding. You asked if Uly would pick her up at the airport."

"Germany?" Alice Maude struggled to remember. "Oh, yes, my Tessie is a reporter. She's on a holiday from the war in the Middle East. She's leaving that war, but she's in danger from the war at home." Alice Maude offered Georgia the splitting maul. Georgia took it, slipping her arm around her friend's shoulders.

"What can I do to help? Do you have her room ready?"

"Oh, no. She can't stay here unless…" Alice Maude pulled away.

Willy trotted up the path. Seeing him, Alice Maude whispered, "Willy is the best boy, but only you and I know why." She stroked the goat's snout. "Willy ended all that torture. Remember, Georgia, it's our secret. I made him a very special breakfast this morning. I have so much to thank him for."

"Willy loves you, Maudey. And Tess is safe now."

Snatching the maul, Alice Maude contradicted Georgia with a violent shake of her head. "Willy's done enough. He can't help with this new thing. It's just too big. Bad things leave trails. They're still here, waiting for her, like rabid dogs, all the things he did to her. If I don't get rid of them, Tess will have to feel all the bad things again. She hates me because I couldn't stop him." Alice Maude lifted her apron to wipe her face then added, frantic, "Tess disappeared so suddenly I thought she turned into a robin and flew out the window. It's what I always longed to do."

With slow sure steps, the women emerged from the sugar bush. Alice Maude surveyed her back field. "But then my sister called from Toronto and told me Tess wasn't a bird at all. She'd gone to stay with Gracie. I didn't see Tess again until she finished university and got her first job. When she did come home, it was to fight with him. To let him see her strength. To frighten him as he'd frightened her." As they walked toward the Vaughan farmhouse, Georgia felt pulled through a force field separating the hidden from the revealed. The women journeyed the rest of the way in silence. Lady Jane disappeared into her other realm. Willy plodded a little behind.

7

"You found a man in a ditch?" Lila cried. "Given all the running I do on the roads around here, you'd think I'd be the one to have that privilege."

"It's a merciful universe," Lola said. "It knows what it's doing when it needs men found before they die of dehydration."

"Piss off," said Lila.

As defense against Uly's icy silence, Georgia concentrated on shelling peas. After several minutes, she looked up from their malachite greenness, startled to hear her own voice. "I should call the hospital to see how my young man is doing."

Lola sat beside Georgia at the table. "I'll finish these," she said. Her hands remained unmoving in her lap. "You know, Mother, whether he turns out to be an ax murderer or saint, your fates are inextricably entwined. He owes you a life now."

"You're nuts," Lila snapped. "The guy didn't ask Ma to save him. If he'd asked and she'd said yes or no, then there'd be something between them, but she volunteered."

"You're wrong, Lila. He owes Georgia a life." She turned to her father. "Isn't that so, Ulysses." It was a statement, not a question.

Uly fastened his eyes on Georgia when he answered. "Yes, Lola, everything is connected whether we give our permission or not." Georgia held her breath, remembering Lila's question about why the boys who'd raped her didn't know they were connected. Uly's voice brought her back to the present. "But Lila's right, too. Responding to a conscious call for help creates a special bond." Georgia knew he was thinking of the men from the city, of their call for help in finding meaningful work. She wanted to run, to Mae's, to the safety of a person who shared her own meaningful work.

Oblivious to the highly charged tension between her parents, Lola sneered. "Here we go, Solomon. To keep the peace, chop another baby in half." Twitching with worry, Georgia left her place at the kitchen table to gaze out the screen door. Still, since finding the young man in the ditch, she felt more hopeful than she had when obsessing over her fight with Uly in infernal heat. She was about to open the door when Lila unwittingly began a fresh quarrel with her sister. In spite of the urge to escape, she felt held in place as witness.

"What was Juan doing out here without you this morning? Was he…" Lola's sudden distress surprised Lila.

"Juan was here this morning? What's going on, Georgia?"

Her mother resented the assumption that she was the more likely parent to pass on necessary information. She did her best to restore calm. "Juan hasn't talked with you?"

"No, he hasn't. We had a date to go over our vows, but he had a rush job for the shop. He's stripping an armoire. It's such a waste of his talent." Lila opened her mouth, then closed it. Lola mistook her sister's compassion for cruelty. "You needn't gloat, Lila. At least I haven't alienated all the men in Essex County."

Lila sat beside her father hoping for a way to undo the unintended snarl in her relationship with younger sister. "Is this a Bowie knife, Dad?" Uly laughed at this absurdity. Lola grew more agitated.

Imperious, she said, "You have to tell me what's going on. I'm going to marry the man in a few days. Was he trying to figure out how to do some special thing at the wedding? Was he getting help with his vows?"

Lila did her best to distract Lola. "I finished the last big Herm last night. Do you want to see it? You can decide how you want to use them on Thursday."

Lola turned on her. "Your sculptures probably horrified Juan."

Uly stood. His knife clattered to the floor. "Lola," he said. "Go home. Talk to Juan. If it were a conversation we could share with you, we would, but this is between you and Juan. You've told us not to interfere and we've respected your wishes. Please respect our decision to stay out of your affairs."

"Affairs!" Lola fastened on the word. "You think we're sleeping together. You think we couldn't honour our decision to abstain from pre-marital sex."

"Who cares whether you have sex or not," said Lila.

"Lila, you're not helping," Georgia said. "You go along, too. This situation needs time and space to sort itself out. Lola, find Juan. Talk with him."

Uly gathered his knives and whetstone and headed for his workshop without meeting Georgia's eyes. From the sanctuary of the cool dark kitchen, Georgia watched Lila put her arm around her younger sister as they walked through the garden. When Lola pulled away, Lila took a moment before trying again. The second time she reached out, Lola relaxed against Lila. The pair walked to the orchard arm-in-arm.

8

When Georgia arrived at Uly's workshop, she found him sitting on his bench, his elbows propped on his worktable's scarred surface. She attempted lightness. "Contemplating your next project?"

"No, Georgia Butte. You know damn well I'm contemplating buying your cousin's farm with people you despise."

She lowered her head, dreading this conversation, knowing they must have it. "Uly, I can't say I'm sorry for my feelings, about the factories, about the men. They're my feelings after all." She struggled to hold back tears. "Those other things…about school… about choices…about being an equal partner…I don't know what to say. You must know how much I love and value you." She sobbed when he turned his face away, took a breath, began again.

"Surely you know I've never wanted to overwhelm or overpower you. And when I made decisions on my own, I never meant to shut you out. You weren't here so much of the time. You said you trusted me with the necessary decisions. You said as much many times."

He sat mute, his fingers playing silent melodies on the surface of his workbench. He cursed her infallible memory. He searched for a defense but found none.

"What if we lose our farm?" she said, her voice quiet, clear. "Can you say we won't if we risk mortgaging it? Seventy is too old to begin again, Uly. If we lost our home, I'd die."

His soft response surprised her. "I would too, Gee." For a moment he surveyed the order he'd created in his work space. "But what would be so bad about dying? At least we'd die trying to do something worthwhile." He turned hard eyes on her. "You've had the best of everything out here on this farm, Georgia.

While people have been breathing bad air, drinking bad water, working at jobs that kill the life in them, you've been living the life you wanted to live, eating good food and only now and then feeling the direct effects of people who don't know how to live lightly on this beautiful Earth. I think I might be ready to die for a good cause, but I'm damned sure I'm not ready to live next to some experimental lab that douses poisons on plants and animals and calls it research. Are you?"

She dragged one of the straw bales they used for mulching to the doorway and sat, a faraway look in her eyes. "Have you dowsed about this?"

His voice bloomed disgust. "I don't have to dowse about this. It's very simple. Either we buy the land next door or we let TriChem buy it and stand by while everything we love, every blade of grass, every tree, every bird, every insect, every animal, and yes, every person, is poisoned. You know damn well I don't have to dowse for this, Georgia, and you don't have to be clairvoyant to know I'm right."

She fought scalding tears. "But I don't want to lose this place. I hold its Soul as it holds mine. Uly, this farm is as much my partner as you are."

"More so, I'd say." When she flinched, he relented. "Here's the thing, Gee. If we want to hold on to this little patch of green, we have to fight for it. Doing it with the men from the plant is a chance for them to create something good, away from the heat and noise and work that wears out their fingers and knees and shoulders. This isn't some crazy scheme, Georgia. It's responsible. It's what I've been led to do."

"I haven't been led to do it."

His voice trembled with indignation. "I recall when you

opened this house to those troubled kids to help them connect with the natural world because you knew we were part of something bigger than both of us here, something that could heal people, I supported your vision. Having kids like Wayne visit is no different than having the men from the plant here. This current vision isn't any different from the one you had all those years ago. Except this vision is mine."

"The scale is different. We don't risk losing a thing when we have troubled young people here."

He looked at her long and hard before he spoke. "We've risked a good deal, Georgia. Not in money, I'll grant you, but in safety. I felt anger from some of those kids so big it could knock me off my feet and slit your throat. I've seen Lila look as if she were putting her head into the lion's mouth whenever an adolescent boy considered her with appetite instead of friendship. We've risked living across from Professor Vaughan. Now, we both know we risk living across from his widow. She's got so many cracks in her even she doesn't know what might leak out." Georgia closed her eyes, Alice Maude's splitting maul glinting in her imagination.

Uly waited for her to speak. When she didn't, he said, "We've risked having our own children, having them hurt, like Lila, die, like little Wendell. Hell, you've risked growing organic when most of the farmers around here laughed and waited for you to fail. It's only been in the last few years that the men in this county have spoken of what you do with any respect. You risked being wrong for forty years before that, Georgia, and I supported you. Don't say we haven't taken risks."

"Yes, you're right. We have."

Giddy with victory, he pulled her to her feet, returned the embrace he couldn't return earlier that morning. "Life has been one adventure after another because of what you see that others can't. I've learned more than I ever counted on in this marriage. But we can't rest on past triumphs, Gee. We can't let TriChem happen. And we can't pretend the two of us can handle a corporate giant alone. We can't let that company buy Webster's land and ruin your old farm along with every farm in this county."

She thought of her plan to ask her mother to buy Webster's farm, opened her mouth to tell him, but he ignored her.

"Remember what our daughters said during their little skirmish earlier today. Everything is connected. As soon as they start killing things at Webster's, they're killing them here and everywhere else."

"I know." To avoid more strife, she kept her plan to have her mother buy Webster's farm to herself. She shook her head to relieve her sorrow. "I thought we'd have both farms to leave to the girls. And their children."

He laughed. "You, who've counseled against having children just because of cultural expectations? Who lives every day of your life painfully aware of the burden of the human population on this planet? Who regularly says the pinnacle of evolution is the worm? Georgia, you of all people can't use the legacy argument, at least with any credibility."

Uly held her close. Together they stood in the rectangle of ripe afternoon sunlight shouldering its way through the open workshop doors. "Tomorrow is Monday," he said. "The bank opens at ten."

She pulled away.

"If I said I won't do it until you're sure and my hesitation cost us this chance to beat TriChem, I would lose respect for both of us. We've never been indecisive in a crisis. We've always found common ground. I want you with me in this." His excitement grew. He became garrulous. "When I went to work at the plant, even though you didn't like it, you told me to do what I had to do. It's what we've always done, what we feel called to do. Together. Apart."

"Don't you see?" she said, desperate to be honest with him. "This scheme of yours risks our home. You want to farm not one but two farms with city men who..."

Something troubling clouded his eyes but cleared too quickly for her to name. While she heard his words clearly, she knew in her bones he held back something vital from her. "We've already lost this farm if TriChem is successful in getting Webster's land. With the men from work, we have a chance to protect the whole county. We have a chance to keep out something destructive and create something good."

It hit her then. They weren't going to farm Web's place. "What kind of 'something good'?"

He looked away. "We haven't worked it all out yet."

She put her hand on his chest. "Tell me, Uly. What are you and the city men planning?"

"Leave it, Georgia. We're still working on it." He pulled her close again, this time to hide his face. "We'll figure it out as we go along. We'll ask for guidance, just as you and I do for the hundred-and-one little things we do on this farm every day."

Stepping away from her, he gestured to the wide clear sky. "Look at all this light. I can't believe it's after four. Let's go for a swim."

Numb, she followed him into the meadow's chattering grasses. A breeze ushered in crow talk from a secret convention in Mae's back woods. Georgia stopped to listen to the cacophonous black horde. Uly walked ahead. When the crows finished with her, she resumed her walk, her eyes settling on his diminishing figure. Time continued to whittle away at him. His stooping posture made her weep.

9

An hour later, on their walk from the pond to the house, Uly suggested they thaw chili for their supper. "We have lots of potatoes," he said, making no sign that her silence troubled him. "I'll make hash browns and a salad to go with…" He stopped. Georgia looked up from her foot-path preoccupations to see Lola and Juan, stony faced, on opposite sides of the platform swing. Georgia marveled at the easy way her husband of fifty years pretended all was fine. She stood back as he hugged Juan, kissed him on both cheeks, then embraced Lola. Her resistance telegraphed more trouble.

"I would like very much to eat here with you again," Juan said. Georgia heard a secret plea in the young man's voice.

When the men left for the kitchen, Georgia took Lola's hand. "I'm glad you're here, Beauty." She stroked the curls springing to life around Lola's face. "It's so humid your hair is curling." She paused before asking what she had to ask. "Have you talked with Juan?"

Lola's face crumpled. "He wants me to move to El Salvador…to give up everything here… Who knows?" she cried. "Maybe he doesn't really want a wedding at all. Maybe he expects me to live in sin."

"Lola, you know very well this nonsense about sin and sex is alien to nine tenths of the world." She paused to swallow her anger but couldn't prevent the sarcasm in her voice when she pointed out that Lola was a very recent convert to the notion of sex as sinful before marriage.

"You and Daddy got married. You didn't have sex before."

Georgia pushed down the sense memory of her calculated loss of virginity with her cousin Webster. "Your father and I were raised in different times. But long before we went to Judge Hart, we were as married as people can be. We felt the bond between us when we weren't much more than children." She took a moment to savour this truth. "The marriage ceremony came after the real thing – our spiritual connection – as a belated celebration." She resisted adding that their official marriage had done nothing to prevent Uly's numerous extra-marital affairs and her experiment with her cousin, one that led the way to pleasurable college experiences and insured she was anything but inexperienced when she did marry Ulysses Butte.

Lola tucked rebellious curls behind her ears. "I don't believe that. I think saying the marriage ceremony is just an afterthought in a real marriage is a way to prettify lust. I could marry anybody and make it last. I propose every year and all kinds of people want to marry me. But I want to marry Juan, because he's made my house beautiful, and because he's so public with his devotion." She smiled her dreamy, kewpie-doll smile. "The whole city knows someone thinks I'm special." The kewpie doll vanished as suddenly as she appeared. "Don't you see, Mother? He transformed the commonplace into something rare. Anyone can see this rarity when they see the beauty he created for my home."

Georgia weighed the pros and cons of expressing the tirade bubbling up from her roiling gut. She'd been worn down by the unresolved situation with Uly and her frustration leapt out with a life of its own. "In spite of all your education, you seem determined to act on all kinds of delusions, Lola. You know perfectly well that in this day and age the ceremony of marriage and the ad-driven courtship that precedes it is a patriarchal concept that's been used for centuries to legitimize and delegitimize children, imprison women, hoard property, and generally objectify what should be loved. You are a very intelligent woman. I don't know how all you've learned, about the Inquisition and the Burning Times, allows you for one moment to entertain a belief in church-state sanctioned marriage as the one true way."

Lola turned pleading eyes on her mother. "You say that because you've always had the luxury of believing whatever you want. Raising Lala and Lela and Lila to be non-conformists, treating Willy like a member of the family. Don't you care what they say about us? Don't you want at least one of us to be normal?"

Georgia suppressed a horrified laugh. "Lola, what's gotten into you? Normal never used to matter to you, a girl who's always shared her genius for learning about the world. You never cared about others' opinions of us. What's changed?"

"I'm thirty-three," Lola wailed. "I want my own family. I want to walk down the street and not have people whisper about me."

Georgia grasped Lola's hands, cold despite the hot, humid day. She thought of all the things she and Uly had done differently from other people, as a couple, as farmers, as parents. Refusing the lavish wedding her mother wanted for her. Refusing to farm with chemicals developed for warfare. Schooling the three older girls at home and starting the Saturday School for county children when Lola decided to attend a "real" school. All through her school years, Lola had repeated many of her classmates' tales about her 'weird' family but seemed to wear their gossip as a badge of honour. "It's important to be weird," Georgia cried, startling Lola. "Everyone has the capacity to develop a wild uniqueness. Most people cling to conformity because they're afraid of the magic all about us."

"No one is ever going to love me," Lola wailed. "Out here I'm always going to be that big-breasted brainer, Smart Food, from the Butte farm. Where people dance naked in the woods and drink blood."

Georgia couldn't help but laugh. "Who says we drink blood?"

"It doesn't matter if it's true or not. It's what people say because they don't understand what you're doing. Or why."

When Juan and Ulysses completed supper preparations, to prevent supper from being completely silent, the father of the bride encouraged the groom to describe the foods he liked to cook. Listening with polite interest until the end of their meal, Lola insisted she do the dishes alone. As she studied her youngest daughter on her walk to the house, Georgia knew that Lola's anger, like her father's, had been brewing for a very long time. Listening to Uly and Juan make their polite conversation about tortillas and spinach salsa, Georgia longed to visit with Mae. They would laugh together and their problems would shrink. When the gate rattled, Georgia half expected to see Essex County's Black Madonna, her arms laden with apple mint, walking toward her. But it was Alice Maude who appeared, followed by a preening, prancing Willy. Their neighbour had dressed him in what had been in its day a dapper tweed jacket. The tan trousers she'd chosen were cinched around Willy's sinuous belly with green garden twine. In a large basket, she carried the goat's shorn mohair.

"Oh, my," said Uly, groping for Georgia's hand.

"You two have been busy," Georgia said. "You're in time for dessert, Alice Maude. I believe you know Juan, Lola's..."

"He told me to do it," Alice Maude said, ignoring Juan and thrusting the basket at Georgia. "He just wouldn't leave me alone until I sheared it all off. He picked out the suit. It belonged to the professor, but don't worry, I beat every last bit of him out of the jacket and the trousers. Then I washed them in the washing machine and dried them in the sun. I have to go now. Tess might call again." All three of them watched Alice Maude glide shadow-like through the gate toward home.

Willy cantered around the swing, tossing his head and biting proudly at the lapel of the tweed jacket. "Where's your tie?" Uly asked. "Do you have a date?"

From the kitchen doorway, Lola uttered a blood curdling cry. "This does it," she said, rushing from the house. "Juan, you can come with me now or you can get a ride into town with Ulysses tomorrow morning." Juan leapt to attention.

"It was the good supper, Mr. Ulysses," the young man called over his shoulder. "I am liking so very much the home-cooking chili sauce on the potatoes." These were his last words before buckling himself into Lola's thundering car.

When they were alone, Georgia unbuttoned Willy's coat. "She doesn't seem to have cut him."

"I'd be surprised if she cut him. Alice Maude sheared sheep for decades."

"I know, but I can't say I like the idea of her carrying around sharp objects these days."

As she spoke, Georgia caught another glimpse of Alice Maude's small, deadly splitting maul hovering in the air above her head.

10

With the blisteringly hot evening pressing close around her, Georgia sat in the garden summoning revelations that refused to come. Her stomach knotted. At the sound of hammering, she glanced toward the house. Inside, Uly tackled their summer-kitchen ventilation system's obstinate refusal to work. Earlier, he speculated that something blocked the main exhaust and set to discovering what the something might be. A scent diverted Georgia's attention, some floral mix that made her temporarily forget her challenges with Uly and Lola.

"I can't see which way to go," she told the deepening dusk. "I'm lost, utterly lost." She heard footsteps coming up the path from the pond and hoped Lila would be gentle with her, but no one appeared.

"I don't want to give a damn about losing you," she told the farm. "I know you're not really mine. But why do we have to be taking risks all the time? I want someone else to make this problem go away."

She felt as alone as when she'd left the city to make a life with Uly on the Butte farm. The woods, the meadows, the pond, she already loved and felt part of, but the daunting task of coaxing food out of the soil frightened her. It had been Uly's mother, Spring, who'd coached her through that first tumultuous year before she and Jason left with the traveling Hilberry Theater troupe to crisscross the globe lamenting the universal tragedies of life.

Uly's voice ended her reverie. "Phone for you, Georgia," he called. She wanted to tell him she needed to be in the garden, to assure and be assured she and the farm would remain together no matter what fate sent their way. Dutifully, she walked to the house.

"Hello, Mrs. Butte?" a soft, rasping voice said.

"Yes?"

"I want to thank you."

Her impatience at being interrupted leapt up. "Who is this? Thank me for what?"

"You don't know me, Ma'am, but you saved my life today." Georgia saw again the dusty, fragile foot. "Ma'am?"

"Yes, I'm here," she said, cradling the phone between her

shoulder and ear to smooth her hair, as if he could see her, angry, sweaty, unkempt. "You must be the young man in the ditch."

"The young man in the hospital bed now, but earlier today, yes, the young man in the ditch." She heard him struggle for breath. "They tell me I have you to thank for being able to watch the sunset tonight."

Her eyes took in the swatch of sky framed by the window over the sink. Layers and layers of hot-pink and lemon-yellow extravagance stratified blue-black velvet. It was what Lila called their K-Mart sky, because it was so much like a dime-store painting. "I'm so glad you're feeling better," she said, grateful to share the sky's temporary garishness with this stranger.

"Oh, I'm feeling pretty awful." His attempted laughter became a cough. "But I'm feeling well enough to call and thank you, Mrs. Butte."

"What's your name?" she asked. Not hearing her, he ended the call.

She called to Uly. "My young man from the ditch. He's alive."

"I'm glad to hear one very good thing happened today."

"Now he's shorn, I'm going to give Willy a bath."

"I don't know why you bother. It's the mohair that stinks."

Georgia smiled, held back her opinion of Willy's old male body. After Uly's earlier rage about working class boys and men being devalued, she did not want to be lumped with schools and their hatred of male smells and sounds.

11

Comforted by echoes of the young man's phone call, Georgia hummed on her walk toward the amber light winking out from Mae's living room window. The air, cool and fresh now, carried the scent of Mae's apple mint. Georgia moved into the fragrance, relished its caress on her skin, her hair. She would pick a sprig to tuck behind her ear. Aging ears were always so smelly. Mae's mint provided the perfect antidote.

At the half-way point, she stopped to look for the old sign warning of tractor dangers among the leafy hedgerow branches at the farm's northern boundary. Finding it, she traced the weathered marks, awareness creeping up her spine. "Danger, Hidden Driveway. Drive Slowly. Farm Wagons Turning," now announced the farm's current life, "Dance/ ////// //////// ///// Slow//Farm ////// ///////," the illegible letters transforming into dancers gathering each Friday night in the farm's Dance Temple. "Oh," she whispered, knowing how this synchronicity would please Uly.

Behind her, a car made the turn onto the shoulder of the road in front of the Butte farm. She turned, retraced her steps, hoping Lola had come back to make peace. But it was not Lola who'd arrived at the farm.

"Hey, Gee." The familiar voice shocked Georgia. She searched the darkness until Wayne stepped from leafy roadside shadows. She rushed to embrace him.

"You've come home. Who brought you? How long can you stay?" To these questions, Wayne shrugged his best teen shrug.

They walked side by side, intentionally bumping shoulders. "I brought a surprise for you," he said. "A big surprise." The car lights she'd seen belonged to an old Honda Civic with almost as many bumper stickers as Uly's truck.

"Whose car is this?"

Wayne's grin broadened. "You'll see. You'll meet her. She's part of the surprise."

By the time Georgia and Wayne arrived, Uly had settled their guests in the living room. A middle-aged woman, two small girls, and a young woman all jumped to their feet when Georgia joined them. "Georgia," Uly said, leading her to the younger woman. "This is Sadra, Wayne's mother."

Georgia grasped the young woman's hands. Shy, Sadra nodded at Georgia before locking her eyes on the floor. Wayne pushed the little girls toward Georgia. "These are my sisters, Kim, and Karen."

"Wow, such Canadian names," Georgia said. "I suspect they got them from the same Canuks who christened you."

Wayne laughed. "And this here is Ms Welding. She was my settlement worker when I first got to Kitchener."

Ms Welding embraced Georgia. "I am so happy to meet you, Mrs. Butte. Wayne's told me so much about you, about his time on this farm. Before the judge sent him to you, he participated in my Welcome-to-Canada classes."

Wayne took Georgia's hand. "Ms Welding read me stories and let me draw. She found us in Hamilton this morning."

"I asked the judge to send Wayne to you when he was arrested last year for taking items from unlocked vehicles. I knew lockup wouldn't do him any good. Thankfully, his judge agreed."

"It's good at least a few judges are using opportunities for learning instead of punishment," Georgia said, delighted by this new development in the farm's life.

"I still don't get it," Wayne said. "Back home when I found stuff, I was a hero. I found things nobody else could find. Even wood."

Uly carried in a tray of tea and grape juice. "Did Wayne tell you about Willy?" Uly asked the girls.

Whatever he said, Wayne's translation made his entire family giggle. "Where is he, Uly?"

"I think he might be hiding," Uly said. "He got a haircut today. He was fine when he wore the suit Alice Maude dressed him in, but when it came off for his bath, he seemed embarrassed. He may not want to meet new people just now."

"Can I talk to him? Is he upstairs?"

"You might find him nesting on the shoes in our closet," Georgia said. "That's his favourite place to be sad."

Wayne retrieved an ancient view master and slides from the wooden box of toys behind the sofa and took a moment to show his sisters how to work the contraption then took the stairs two at a time. Georgia watched him go, marveling at the ease with which this young boy wove himself into the fabric of their family.

Ms Welding inclined her head in the direction of Wayne's mother's soft whispers. "Sadra is very grateful to you. She says Wayne begged her to let him stay last September, but she wanted him to start a new life with her and his sisters when his probation was over. Hamilton seemed the very best place to do this. It was her husband's brother who sponsored them after her husband was killed in one of the camps. The brother lives in Hamilton. Initially, they were settled in Kitchener, on their own, but after Wayne got into trouble, this brother thought it best to move the family in with him." When she paused, Georgia encouraged her to go on.

"You know the story, I'm sure, Mrs. Butte. Her brother-in-law insisted her children needed a firm hand when challenged to justify his physical punishments and restrictions on their movements." Sadra whispered to Ms Welding.

"Sadra wants me to tell you that he didn't permit the children to go to school and forced them to work the night shifts for his cleaning business. After cleaning offices all night, they slept during the day, virtual prisoners in his tiny apartment." Georgia leaned forward to better hear Ms Welding's lowered voice. "Sadra," she said, nodding at Wayne's mother, "said he tried to coerce her into prostitution. She suspected he made plans to make the girls and Wayne do more than clean." Georgia reached for the young mother's hands. "When I got Wayne's call early this morning, I drove to Hamilton for them. I'm sorry we didn't call first, but Judge McQuarry was out of town for the weekend and I no longer had your contact information because I'd sent it on to their Hamilton school. Wayne managed to remember how to get here."

"Really?" Georgia said.

Ms Welding laughed. "We've been exploring the roads for a while."

"You must be exhausted," Georgia said, her briskness an attempt to calm her outrage on the family's behalf. "We'll make up the bunkhouse for Sadra and the girls tonight, and then tomorrow we'll make more permanent arrangements."

Embarrassed, Ms Welding smiled. "I know it's odd, but it's her wish that she be called 'Wayne's Mother,' for now. Wayne's broken with tradition in so many ways, changing his name, his language, his clothes. She wants to remind him of her authority."

12

Once Georgia made a rapid mental calculation of suitable beds, she said, "Ms Welding, you and Wayne can stay upstairs. I imagine Wayne will want to stay in the studio after tonight."

"The studio?"

"My daughter lives in a studio on the other side of the woods. She and Wayne became quite a team when he was here last year. She's been expecting him, as a matter of fact."

"Your daughter Lila is the artist."

"Yes," said Georgia. "Wayne told you about her?"

"He tells people she's a 'Sister from a different Mister,' that you and Mr. Butte are his Canadian grandparents, and that this farm is his real home."

Blinded by tears, Georgia excused herself to call Wayne. When he didn't answer, she climbed the stairs, blotting her tears as she went. She opened the door to Lola's old room. Light splashed over Wayne, asleep, his bare chest above the sheet, his left arm beneath Willy's head.

Willy opened his eyes. "It will grow back, Beauty," she whispered. Willy turned away. "I'll leave the screen door unlatched," she said, hoping to lift his spirits with thoughts of a cool night in his special nesting place by the barn. With a quick look, he let her know he was beyond such solace.

Downstairs, Uly gathered bedding for the bunkhouse. Georgia handed out flashlights and asked the girls to blaze a trail for their mother. They set out in the dark, talking and laughing, their beams exploring the branches overhead.

Opening the bunkhouse door, Georgia held her breath as a young foot disappeared over the top bunk. It was Lila's, she felt sure. Kim and Karen explored the room with their flashlight beams. Georgia flicked on the light.

"You and your sister can sleep on the top bunks," Georgia said, showing them the ladders, flipping the mattress on one of the beds, making it up quickly. "It's a beautiful night. You can count the stars." She pointed to the skylights not knowing how much English they understood. Wayne's linguistic abilities were extraordinary, but these young girls hadn't had his freedom on city streets.

As Georgia made up the second top bunk, Sadra made up the opposite bottom bunk in the efficient way of people used to a nomadic life. When their beds were made, she led Sadra and her daughters to the nearby barn, first introducing them to its kitchen and supplies, then to the bathroom. The girls chose new toothbrushes from the Butte stash, along with bright pink towels. While the family bathed, Georgia wandered the barn's lower rooms, checked on her water-lily purifying tank in the spacious greenhouse Uly and Max and Lila built when the barn's inner rooms were completed. When Sadra and her daughters emerged in their nightgowns, they embraced Georgia in a family hug.

Back at the bunkie, Georgia took stock. "If you need anything at all, just come to the house." She moved to the doorway and pointed to the farmhouse lighted windows across the garden. "Are you hungry? Have you had enough to eat?" She made an eating gesture. Sadra pulled a bag of chips from her large bag, offered it to Georgia.

"I have soup," Georgia said, wondering how to convey the wholesomeness of the food she had in mind. Sadra shook her head, brought her hands together at her breast, bowed. Georgia returned the bow and as she did, felt bound to this woman through an ancient and indestructible grace.

Back in the house with Ruth Welding, the new friends chatted, sipped soup, clucked over the insanity that made refugee camps necessary. When Ruth yawned, Georgia provided towels and left the younger woman to make herself comfortable in Lila's old room. On her way downstairs, she looked in on Wayne. He and Willy slept soundly, their bodies transmitting whatever comfort they needed to forget the cares of the day. Filled with tenderness and gratitude, she hoped Uly might talk, but when she found him in the summer kitchen, his determined focus made clear he'd had enough people excitement for one night. Tinkering with the jammed fan allowed him to unwind, clear out the debris of the day, restore his sense of competence and control. She left him to his bliss.

"All right," she said to the invisible beings ever ready to rescue her from strained connections, "I'll go to bed." The moment she said the words, her lids grew heavy. Her face washed and her hair braided for sleep, she curled beneath a single sheet feeling more like a fetus in the womb of the Universe than a mature, responsible woman so many counted on for food, for shelter, for understanding, for love.

MONDAY

1

Georgia floated to consciousness, the copper piping's water song insisting, ready or not, she acknowledge a new day. With groggy awkwardness, she groped for her flannel robe, protection against the weather's continued caprice. Despite the previous day's hellish heat, this morning she felt sure she'd see her breath before the sun worked its magic. She glanced at Uly, glad to find him sleeping after his late night. She dressed, picked up an extra sweater, headed to the kitchen to wait for Ruth Welding.

Downstairs, she opened the inside door Uly had closed after letting Willy out sometime after midnight. Peering through a screen dotted with moths, she smiled. At four-thirty, the deep night sky, already a fading indigo, made room for this new day. She flicked on the outside light, watched the moths dance. She tore herself away from their beauty to put on the kettle then went out into the garden to greet the dawn.

Dew soaked her ancient runners, chilling her feet and making her glad of extra blankets in the bunkhouse. Mars, ruddy and secure on the eastern horizon, drew her attention from earthly things. A week before, people at the Windsor market talked about the planet's influence on the way things were growing. They feared human and natural activities were held back because the red planet was not moving as it should. "Behave," she whispered to the pale, distant orb. "We need your energy down here. Bless us," she commanded, "with every good thing."

"Georgia?"

She turned to find Ruth Welding standing in the kitchen doorway. Even before she asked, Georgia could see the effects a good night's sleep had on this new friend. "I had such a good rest. No tossing and turning. No anxiety about getting back on time today." Georgia joined her in the kitchen.

"Shall I make breakfast? We have homemade grape juice. And jam. This year's strawberry, last year's currant. Amazing local bread. The best eggs you've ever tasted."

Ms Welding declined. "I'll stop for coffee and a bagel. I saw a Tim Horton's on the highway on the way in." She laughed, acknowledging the absurdity of refusing a homemade meal. "You may not be aware of this, but caffeine runs the educational system in Ontario. I'm as hooked as the next person." Lola's coffee highs and lows, indelibly implanted during exchanges with her youngest daughter, supported Ruth's claim.

The younger woman slipped into the sweater Georgia held for her. "At the end of all my school commitments for this year I'll return this and see how they're doing."

"Stay with us as long as you like. Although I warn you. There will be lots to do to earn your keep. Lots of play, too." Georgia paused, sensing undercurrents. "You seem a bit apprehensive, Ruth, as if we're doing something wrong."

The woman blushed to the roots of her dark hair. "It's funny you should say that. I feel as if we have. I don't know why."

Georgia led the younger woman through the garden. "It's an odd reaction. Let me know what's behind it when you figure it out. Do you have our phone number?" Nodding, Ruth offered Georgia a final hug before getting into her car.

"You'll think I'm naïve for saying this, but thanks for the chance to defy the system and give at least one family a fighting chance at happiness."

"Naïve? Not at all. Optimistic, I'd say. Like me." The women smiled at one another. Georgia stood for some time waving off Wayne's rescuer.

2

Before heading back to the house, Georgia walked along the shoulder of the road, stiff with cold and stewing apprehensions, not seeing the Welding car's diminishing taillights but an angry beast dragged backward at furious speed. She recalled the white ambulance that had borne her young man to Leamington General Hospital and IV drips the day before. A dog began to bark. She looked skyward. Despite the unseasonably cold dawn, the sky promised a beautiful day.

Deep in wonder, she walked the path to the house. Wayne broke the spell weaving her into some story she could not yet identify when he called to her from the kitchen doorway. "I fell asleep with Willy. Is it too early to go to the studio?"

With the joy of his homecoming, Georgia hugged him. Before her stood a growing, flesh-and-blood person. TriChem loomed, but at this point, only as a possibility. She hadn't resolved her quarrel with Uly's plan to buy the Jones farm with his city friends, but Wayne had come home. His reunion with Lila, something she needed to witness as proof of happy middles if not endings, would wait. First, she would make him breakfast.

Wayne wore an old shirt and pair of jeans he'd chosen from the cache of clothes in Lila's closet. They'd be about the same height now. The boy had grown some but was still boy-skinny. Lila's thinness had another cause.

As she scrambled his eggs, he cut the first of his toast into strips, then dipped these in grape juice before wolfing them down. A habit he absorbed during his mealtimes with Lila, he might have been her child so alike were their mannerisms.

"How did you sleep? I hope Willy didn't bother you when he got up to do his night roaming."

"That goat is depressed. And not just a little bit."

Because of the previous evening's surprise visitors, Georgia hadn't given much thought to Willy's reaction to Alice Maude's shearing. She resolved to comfort him when she returned from Lila's studio. "You think so? Because he's been shorn?"

"In case you didn't notice, he's bald." He vibrated with indignation on Willy's behalf. "She didn't leave him enough stubble to rub into a bristle."

"He's been shorn before," Georgia said, knowing the irrelevance of her comment.

Wayne's eyes widened at Georgia's apparent lack of sensitivity. "That don't mean he likes it. My guess is he's gonna be mean as anything 'til it grows back."

Georgia touched Wayne's cheek where it dimpled, placed his eggs before him. "Was he very glad to see you?"

"Not so's I noticed."

"Really?" she said. "I thought he'd be overjoyed. You two got to be such pals." In his rush to see Lila, he inhaled his meal, afterward taking care of his dishes in the balletic choreography he established during his first stay at the farm.

On their way to Lila's studio, they passed the bunkie where his family slept, the barn, and the open paddock where Willy sometimes spent the small hours of the night. This morning, the family goat was nowhere to be seen. A stab of worry distracted Georgia until she caught her first glimpse of the woods path. "Do you remember the way?" She looked from Wayne to Webster's alfalfa, green and dewy.

Wayne bumped hips with her, his high spirits rooting her in the present. "Remember the way? I dream about this farm every night. No matter where I go, I told Mama, I will never forget this place. We went from camps where we had to fight for water and food, for everything, to a big Canadian city. She doesn't know about places like this. I told her, 'Mama, they didn't send me to jail. They sent me to heaven.'"

"Heaven with bugs," Georgia said, wondering how to protect him from her TriChem anxieties. To distract him from sensing her worries, she reminded him of his wild reactions to the occasional spider dropping onto his shoulder from out of nowhere. To shake off these memories, he began to sprint, flinging himself through the air and landing, nearly soundless, before crouching to prepare for another launch. At the edge of the woods, he asked about the chickens.

"May-Bell, Suzie, and Francine are just fine, but Old Dotty died in April."

"Old Dotty died? Ah, that's sad. The girls'll be surprised to see me." He turned to her. "You still don't eat their eggs?"

"I still don't eat them."

"But doesn't your stomach say 'gimme an egg' Gee? Doesn't it howl at you?"

She laughed. "My stomach says the opposite. It says if I give it an egg, it will give me a belly ache." She remembered how astonished he was to discover her food preferences, his experience of vegetarianism one of many deprivations endured in the camps.

"I don't think it's good for you. Them chickens want you to have those eggs. That's why they lay 'em."

She shook her head. "No, they lay them for you, Wayne. They know you need all those minerals and all that protein." He laughed at this notion, but the hens they kept for manure had been secretive layers until Wayne joined them. "I think they wanted to feed you from the moment you sang them your chicken song."

Wayne no longer listened. He walked quickly into the trees looking from side to side as if greeting old friends, slowing his pace only when the back meadow became visible through a lattice of leaves. He stopped to wait for Georgia. Together, they looked down the slight slope to Lila's small retreat. The studio stood within the stand of lilacs Spring and Georgia had planted twenty-odd years before. Like the Jones's lilacs, they'd been glorious this year.

Crouching on his haunches, Wayne duck-walked the slight descent. Surprised, Georgia remained behind to watch him, worrying that he'd forgotten Lila's story and intended to bang open her door. She followed him, her eyes filling when he touched the ground, stroking it as he might a beloved animal.

When he was close enough to touch the studio's silvered cedar shakes, he stood. Georgia stopped, held her breath as he rounded the studio corner. When she caught up with him, she found him sitting on the large flat stone Lila used as a carving seat, his arms crossed over his thin chest. She knew now. He remembered everything.

Joining him, she whispered, "Shall I wake her?"

"Nah. I want to be sitting here when she walks out that door with her mean morning face on, scratching like she's got fleas and rattling that chain." The pair sat motionless, Wayne staring at Lila's door, Georgia absorbing the growing light.

In twenty minutes, Lila opened her door appearing as Wayne had described her. She wore a pair of her father's ratty sweat pants and a sweatshirt. A version of these she always slept in, summer and winter, her armour against bad dreams. In one hand she held her lycra running outfit, in the other, her chain. For a few seconds, she gave nothing away. Then she blinked with the effort of hiding her joy.

"Where have you been, Wiil Waal? We've got back orders for those frog planters of yours." Although he'd instructed Lila under pain of serious retaliation never to use his Somali name, the boy leapt from the large stone and snaked his arms around her, lifting her off the ground and whirling her around until they stumbled to a stop. Lila hugged him back, whooping and kicking.

He broke away to leap into the meadow. Georgia was sure he jumped two feet in the air, his soaring leaps the reason Jason and Spring nicknamed him Fling when they were home for a visit during his previous stay at the farm. Studying him, Lila crowed. "Didn't I tell you, Ma? Didn't I tell you he'd be back?"

"Yes, Beauty, you told me."

The women watched the child leap and land with more pleasure than they'd shared in a long while. Finally, Lila leaned into her mother. "How long's he here for this time? The summer?"

"I think this might be home, at least for now. He's brought his mother and sisters with him." Lila stiffened. "They're in trouble, Lila. They need a safe place to regroup." Lila looked away. Georgia felt the wave of terror stiffening her daughter's body, her fear of growing even more attached to someone who would eventually become a man.

Laughing, Wayne leapt his way over to them. When he stood before her, he took a foot of Lila's chain in his hands. Jiggling it, he pretended to calculate its weight. "I thought you'da given this dirty disgusting weapon to the fireman by now."

Lila snatched the chain from him. "I haven't finished my suit of armor yet."

"It's gonna be awful hot today." The young boy said this as if he'd been predicting the weather his whole life. "You're gonna sweat like a pig."

"Pigs don't sweat, ignorant boy."

A wicked glint appeared in Wayne's eyes. "Okay, then. You're gonna sweat like a man."

All at once, Georgia saw with a clarity that made her breathless a new future for Lila, her traumatized daughter standing on the brink of chainless freedom. "I have to get back," she muttered, walking toward the woods, not wanting Lila to feel the pressure of her mother's longing for her healing. "Willy's depressed because of Alice Maude's shearing," she said, knowing mentioning Willy would end any curiosity Lila might have about her mother's emotional state. "I'm going to ask Mae for help."

"Well, thank you, Alice Maude," Lila said. "Let's hope he smells a whole lot better than he did yesterday." Georgia almost mentioned Lila's frequent stench but thought better of it. She left the pair chattering like magpies and feeling in her bones how good this reunion was for both of them.

3

After countless rings, Mae answered her phone with a low, menacing growl. "This had better be the voice of God Himself."

"I need your help, Mae. Willy needs your help." Georgia listened to Mae's rustlings and plumpings, heard the soft whisper of Mae's delicate turquoise shawl as her friend slid it around her shoulders to ward off this morning's chill.

Her rearrangements complete, Mae spoke her concern in her every day voice. "What is it, Georgia Butte?"

Georgia stifled the urge to howl. "Willy is stark naked. Alice Maude took the shears to him yesterday."

A long silence preceded Mae's decision to risk the truth. "He smelled pretty bad on Friday, Georgia. As much as I hate to think of Alice Maude with sharp objects, I'm sure it's for the best. His coat will grow back."

"Willy doesn't feel it's for the best. He's in a blue funk. Wayne says he's depressed."

"Wayne! Is that gorgeous flying bundle of boy back?"

"With his mother and two younger sisters. I think they're here for the duration."

"And just how long is that?"

"Who knows? Things didn't work out for them in Hamilton. Turns out her brother-in-law believes in child labour. And sex trafficking."

"Have mercy! What's Mama like?"

"She's twenty-four, Mae."

"Gracious, twenty-four with a twelve-year-old? There's young and there's child abuse. What a world." Mae's soothing voice comforted Georgia. "We'll help her out. We'll teach the kids, just like the old days. This time I want the unit on the birds and the bees. You shocked those little Kingsville kids something terrible when you took them down to Joe's to watch the stallion do his stud-horse business."

Georgia embraced the warm, long-ago day that held horse smells, an ardent mare, her more ardent mate, and several Saturday-School children, their eyes wide with the indelible nature of this sex education lesson. "As I recall, we all learned a great deal that day."

Mae snorted. "As I recall, one of the Deerfields said he wanted to do *that* for a living when he grew up. We never did figure out which part of the lesson he meant."

Willy bumped through the screen door. "Willy's here, Mae. Do you have time to make something beautiful? He needs something to wear while his coat is growing in."

"You have got to be joking."

"I know how ridiculous this sounds," Georgia said. "But he's so sad. And we've got company coming for…" She hesitated to say the word wedding but couldn't bear the thought of explaining the current situation with Lola and Juan. "The big day." She was glad Mae couldn't see her liar's face.

"Do you want formal? Or will something casual do?"

"Both, I think. Casual for now. But for the big day, something dressy."

Mae sputtered protests. "I was joking, Georgia. I still have to finish Lola's mantilla. And Lila's shawl. And your hat."

"Forget my hat," Georgia said. "Make something for Willy. I'll wear my straw hat. I'll be fine."

"That beat up old thing you wear in the garden? Lola will have my head. Her instructions were very specific. The mother of the bride must have a periwinkle blue dress with matching hat."

Willy took a few desultory turns around the kitchen before bumping out the door. Georgia waited for him to leave before she said more. "Really Mae. Willy needs something funny to cheer him up."

"How could it not be funny? We're talking about a wig for a goat. For a goat's body! I don't know if I'm up to this nonsense, Georgia Butte. You are sounding like a crazy white lady."

"I know. But it's Willy. This may be his last party." Georgia's voice broke.

"Georgia? Georgia. What's really going on?"

"Uly and I are going to the bank to…"

"No!"

"He's determined Mae. He's sure they'll loan us mortgage money to buy the Jones farm with…some other people."

"What other people?"

"Some of Uly's former co-workers." Mae's silence told Georgia all she needed to know about her friend's opinion of this plan.

After a time, Mae said, "I was hoping it was all just a tempest in a teapot. Are you sure it's come to this? Your farm is such a going concern. And Webster feeds most of the well cared for animals in these parts. It's an awful lot of land to work. To say nothing of the big debt it brings."

"It turns out a chemical company, an outfit called TriChem is romancing Web."

"No!"

"Uly says local farmers are persuaded that agribiz inputs are the only way to go. To increase yields and profits." Georgia's eyes filled. "They're convinced they can have limitless yields with constant production. As if that's sustainable."

"What's Web's place going for, anyway? I know the Joneses are your mother's people, but last I heard mention of the house, it was a wreck. As I recall, when I moved in, everybody couldn't wait to tell me how your Aunt Violet and Uncle Frank didn't meet local housekeeping standards. I heard their kitchen scared away Rusty and Pete when they showed up to paint the place."

"I probably told you that. But Moira got the place shipshape as soon as she and Web married. Besides, the house isn't what TriChem wants. It's the land, for product experiments. On Friday, Hal said he didn't know what Web's asking. No one seems to know if the chemical company has made him an offer yet." Sorrow washed over her. "Web's kids left the farm as soon as they could. They have no affection for the place. My guess is they've been pressuring Web to sell since Moira died." Her throat tightened. "When he dies, it's theirs anyway." She brushed away tears. "Last time Uly heard, farm land around here was going for as much as seven thousand an acre."

Mae whistled. "I bought my place with the money I got when I sold my house in town. Out here, land and house, in great shape I might add, were so much cheaper. I paid less than thirty thousand dollars and got clean air into the bargain."

"But Mae, that was more than twenty years ago."

Mae took a moment to calculate. "It was!" She warmed to the subject. "I'm sitting on a goldmine. At seven thousand an acre, I'm rich." She took in a breath that spoke volumes. Tony, the child she'd hoped would farm with her, was long dead. And Darlene was, like Lola and Erie, citified through and through. "What do you think the bank will loan you? If I'm rich, you and Uly are rolling in it. You've got close to two hundred acres there." She sensed Georgia's terror. "No wonder you're scared to death. If anything should go wrong, you'd lose it all."

4

On the drive into Kingsville for their banking appointment, Georgia asked Uly to stop. He set his jaw, but parked on the road shoulder without argument. "I thought I could go through with this, but as we get closer to the bank, I feel sick, Uly. I want everything clear in my mind before we go any farther." She bristled at his exasperated sigh. "I can't believe you're any easier about mortgaging the farm than I am." She touched his hand. He pulled it away. She tried again to find common ground with him. "We've always managed to stay rooted in the sane. Through all the times when popular opinion said try this new thing or that, we resisted. We've always honoured our land's limits. We've been respectful of…"

"I am still sane," Uly snapped.

She'd been staring at the field to her right. Now she faced him. "No matter what your ego says, or your young friends from the city, we aren't middle-aged anymore. This mortgage could wipe us out." Uly opened his mouth to argue. "Please, Uly. Hear me out." He sat back, sighed his martyr's sigh. With effort, she ignored it. "We're not likely to find others who could step into the breach with millions to bail us out. People attracted to our way of doing things are back-to-the-landers. Young hippies. Homesteaders like us. People who know about the great web of life and feel they're only a part of something miraculous and vast, with no right to ruin or waste or ignore their obligations to the whole." She reached for his hand again, held on to it through his resistance, brought it to her lips.

After a long silence, he took his hand away. He leaned out the open window before turning cold, hard eyes on her. "Take a good deep breath, Georgia. Smell that rotting stench? We're a few miles from home and this field of soybeans is as close as the poisons have come to our farm so far. It's just plain dumb luck that our closest neighbours have been goat herders or city folk playing at farming with a couple of horses and a brood of chickens. There aren't many small-scale farmers like us, managing to grow most of their own food and bartering for the rest in that friendly way life in the county inspires." Seeing tears on her face, he looked away. "Even you have to admit it. Power is shifting away from us because of people like Webster's kids, people who live in their illusions of how the world is rather than in the world itself."

He swallowed his own tears before he continued. "You and I have been blessed, you with your ways of seeing, me with my ways of making. We've always managed to hang on to this sense of being part of something much bigger than our individual lives. Being a part of something greater kept us out of harm's way, out of the malls and banks, out of the churches that preached the world was ours to consume to death." Weary, he rubbed his eyes. "I know we're not alone anymore. I know we have connections with people all over the world who feel as we do. But, Georgia, even you have to see there are very few of us standing on Essex County roads against TriChem and the army of beaten down farmers selling out to big agriculture." He weighed the pros and cons of his next admission. "And the men in town are ready for a stake in something…"

With a sudden flash, she knew he and his city friends had plans for Webster's land that had nothing to do with farming. He'd been holding back from her as she'd held back her plan to have her mother buy the Jones farm. "What kind of something?" She stiffened, ready to attack whatever it was he'd agreed to without telling her.

He expelled a gust of air. "Gord and the others know how much farming means to you, to us, but…"

"Just get to it, Uly. What kind of something?"

"They're researching a couple of things that will attract investors. Right now, they like extraction possibilities – lumber, sand, gravel. The investors we've approached like these ideas, too. The numbers are good."

Georgia felt the air leave her lungs. At first, she had no words. When they finally came, they were etched in acid. "Why not a chicken or pig CAFO? Hell, why not both?"

He couldn't look at her. He knew she wouldn't like any options other than farming, but as he spoke the words aloud, he knew he was very close to agreeing to betray her way of life, their way of life. When he was with the men, the plan seemed practical. Sitting with her, breathing in pesticide-fouled air and staring at GMO'd soybeans, he felt the danger of losing one thing to gain something far less sure. What this something was, he couldn't say.

He did his best to cultivate the goodwill he needed if they were to continue this conversation "These business ventures would pay off the mortgage, Georgia. Everyone agreed the final plan should be some paying, food enterprise." He thought of his boyhood, fishing on Lake Erie before Detroit industries used the river as a sewage dump. "Almost everyone grew up fishing, so maybe we could…"

"Farm fish? After you clear cut? You're breaking my heart."

He reached for her hand. "Georgia, whatever grudge you have against the men, it's time to let it go. I can't work with them if you're against it." He shook his head, angry that he had to plead with her. "No matter how much you see into that other world, you just can't seem to see this one. We need the men to save our farm."

She dried her eyes. "What I know is that we're in a battle between those who understand that we're a part of the web of life on this beautiful planet and those who are convinced humans are the only part that matters." She had a flash of insight. His yearning to bring the men into their future was as honourable as her impulse to include Wayne, Sadra, and the girls. This insight softened her.

She looked away from him to the tidy, engineered crop. "Can we at least agree we won't sign anything today? That we'll use this beautiful morning to see what kind of mortgage they'll give us to buy Grandma Jones's…Web's place?"

Relieved, he touched her cheek. "We'll call this trip our first reconnaissance."

"I should have worn my battle fatigues."

He laughed, kissed her palms. "I don't feel old yet, Georgia. I don't think you do, either."

Georgia smiled. "No, I don't feel old. Maybe one day it will sneak up on me and I won't be able to get up after spending the morning on my knees in the garden. But it hasn't happened yet."

"Maybe this is just more of what life has always expected from us. Maybe this TriChem business is a sign that the land wants more of us. It's not like we've ever lived in isolation. Don't you always feel loved, protected out here?"

Georgia closed her eyes. A fleeting, kaleidoscopic ordering of woods and garden, pond and sky danced across her mind's eye. Into this ordering she, Uly, their children had been woven through time and place. "Yes," she whispered. "I do. I always have."

"Well, then. How can we let them make more mischief? If we sit back and complain about the terrible events going on in the world and do nothing to improve our small part of the web, aren't we as much to blame as this chemical company?" He looked out at the perfect rows of soy beans. "We have to find a way to protect our home. Everyone's home." With effort, he summoned tenderness. "I never pretended to understand Web's parents, but I always knew Frank and Vi were crazy in a good way. Maybe caught in a time warp, letting their young chicks have the run of the kitchen, and that new calf sleep under the grand piano."

"You should talk, Ulysses Butte," Georgia said, pretending playfulness. "You live with a goat." They exchanged diplomatic smiles. "Let's go," she said. "We've got a big meeting ahead of us."

She watched him start the old truck, touching the dash before he eased it into first, his way of thanking it for taking them where they needed to go. The gesture shocked her with the sobering knowledge that while she could hate his sneaky ways with the men in town, she also experienced countless moments of his gentle presence to what is and what wanted to be. These moments filled her with irrepressible love for him. Love and hate, she pondered, dancing, always dancing together. She wanted always to remember this.

5

Harold Shuttleworth, manager of the Kingsville Farmers First Bank, looked over his comfortable paunch at Ulysses Butte. "Well, I have to say I was very surprised to get your call, Uly. And pleased. Have you decided to get rid of that northern woodlot and plant a cash crop? Is this about a tractor loan?"

Suppressing the urge to mimic his smug tone, Georgia said, "We're thinking of buying more property, Mr. Shuttleworth."

The bank manager's eyes didn't leave Ulysses Butte. "Really? Any place in particular?"

"We're interested in the Jones place," Uly answered. "We want to see about buying it before Webster's too far gone to do business."

Harold Shuttleworth broke into a laugh. "I guess you know you've already missed the boat on that one." He cleared his throat, remembering Georgia's blood connection to Webster. "No offence, Ma'am," he said, glancing at her.

"Oh, none taken, Mr. Shuttleworth," Georgia said. "Is your wife still with the weavers' guild?"

The banker rubbed the fabric of his suit coat with obvious pride. "She is, she is," he said, shifting his eyes from Uly to Georgia and back again.

"I have some mohair for her. Let her know it's at the farm if she'd like it." Harold smiled his thanks, carefully avoiding mention of the infamous Butte goat.

Uly slipped into the roomy silence Georgia's graciousness created. "The last time I spoke with Milo Nadrofsky, he said farm land in these parts was going for about seven thousand an acre."

Harold immediately closed the door on his wife's accomplishments. "Milo is behind the times if you spoke with him recently. More like thirteen thousand at the low end and twenty at the high in the current market. But that's cleared land, workable land, in a prime location, a site that lends itself to greenhouses. As I recall, your place has more trees than Carter's has pills. If you want to get top dollar for your place, you'll have to get those trees down and cultivate."

"We aren't interested in selling our place," Georgia said. "We're here to inquire about a mortgage, so if we decide to do so, we can buy the Jones farm."

The bank manager grasped a pale green writing tablet to record details. "How many acres have you got there, Ulysses?"

"Georgia owns the farm, too," Uly answered, knowing how the clubby men's bond Harold wanted to establish would rankle Georgia. "She worked it mostly on her own until I retired a few years ago. We have two hundred and twenty acres, more or less."

Grudgingly acknowledging the rebuke, Harold turned to Georgia. "How much is farmed, Ms Butte?"

"Now? Only about a fifth. But a third is cleared and has been farmed. And it's all certified organic by COG." Harold's questioning look prompted her to add, "the Canadian Organic Growers. They only require seven years, but our farm has been clean for a century." She gave Uly an apologetic look then added, "I've been researching how to apply for a hemp license for the back field, out by the amphitheatre. Getting the license is a long shot, but industrial hemp is a viable cash crop and it's good for crop rotation. I'd like to expand our orchard, as well." She reached for Uly's hand, hoping he'd forgive her for not talking with him about growing hemp and expanding the orchards before mentioning them to the banker. Uly covered a feeble cough to avoid her touch.

As he began his calculations, Harold Shuttleworth's pupils contracted. "Science says we can forget about the organic claim counting for much now it's proven we live in a closed system. What neighbours spray on their tomatoes falls with the rain on your land, too." In the interests of bank business, he held himself back from full blown argumentativeness. "I know, I know. It's all a matter of degree. Organic or not, that's a good-sized farm you've got there. I didn't realize. How many acres does Webster Jones have? Fifty? A hundred?"

Georgia held onto her anger as she would a snarling dog. "Two hundred and some as well. Two fifty, as I recall."

"What on earth would you two do with all that land when you're doing so little farming on your own place?"

Uly opened his mouth but it was Georgia who answered. "We want the Jones farm for sentimental reasons, Mr. Shuttleworth. We have four daughters. We'd like to leave each of them a little place." She enjoyed lying to the banker, enjoyed pretending she was following the legacy guidebook most people in the county believed was the best way forward for small farms.

"You'd have to see about the zoning possibilities. But you could create ten or fifteen very nice parcels. They'd fetch top dollar."

"That's true," Uly said, "but we're interested in leaving the farms to the girls jointly, to share as they currently exist."

Harold Shuttleworth was not an intelligent man, but he could focus on a goal with laser-like precision. "Let's see now," he said. "You want to know what we'll loan you for the Jones place, based on your current holdings. What debts do you have?"

"None," said Uly.

"No car payments?"

"No."

"No short- or long-term loans?"

"No."

"No farm equipment loans?"

"No."

The bank manager did his best to hide his disappointment. "And what about your assets?"

"The farm," Georgia said.

"My pension," Uly added. "Forty-three thousand a year."

"Gross?"

"After taxes."

"My business," Georgia continued. "We make about forty-thousand during a good year, thirty during a shaky one. That would increase with hemp and more fruit."

"My truck."

"What year?"

"It's a nineteen seventy-four Dodge Ram, converted to a combination of solar cells and propane. It runs for about three dollars a month in summer, a little more in winter because of snow tires." Uly searched for the words that would wipe the smirk off the manager's face. "By the end of the summer I'll have worked out the conversion to vegetable oil. I'm modifying Green Peace plans. Patent companies are interested." Georgia's face registered her surprise. Ulysses pretended not to notice.

"Part of the save-the-planet revolution, eh?" The banker's dismissive tone tempted Georgia to let her snarling anger have its way.

"Part of what protects the earth and keeps it safe for your grandchildren." Uly's mild response brought tears to Georgia's eyes. The banker's implacable face assured her Uly wasted his breath. They might get money from this man, but they'd be fools to look for understanding.

"You folks leave this with me. I'll call a couple of contacts in the rural real estate business, put my ear to the ground, literally," he said, delighted with himself, "see what kind of deal we can come up with." He stood. "Are you in a rush?"

"No," Uly said, hoping Harold Shuttleworth would not hear the lie in his voice.

"Good. This will take a bit of doing. Your property's a very nice piece, but I have to be honest with you. The size of your farm is against you. The larger the parcel, the lower the price per acre if it's not entirely under production. It's best to be frank. Your age is against you, as well. And you have no sons."

"We have four daughters, all gainfully employed, one a doctor, one a community organizer, one a teacher, and one whose art work is in the National Gallery, Mr. Shuttleworth." Georgia smiled her own version of smug.

"In the National Gallery you say." She was pleased to impress him. "I had no idea your…youngest?"

"Lila is our third daughter, Mr. Shuttleworth. She is the woman who runs the back roads sporting a chain you've no-doubt seen evidence of on the hoods of cars belonging to men who bother her."

Visibly embarrassed, the bank manager grasped Uly's hand and with it a lifeline to the world of men and commerce. "It's been a pleasure, Ulysses. I hope we can do business."

Georgia thrust out her brown calloused hand, discouraged by how very little life in the county had changed. In spite of her desire for things to be otherwise, she knew the truth. Harold Shuttleworth and the armies of men just like him were still in charge. She smiled a small, tight smile. "Don't forget to tell your wife about the mohair. And be sure to mention how much I admire your suit."

Uly took his turn with the bank manager, saying something in a low voice that made the manager laugh that insider laugh Georgia knew all too well. Reading guilt in his expression when he turned to her, she suspected her husband of saying something about her to appease the banker. In spite of her earlier feelings of love, in this moment Georgia felt only hate for him.

6

They spoke little on the drive home, the public revelations of their different plans eroding the last of this day's goodwill toward one another. With a sense of obligation, Georgia opened her mouth to apologize for blindsiding Uly with her hemp license and orchard-expansion plans. Remembering it was Uly who insisted on the bank trip, who apparently agreed with the men from the city to clear-cut her old farm and create a gravel pit, she silenced herself. Her heart ached over his apparent willingness to reduce the Jones farm to an extraction economic venture so he could continue as the great rescuer of his city boys. For his part, Uly felt it was more of the same from his wife of fifty years. She already discounted his ideas, had plans in place before he even addressed the possible ways in which to pay off a bank debt and get his friends out of the factory and onto the land. He didn't try to hide his anger, felt justified in his outrage, couldn't wait to escape into his workshop.

By the time the elder Buttes reached home, Sadra had transplanted several pots of nasturtiums among the rows of vegetables. "So many flowers," Georgia said, relieved to focus on beauty. "They're lovely. And they'll attract bees." She buzzed. The women smiled at one another. "We eat them, too," Georgia said.

"Eedem?" echoed Sadra.

Georgia pantomimed eating then picked a flower, chewed, and swallowed it. She offered a blossom to Wayne's mother. The young woman put her hands over her mouth, laughing. Then she took the blossom, chewed, reflected, smiled as she swallowed. "We put them in salads," Georgia told her, pointing to the spirals of lettuce varieties. "They add a peppery taste." She fanned her mouth in mock distress.

The young woman's eyes filled. Georgia understood. Food as beauty, beauty as food, the ordinary abundance of the Butte farm overwhelmed Sadra after her hardships. With a worried expression, the young woman opened an empty pocket. Georgia dropped a finger-tip kiss into it. "What you've done this morning is worth a whole pocket full of money, and kisses, too," she told the young mother. "You'll get your first pay cheque at the end of this week. Room and board come with the work. You're all a blessing to us." Sadra retrieved the kiss, held it to her heart.

Watching this unfolding friendship and feeling resentful and small and mean spirited, Uly pretended indifference. Out of spite, he'd been rehearsing his challenge to Georgia's hemp plans. Instead of taking up the argument he longed to make, he walked away from the women without a word.

Georgia watched him go with tit-for-tat, adolescent satisfaction. Turning to Sadra, she said, "We're so glad Wayne brought you here. We love him very much. Lila says he's a fine artist. She's helping him develop his drawing skills."

"Drawing not good," the younger woman contradicted. With an expression of disgust, she scribbled with her toe in the dirt.

Glad to have this small crisis replace her larger one with Uly, Georgia touched the young mother's hand. "His drawing is a good thing, Sadra. There'll be time for letters and numbers later. Right now, he needs to move, to run, to jump, to make things. He needs safe places to express his feelings." She thought of Uly and his sense of inferiority, a feeling she only recently discovered she provoked simply by being herself. She blinked back tears. "Drawing helps Wayne understand himself, who he is, what he feels, what he wants to create. He and Uly did some very fine repair work last year. Uly says he's got a maker's knack."

"Knack?" Sadra repeated.

With her hands, Georgia built a castle in the air. "When our bodies know something and just do it, without much explanation. It's in us."

The young woman offered Georgia a shy smile. "Knack," she repeated, taking up the hem of her woven skirt.

"You're a weaver?"

"Aweaver." The young woman repeated.

"On a loom?" Georgia sent an imaginary shuttle flying between them.

"Aweaver. Ondaloon."

A persistent car horn interrupted them. "For heaven's sake," Georgia grumbled. "City folks expect everything to be done in double time." With smiles, she left Sadra to consider the value of art.

7

In front of the Butte gate, a black limousine idled in the noonday sun, its tinted windows impenetrable. Still, Georgia knew. Clytemnestra Butte had come home.

Always a lover of drama, her sister-in-law lowered the back window a crack, revealing only Maria-Callas eyes. "Clytie," Georgia cried. "Tell your driver to turn off the engine and get out of that hearse so I can hug you."

The liveried driver turned off the engine, stepped from the car, and opened the door for his passenger. Like the queen she'd been named for, Uly's younger sister stepped upon Essex County rich black soil fully aware of the impression she created. Seeing her red, stiletto heels, Georgia cried, "My goodness, you'll kill yourself in those." Her sister-in-law's beautifully sculpted, tanned legs seemed a mile long. "What on earth have you got on?" After several smoothings of hair and dress, Clytemnestra stood before her in a red sleeveless sheath. "Well, look at you," Georgia said to this vaguely familiar apparition. "How did you roll back time?"

"Georgeous!" Clytemnestra cried. "You don't need all this. You're beautiful just the way you are." Issuing directives to her driver, Uly's sister caught sight of Kim and Karen peeking out the open gate. "Who's this? Come and meet your new Auntie. She's brought presents."

Georgia introduced Wayne's wary family, tossing names across the drainage ditch and praying the farm's most recent arrival wouldn't sour Sadra on making the farm her home. Georgia knew all too well how Clytemnestra appeared to strangers. If the city and its evils could be packaged in a single woman, the good Christian ladies of Kingsville would say she just arrived, special delivery, on the Second Concession Road in Essex County.

Georgia nodded to Karen, Kim, and Sadra. "They've come from hard times in Somalia, and harder times in Hamilton. They have very little English as yet, but great emotional and physical understanding. This is their first day with us. They're tuning in to the rhythm of the place." Empathy transformed Clytemnestra's face. She nodded and exchanged smiles with the family then linked arms with Georgia on their way to the house. The limo driver followed with several pieces of luggage.

Once seated in the familiar kitchen, Uly's sister grinned. "Are you surprised? I'm sure I told you I wasn't coming until Wednesday." She thanked and paid her driver. When they were alone, she said, "I'm so glad to be home, Georgeous. Everything looks even healthier than I remember." She kicked off her shoes. Georgia picked them up. Clytemnestra took them from her, then pitched one after the other into the dining room. "We'll do all this later. I want tea. And news. How's our Lila? Has she gotten rid of that nasty chain?"

Georgia filled the kettle then went outside with towels, suggesting Sadra and the girls join them for tea or have a swim. She pantomimed pouring tea and then the breast stroke. With smiles they took the towels and headed for the pond. In the time it took for her to turn to the house, she saw each of them age and blossom and transform into glorious, powerful women. "You're behind this," she said to the ground beneath her feet. "You called them here." Hearing her own words, her flesh tingled. On her way to the house, she shook her head to dispel the mystical trance threatening to take her out of the everyday and into the vision playing at the edge of her consciousness. Opening the kitchen door grounded her. Clytemnestra looked up, happy.

"Where's the gin, Georgeous?"

"There's never been any gin, Clytie. You've got your relatives mixed up."

Her sister-in-law laughed. "Is that a crack about Dad's Retsina habit?"

Georgia embraced Clytemnestra again, then held her at arm's length. "It's so good to see you. I forget how outrageous you are until you come sauntering up the path like a character out of the movies."

The younger woman held out a leg. "Very good sauntering, huh? I've been walking, five miles a day, seven days a week, on the Aegean's fine white sand. It does wonders for the butt."

"I'm sure," said Georgia. "Where's Nikos? Why isn't he here to admire your butt?"

Worry flitted across Clytemnestra's handsome face. "He's in Marseilles. I finished my work there, but he had to do some negotiating with the Swiss." She bit into the cracker she'd smeared with goat cheese. "Will I have a good time while I'm here? France was hard work. My French is appalling and Nikos is always grumpy these days."

"A good time at the wedding?" Georgia asked, feeling undercurrents.

"Yes, at the wedding. I haven't been to one in so long." The sound of Willy's bleat prompted Clytemnestra to rush to the door.

"Is that you, William?" Willy bumped through the door before Clytemnestra could open it. Someone had draped him in an old sheet, toga style. "What on earth?" Clytemnestra kissed each nubby horn. "Willy! What's happened to you?" Willy shook his head vigorously before eyeing the crackers on the table. Georgia coaxed his head away, then offered him one with a conciliatory pat.

"You've been shorn," Clytemnestra observed. "I am indignant on your behalf."

"Alice Maude decided he needed a haircut yesterday. He'll be in a funk for a while."

"Really, Gee. That woman." She stroked Willy's nose. He responded with soft bleating whimpers. "Don't worry, Will. We'll find you something spectacular for the wedding."

"Mae's already working on his outfit."

"Good. We'll be in chiffon together." She kissed Willy's nose. "Now run along so the grownups can talk. I'll give you your treats later."

Willy skipped out of the back door, his good humour restored by a few crackers and his aunt's affection. Georgia was about to comment on his change in mood when her sister-in-law launched into a description of her recent beauty enhancements. "How do you like the hair?" Without giving Georgia time to answer, she said, "Extensions. I entertained dreads for Lola's wedding, but opted for sleek in the end. I thought I'd just do the long black straight look. You know, elegant, Princess Grace-y."

"She was blonde," said Georgia.

"I know. I'm talking about a general style, Georgeous." Georgia laughed. Her sister-in-law poured tea before settling in to play oracle. "Something's up. And I know it's not boredom with my superficiality. It's way too early for that. Tell me. You know I can smell trouble a mile away when it comes to my family."

Georgia wondered where to begin. "Well, we've got a few things to choose from, Clytie. For starters, Lola's groom only just announced his plans to leave Canada. He wants Lo to live in El Salvador."

"How can he suggest such a thing?"

"She's thirty-three, Clytie, and apparently so desperate to marry she makes yearly group proposals in all her classes. She's chosen a young idealist, one who wants to go home, to make a difference."

"Who is this young man?"

"Juan. Juan Elias."

"Juan and Auntie C will have a little talk."

"Don't be absurd, Clytie. He cares about his country, his culture, his heritage. You aren't going to reduce him to jelly with your long legs and firm bottom if that's what you have in mind. He needs to go home. To be honest, I think it would do Lola the world of good to get out of this culture for a while. She's far too conventional. And privileged."

"Oh, right," Clytemnestra snapped. "We have to make sure they all do their best to avoid appearing as if they were born into a human family. Now Lola can pretend she was raised by wolves as well."

Georgia laughed. "You're the one who introduced livestock into this family."

"Livestock, yes. Not creatures from the wild. Is Lila using words these days? Does she carve symbols on trees to communicate?"

Georgia took Clytemnestra's hands. "Lila is doing well. In fact, I think she may be on the brink of joining the ranks of the vulnerable."

"Well, that's a mistake. She needs to be armed. She simply has to choose a subtler form of protection than that damn chain."

"Like you?" She pointed to the red shoes on the dining room floor. "We both know what those heels are really for."

Clytemnestra grew thoughtful. "I've changed, Georgia, I really have, thanks to progesterone and herbal therapies. Just ask Nikos. I've transformed from tiger to sweet little pussy cat. No more plates thrown out windows. No more cars driven through garage doors. I'm kind and mild and very, very nice to everyone."

"I'm sure the limo driver will attest to that."

"He's on Nikos's payroll, Georgia. He knows his place."

"Under your bright stiletto heel?"

"Let's plan a little back-up party in case Juan can't be made to see the joys of living in Windsor with the extraordinary Lola Butte." When Georgia didn't laugh, Clytemnestra asked, "What's really got you worried?"

"Webster's kids have got a big pesticide company interested in the Jones farm."

"No. Not that stuff. Not out here on your old farm."

To honour sibling loyalties, Georgia refrained from mentioning her own plan. "Uly's researching possibilities with men from work. I'm sure he'll tell you about it at supper."

The younger woman leaned across the table to stroke Georgia's cheek. "You are far too cheerful for a woman who's entertaining a non-wedding and a chemical nightmare. I hope that's all that's going on."

"A Windsor woman whose daughter was thought to have been murdered by Uly's co-worker has come out to connect with Alice Maude. You might remember her. Erie Woodburn?"

"How could I forget? Her daughter was one of the six not

named by that madman." She frowned. "What was his name?"

"David Daniel Lawson," Georgia said. "Erie's mother and grandmother used to buy from us regularly. For their catering business."

"I remember. Lillie Woodburn and Gertrude Bradshaw. They created 'Love Bites.'" Clytemnestra warmed to the memory of their shared past. "They were the first local catering service to advertise the nutritional value of local, seasonal food grown without chemicals. They helped you expand the organic food trend." Clytemnestra inched her chair closer to Georgia's. "Did they ever find Persephone's body?"

"No. In fact, I think Erie is visiting Alice Maude because she thinks her daughter may be alive. Alice Maude says she's been hearing Persephone's dead father sing in the Miner feeding field. She called Erie after that man was murdered in prison. Alice Maude thinks George may be trying to tell Erie something about their daughter."

"This is why I come home, Georgeous! Have you done a reading for Erie?"

"Clytie, you know I don't do readings."

"Okay. Have you held a session to look into the future?"

"You know perfectly well I don't do that either," Georgia said. "I only wish I could." She recalled her recent surprising ruptures with Uly. "Sometimes I can barely see beyond my nose."

"Georgeous, that's false modesty talking. I remember when you saw Dad's stroke coming. If you hadn't warned him, he wouldn't have gone for a checkup and got his blood thinning meds."

Georgia shook her head, unnerved by the turn in their conversation. "That wasn't clairvoyance. He was a terrible colour, Clytie. Anybody would have told him to see a doctor." While she wanted to believe this, Georgia knew it wasn't true. Before she'd urged Jason to see a doctor, she had been hearing loud popping sounds whenever she thought of him. After hearing the popping, she saw the colours surrounding him grow pale, almost transparent. At times she actually could see and predict. Still, she was terrified by the idea of people seeing her as some kind of fixer. The responsibility felt overwhelming. And her experience with Lila convinced her long ago that life wasn't to be fixed. It was to be lived – with all its joys, all its traumas – most often in the dark. She flushed with sudden insight. "You've picked up on our troubles because of your own. What is it, Clytie?"

The younger woman stood, stretched, took her plate and mug to the sink. "Not now, Georgeous. You know me, Greek tragedian par excellence. Mama and Papa taught me well. I'm going up for a shower. May I have my old room?"

"Always and forever."

8

Looking out at the bright sunshine, Georgia guessed it was a little after one. She was glad to harvest a batch of oregano, gladder still to give Wayne's family an enjoyable task after they'd played in the pond, explored the farm, and met Wayne's chicken fan club. She moved into the summer kitchen remembering how, almost as soon as they'd taken over the farm, Uly transformed his mother's walk-in pantry into this sunny haven. She wanted, needed to remember his virtues.

To ensure its warmth, Uly built a berm around this part of the house. When he completed the berm, Georgia terraced it, planting Sweet Woodruff, Shiso, Thyme, Tarragon, Chives, perennials that flourished in partial shade and anchored the soil. Sometimes at night when the room was completely dark, it became a dusky womb, a place where she could confirm a hunch. "You know my secret," she said to the room's shifting shadows. "Sometimes I can see what I need to see only when I'm in the dark." The telephone interrupted her mutterings. She answered without her usual softness, afraid it might be Harold Shuttleworth, eager to give them a mortgage.

"I hope I haven't called at a bad time," the unfamiliar voice whispered.

"Is this…"

"I am the man who owes you a life, Mrs. Butte."

He was only a little less hoarse than the previous evening. When he spoke, Georgia felt in her own throat the pressure of the tubes they'd used to keep him alive. "Are you feeling any better?"

"They say I can go home soon. Maybe even today."

"I'm so glad." Georgia waited, thinking he wanted to say something more, but the young mystery man remained silent. "I'm very happy to hear you're improving," she said finally. "I'd better get back to my garden." He said nothing. "Hello? Are you there?" A wave of intense tenderness flooded her heart. He broke their connection.

On her way to pick peas, the phone rang a second time. She rushed inside thinking the young man had ended the call accidentally. "Hello?"

"Georgia? It's Hal." Her heart skipped several beats. She prayed this wasn't bad news about TriChem. "I'm organizing the next meeting of Friends of Essex County. Mark your calendar for a week from today, seven o'clock, my place. We'll be focusing on the reforestation project we're launching on farms around Leamington and Kingsville. And we've got some special Point Pelee business to take care of. The

E. coli warnings are helping by keeping people away from the fragile beaches near the Point, but we still need to protect the marshes at the entrance of the park from too much foot traffic."

"Have you talked to anyone else about the Jones place?"

"No. Why?"

"Maybe we better put the Jones farm on the agenda. Just to see what other people think about what we might be able to do."

"I thought the sale was a done deal. I'm glad to be wrong."

Although he hadn't mentioned the incident, Georgia blushed over what happened between Lila and Hal early Friday morning. The incident couldn't be avoided when Hal asked, "How's Lila?"

"In spite of her recent attack on your truck, she's doing well. Be sure to send us the bill for your paint job." She thought for a moment. "Oh, yes. Wayne's back. I'm pretty sure he'll help her with the process of disarming."

There was an awkward cough at the other end of the line. "Well, I guess I'm not the only guy in these parts who thinks that would be a good thing. Give her my best. And tell Uly we hope to see you both at the meeting next Monday."

Monday, Georgia thought. Next Monday, whatever may happen on Thursday will be a thing of the past. "We'll see you then, Hal," she said, thinking it fortuitous that one of the meeting topics was deforestation. Uly needed to hear whatever might be said before he supported any clearcutting venture. Standing in her cool, fragrant kitchen, Georgia convinced herself her mother had already bought the Jones farm.

Preoccupied with Uly concerns, Georgia returned to her garden tasks. Sometime in the midst of picking more peas, the perfection of the moment took hold of her. Despite the erratic weather, the wedding's ambiguities, and the divide with Uly, despite TriChem horrors and Alice Maude's bizarre episodes, everything was thriving. She looked at the fat green sugar snaps. In less than two months, the farm had given them this bounty. Beyond the peas, the cucumbers had begun their impertinent imitations of fat little penises, and the outer cabbage leaves, as blue-green as Clytemnestra's Adriatic Sea, sang lullabies to the tight little heads nesting within them. Georgia closed her eyes, amazed at how her human concerns could trick her into forgetting the perfection that held them all.

After a little more picking and weeding, she shucked off her hat and gloves to wander into the orchard. There, miniscule pears and apples appeared to swell under her gaze. From the farthest reaches of the meadow, she heard their newest family members shrieking and splashing in the pond. From farther off came the sounds of Lila and Wayne hammering away on some secret project somewhere near the studio. She bowed her head, overcome with gratitude for the goodness of her life. Breathing, slowly, deliberately, she felt the community of trees breathe with her. In the profound stillness that followed her wordless prayers, she felt the orchard transporting them to some ever-listening Ear. Invisible hands guided her to lay on her belly in the meadow grasses, head to one side, arms spread wide. The Being she called 'the farm' returned her embrace.

9

Moments or hours later, Georgia found herself standing in the kitchen, the phone in her hand. Alice Maude, a stranger to the telephone for the past year, was shouting at her over the line, insisting she come over. Georgia wandered across the road infused with garden bliss, aware of a swirl of golden flecks surrounding her as she walked.

"Alice Maude," she called when she reached driveway. "Alice Maude?" Her neighbour called to her from the back garden. Georgia found her standing at her sawhorse with her hack saw poised. Georgia nodded at this new, potential weapon. "Can I help you build something?" Alice Maude shook her head. Georgia stepped forward. Alice Maude held her up her free hand.

"Do you know why George Three Feather dances here?" She didn't wait for Georgia's answer. "He told me last night. He's been protecting us."

All at once, Georgia heard faint singing. "What from?"

Alice Maude pointed to her barn. "He knows what the professor does in there. He knows all about the terrible things he does to Tess…"

"Alice Maude," Georgia began, gentle. "The professor is dead. You remember how Willy…"

"No, no, no," she cried, rushing at Georgia and yanking her into the barn's stifling interior.

"You feel it, don't you?" Alice Maude cried. "I knew you would. I knew you'd feel it, too." The women stood together, the rasping sound of their breathing echoing in the empty, fetid space. Georgia searched the shadows. On the other side of the barn, something rustled.

"Who's there?" she called, leaning into the darkness. She waited a moment. Then she knew. Like Lady Jane, the professor and his deeds lived beyond his human life. She heard her own cry as some alien voice. "What can I do, Maudey? How can I help?"

"Keep Tess away from here. Don't let her come until I've done what's needed. Keep my girl away until he's gone. He'll hurt her again if she comes back before I'm finished with him."

10

Uly and Clytemnestra held hands long after the family finished singing their raucous, 'Yum, yum, yummy, yum, yum,' grace. Touched by their reunion and grateful to have this collective joy replace the fear she'd been carrying since visiting Alice Maude's barn, Georgia couldn't help but smile. She listened to the conversations spinning out around her as people got to know one another. At some point, everyone's attention gravitated to Wayne's new project. His secret was out. He was creating a horse from found wood.

"Today, I went looking for the tail. Tomorrow, I'm gonna find the legs."

"What about the body," Clytemnestra asked. "Surely you need to find a body first, and stick the other things on it?"

Lila blew her aunt a kiss. "You'd think. But a body has too much that's hidden. I'm teaching Wayne to look for bare essentials first. The tail and legs are easiest to recognize. They don't have many secrets."

Studying Lila, Georgia was sure her daughter was speaking in code and that if she crossed her eyes perhaps, or brought her hands to opposite shoulders, Lila's hidden message would reveal itself. Instead, she kept her eyes uncrossed and her hands on her salad bowl, reminding herself that Lila had a right to her secrets.

In mid-horse talk, Wayne's mother wiped the crumbs from her son's mouth. He accepted her fussing stoically. When she'd finished her mothering, he said, "I wanna make a full sized one, a shadow horse. All outta those silvery logs."

"Cedar," said Georgia, surprised to hear her own contribution to their conversation.

"Yes, cedar." Lila's eyes shone with a mentor's pride.

"Just like that horse I've been seein' around here since I first came to live with you."

Georgia's heart danced a jig. "What horse?" she asked, wondering if clairvoyance could be caught, like a cold.

"That big white one that stands down there in the creek sometimes."

"Wayne sees ghosts?" Uly asked.

"Ghost?" Sadra jerked her attention away from her bowl of nasturtium-dotted greens. "No ghosts!" It was apparent ghost was a word Sadra not only heard before but understood as something terrifying.

"I'm gonna make just one horse to start with," Wayne said, untroubled by his mother's distress. "Maybe more if it turns out good."

"*Well*," said Lila. "If it turns out *well*." Georgia left off worrying about infecting Wayne with the gift of sight to admit the absurdity of irreverent, inventive Lila Butte passing on Scratch grammar expectations to a Somali child. "Hey, Dad, I'm taking the kids in to the mousetrap for a special end-of-school movie. Can I borrow the truck?"

"*May* I borrow the truck," said her father.

Lila elbowed Wayne. "There. This is what I've been talking about. This is Karma. You get what you give. Even grammar lessons."

Sensing Clytemnestra detach from this playful talk, Georgia wondered again what troubles pursued her sister-in-law halfway around the world.

"You *may*," her father answered. "What movie are they showing at the school?"

"The best launch into an Essex County summer. *Charlotte's Web*. Wayne has no idea what's waiting for him in that hot, crowded little gym." Fascinated, Georgia studied Lila's motherly attention to Wayne's small, giggling sisters.

"Children movie only!" Sadra said, impressing everyone with her vocabulary and her knowledge of cinematic evils.

Wayne helped himself to more mashed potatoes, an aid to finishing his peas. Georgia noticed this ploy at the same moment Lila did. "Look at that, Ma," she whispered. "I told you we were related."

After supper, Clytemnestra ran hot water into the old porcelain sink. She turned to Uly. "It does my heart good to see Lila so engaged with people despite her need for that damn chain." She stretched, yawned a jet lag yawn. "I haven't seen her look this happy in years."

"It's been decades," Uly said, packing up leftovers.

"Since the gang rape," Georgia added. This evening, she felt called to give every single thing its proper name. She studied her husband's hands as they snapped lids into place. Such competent hands, they should have been utterly familiar, yet in this moment of strained domesticity, she felt they might belong to any number of strangers.

She turned to Clytemnestra. Her sister-in-law had exchanged her travel clothes for a long cotton shift and rearranged her recently acquired hair in a single braid. With her face scrubbed and her feet bare, she looked as if she'd spent every waking minute of her life on the farm. "What's changed for our Lila?" As she waited for answers, Clytemnestra went through the composting and dishwashing rituals learned during her childhood.

Taking in everything her sister-in-law did, Georgia answered with detached curiosity. "I don't have any idea." Her voice broke out of her mouth after working its way up from a deep fissure in her chest. She wondered if Uly and his sister noticed how odd she sounded, but the pair went about their tasks apparently finding nothing remarkable in what she said or how she said it. That voice continued like some ancient oracle. "We've seen occasional changes over the last few months, but they appear to be accelerating now." She paused, then added a thought that described her more than Lila. "Perhaps Lila has found what she needs to break out of her protective cocoon."

As if Georgia hadn't spoken, Uly said, "We've had a wonderful Spring. Everything's ahead of schedule. Lila's been healing for a long time, Clytie." He brought tea cups from the table, returned for the pot, absently composted the herbs they'd brewed. He nudged his sister. "Wouldn't it be great if we could all see our chains the way Lila can?" His potent stare landed on Georgia like a blow.

Clytemnestra eyed first Uly then Georgia before returning to her dishwashing, knowing better than to get between the pair. Several cups later, she said, "Something we all learned from Mom and Dad on this farm, and the Greeks I've been living with confirm – all the gods and goddesses are omnipresent. Whether we're believers or not, there is always the energy available to ask for guidance, to open to answers."

Georgia breathed, out, in, and out once more, her experience of being heard by the farm's ever-listening Ear washing over her again. Looking through the kitchen window to the sun, still bright and only a little inclined toward the west, she knew its setting would feel especially swift this evening. For now, it pleased her to see it riding high and brilliant above the woods Harold Shuttleworth suggested they replace with a cash crop, one indistinguishable from Jones farm woods Uly and his city friends considered sacrificing to meet mortgage payments. Her mouth went dry with rage. "I am in need of a walk," she said. "I'll leave you two to visit."

11

In a cloud of unknowing, Georgia took the path to Lila's studio. As she walked through a landscape as familiar to her as her own body, she heard unfamiliar mutterings. "What is it?" she asked. "What's happening to Uly? To me? To us?"

Fear had never been a companion of her gift, but she could be startled by sudden, unexpected revelations. Still, she'd been very frightened earlier, in Alice Maude's barn. Bird song took her out of that memory and into her senses. Sunlight found its way through the canopy, gilding her hair and shoulders. Then, she was in the truck on the way to the bank. In his mildest voice, Uly revealed his plan to cut trees, extract sand and gravel, to save the Jones farm. She doubled over, retched, took a moment to come back to herself. She straightened her shoulders, walked through the trees whispering, whispering, asking, waiting for answers, walking toward the light beyond the woods.

When she reached Lila's studio, Wayne's search for perfect horse parts caught her attention. Twigs and sticks of various lengths and thicknesses lay in groups, a hodge-podge pile by the large flat stone in front of the studio door waited for later sorting. She felt a building joy because of Wayne's return, absorbed the early evening light and with it, returning peace. A soft nicker traveled up her spine. She raised her head. Lady Jane stepped from the woods, walked down the slope toward her. Lila's carving tools flared in sunlight then winked out in growing shadows.

Georgia sat on the large, warm stone in front of Lila's studio. Lady Jane stopped to stomp away flies and toss her head against an assault of gnats. At the edge of the wood, several copper beeches called to Georgia, their leaves garnets among the emerald hues of ginkgo and birch, their trunks wise old elephant legs. A heron winged lazily from the lake, banked over the distant pond, disappeared into the trees. Bergamot and mallow Georgia had planted for Lila long ago, torches of pink and scarlet to light her dark time, flashed incandescent before shadows swallowed them. A hummingbird vibrated at Lila's feeder.

Into this tableau stepped a doe and her fawn. I've been brought here for this, Georgia thought. I've been brought here to witness some life affirming ritual. She half expected a stag to leap from the shadows although she knew that buck and doe lived separate lives after the fall rutting season. The doe bent to graze, her ears flickering forward and back, her tail down and up and down again, the fawn nursing as it could.

Lady Jane nickered. The doe raised her head, assessed her surroundings, then bent to graze again. She raised her head a second time, looked directly at Georgia, then nudged her fawn away and began the walk to the amphitheatre. Looking back once to make certain her fawn followed, the doe looked a third time at Georgia. Georgia stood. Lady Jane nudged her forward. Together they followed the doe.

When she reached the lip of the amphitheatre, revelation electrified Georgia's senses. For the first time, she felt the full force of the meteor's catastrophic smashing into Earth. She felt the fire, the displacement, the open wound. Then, she felt its healing through time and the many species who made a home in its aftermath, who made meaning out of its chaotic arrival. She looked around. Overgrown with vetch and wild carrot, the hollow seemed an insignificant depression. She took her descent in slow careful steps, feeling the time before time pass through her cells. She reached its floor, the stage where they'd performed so many plays, looked up. Echoes of their performances reverberated in the air, dire warnings against the perils of resisting one's fate, of indulging in hubris, of ignoring the messages perpetually offered by the unseen world. Time had rewritten the gaping wound into coherent story. Standing in the aftermath of that earlier catastrophe, she felt how, yet again, because of a different sort of cataclysm, they were birthing something new. She, all of them, were time's dancing, shaping energies, serving the farm, the county, the massive glacial gift of fresh water and rich loam and swamp decay.

Swallows fed on the swarm of gnats her arrival stirred into flight. Lake Erie's fishy perfume permeated the air. Lady Jane blew warm, salty air into the hollow between Georgia's neck and her shoulder. On the slope a little above her, the doe grazed and her fawn nursed. Woman and doe looked to the tree tops above the vast depression.

She became aware of Webster's woods, her childhood refuge from city expectations. She knew every path, every toe-stubbing root. She recalled the sacred archway she and her cousin formed after they learned about pleaching techniques. Beneath those woven branches she and Webster promised friendship forever.

Led by a swoop of swallows, Georgia retraced her steps. She sang to the birds until the sound of her own voice oppressed her. She stopped, a fresh silence enveloping her. She sat on one of the theatre's natural benches until she felt called to climb once again. Doe and fawn followed her progress with large, kind eyes that told her she'd tricked herself into believing she understood Webster's intentions.

Because of her adolescent guilt over initiating their sexual experimentation, she'd avoided the difficult business of talking with him about TriChem. When she turned toward home, she knew what to do. She knew it was time to call on Webster.

12

"Where have you been, Gee? No reading for two whole nights. We want a story. Read about Harry and Hermione." Uly sprawled beside his sister on the swing, the picture of perennial boyhood.

"You two don't need me for Harry." The urgent need to speak with Webster made her harsh. "Clytie can read that one all by herself."

Clytemnestra sided with Uly. "I can't read, Georgeous. I've got jet lag. I'm toast. Come on. It's been too long since you told me a story." She patted the swing. "You sit here. I'll get the book."

Georgia watched her sister-in-law disappear into the house. "Where's Willy? I haven't seen him since supper."

"Clytie gave him a bath, with special imported Greek bubbles. He's preening."

"But I just gave him one. He'll peel for sure. Where is he now?"

He ignored her concern. "At the pond, I think."

Georgia stared into the distance. When her words finally came, she felt relief. "I've been thinking about Webster, Uly. I'm going to talk with him. I need to hear whether TriChem is a real threat or just town gossip."

"What brought this on?"

She didn't speak of the amphitheatre, of the sense of being woven into the healing following a cataclysm no one could yet articulate. Instead, she spoke a different truth. "We're not the only people who care for this land. Webster has always done his part. I can't believe he wants TriChem to kill everything here, or anywhere…" She thought a moment, then added with heat, "or that he'd countenance you and your friends cutting down his trees and destroying the understory by digging for sand and gravel. All in some misguided attempt to save the land."

Before he could react, Clytemnestra returned with the Potter book. "Clytie, you'll have to do the honours, jet lag or no. Georgia is calling on Webster." He couldn't meet Georgia's eyes.

13

On the bank of the stream, Georgia removed her sandals and threw them one after the other to the opposite bank. She waded in to the shallow water, bent low, cupped her hands. She drank, splashed cold water on her face and neck, willed away her anger at Uly.

"You are an absolute fool to be drinking that water." Webster Jones stood in the shadows cast by the family of cedars on his side of the creek.

After a few moments of agitated excitement, Georgia smiled up at him. "There's nothing around here that could poison it. You don't spray. We don't. And I'm pretty sure there isn't a good-sized herd of cattle or poisoned crop for miles around."

"Hold on there, Gee. What about airborne particulate matter?" Flustered by Harold Shuttleworth echoes, Georgia waded out of the water and stooped to fasten her sandals. When she straightened, she found Webster only a couple of feet away, his hand held out to help her up the uneven slope. When their hands clasped, she felt the unmistakable flesh of kin.

"When did you get to be such an expert on dirt?" she asked.

He laughed easily. "Those garrulous house painters, Rusty and Pete, will tell you all about the source of my expertise. I believe my mother-and-father housekeeping stories are their single source of social capital." Grinning, Webster looked at Georgia full on. "But you should talk. Norman down at the gas station tells me you're still letting your goat have the run of the house."

"Willy's a member of the family. Grandma Jones and your mother taught me well." She walked a little way along the path bordering his alfalfa before pointing to his house. "How about asking me in for tea, so I can see how well you're doing in the dirt department."

"You don't want to be going into my house."

Aware he might have misinterpreted her meaning she regretted her joke. "No," she said. She laid her hand on his arm. "I came to talk to you about…"

"You've heard about my kids pestering me to sell. You've heard about TriChem. I figured it was just a matter of time before I went to you or you came to me."

Georgia looked into eyes very much like her own. "Yes," she said. "I'm glad we don't have to pretend. Are you really considering selling to them, Webby?"

Webster Jones, she knew in her bones, to be a good man. She also knew her love of nature and her knack for seeing and feeling beyond her ordinary senses were proclivities she'd inherited from the Jones side of the family, Webster's family, despite her mother's denial and lofty ways. "It can't be easy to resist a bundle of cash, even if it comes from a company that will destroy the place."

Relief at finally being able to talk about his current quandaries softened his broad, weathered face. "I wish I could tell you I haven't considered it, Gee. But the truth is, I'm thinking about it." He paused, his silence conveying his agony. "In fact, I seem to spend my days thinking about nothing else." He rubbed his eyes, then smiled the sorrowful smile she knew well. "My kids need the money. They've made it pretty clear it's all they want from me." Regretting his self-pity, he said, "You know how it is, Gee. They've got mortgages. And the grandkids will be needing college money soon." He looked into the sky. Georgia followed his gaze. Both watched a heron fly in the easy untroubled way of large birds in flight. "She's on her way home, to the Pelee marsh. Every time I see one, I get the shivers."

"Grandma Jones always said, 'Great Blue Goddess.' Remember?"

"I've been seeing her." He said it simply, taking her understanding for granted.

Georgia nodded toward the house. "Is she in there with the chickens?" Webster laughed, shook his head.

"If she were, she'd tell me to wash my supper dishes before taking my evening constitutional."

"Do you see Lady Jane?"

"Spring's horse? Now and again. You?"

"Almost every day. I think Lila may, too, although she doesn't say. She's busy with Wayne, the young boy you met last year. Wayne sees her." She marveled at how their feet knew where to take them. "Did your kids ever see her?"

"No. My kids take after Moira. 'Just the facts, Ma'am. Just the facts.'" He laughed at his imitation of TV Detective Joe Friday.

"Uly and I went to the bank this morning. He's pushing to get a loan, using our farm as collateral, so he can buy yours with some of his city friends."

Webster whistled. "That's not quite as crazy as my kids wanting me to sell to TriChem, but it's pretty close."

"You think so?"

"They'll give you the money all right. But how will you pay it back? If you lose your farm, nobody'll care for it like you do."

Georgia snapped. "Then why force us to consider it? How can you entertain notions of selling our family's farm to a bunch of…"

Webster stepped back from her. "You don't have any right to be telling me about family matters when you just slam the door on my love without so much as a single conversation."

"Webby! That was fifty years ago." She pointed to the path they followed. "I guess we both know where we're going."

They walked in silence, Webster releasing his indignation and taking the lead when the path narrowed, Georgia studying him as she'd studied Uly when he carried the dead rabbit to its final resting place. What is a man, she thought, that you can cause such heartache? As she stared at the slope of his shoulders, she felt he, like Uly, carried the history of the world's love and sorrow in his beautiful, disappearing body.

"There," Webster said, pointing. She looked past him to the massive boulder barely visible through the dense wood. As she looked, a jolt of recognition shot out from the stone. She felt claimed.

"I haven't been here for years and years," she whispered, moving through the trees, crossing the small clearing, pausing, then touching the massive stone.

"I come every week or so."

Delight rippled through her. "You do? Why?"

Her cousin thought for a moment. "I'm not sure. It's kind of like church is for others. Coming here is just something the reverent part of me has to do."

The boulder stood within a circle at the heart of the Jones northern woodlot, its twin in a similar circle on Butte land, the surrounding trees on both farms giving these massive, ancient Beings room to do whatever it is such Beings do. Georgia didn't remember the Jones circle as quite so generous or the solitary boulder as quite so large. She bowed her head before resting both hands on the stone's warm surface. As soon as she made contact, she felt her hands on its twin the morning before.

The stone's vibrant green moss responded to her touch. She brought her fingers to her lips, whispered, "Sacrament." Waning sunlight bathed the stone in warm yellow light. She relaxed, leaned her body against this ancient friend.

Her cousin walked to her side, not giving his weight to the stone but facing the same direction as she, each taking in a dead cedar's bird visitors and the last of the sunshine on the far side of the circle. As they watched, a ruby-throated hummingbird perched on one of the snag's branches. His mate soon joined him. The birds cleaned their bills on the cedar, preened their feathers, then cleaned their bills a second time. In slow motion, Webster lifted his hand so his right thumb was visible to Georgia. She knew what his signal meant, heard echoes of his boyish, delighted whisper, 'no bigger than my thumb, these birds, their wings no bigger than my thumb nail.' He cleared his throat. The hummers flew off.

Turning to her, his eyes moist with wonder, he invited her into his private world. "I saw a talk show that helped me understand my kids." Georgia's eyes filled at the sight of tears on his cheeks. She remembered the neighbourhood excitement when, in the mid-fifties, he erected a thirty-foot tower and antenna to improve the reception of a twelve-inch black and white TV set.

"You watch a lot of TV?"

He dried his face. "Not a lot, but I have my favourites. CTV news. Oprah. It might have been on her show that I heard about a book," he interrupted himself to offer her a shy smile. "It was all about you, Georgia."

"About me?"

"About you if you were living in the states. You and fifty million people just like you. The writers called you 'cultural creatives'…people who love the earth and work for peace and justice. People who spread the word about sustainability."

"Fifty million of us? With the world the way it is, how can that be true?"

"That's what their book is about. My kids belong to another group, or aspire to – the 'Moderns.' They want lots of money and the freedom to spend it on whatever they want. They believe creative, land loving types like you are crazy, you know, just tree huggers and dirt worshippers standing in the way of progress. To them, you're deluded about what life's really about."

She laughed. "I've heard that before. What about you? Where do you fit in?"

"You probably won't believe this, but I've thought a lot about where I fit in. I'll admit I tried to fit into your group, but I've got too much inertia to make it stick. I love the land, but I have a lot of resistance to social reform. Like those kids you bring out here. I believe in jail, Georgia. And you believe in…"

"Growing things." His laughter, explosive and unexpected, startled her. He raised his hand to gentle her, then thought better of this intimacy. After a moment, he returned his hand to the massive stone.

"Webster," she said. "You know I love you, have always loved you."

"Don't."

"I have to say it."

"It's too late, Georgia."

"I don't believe that." She blinked away tears. "The thing with Uly, it was unstoppable. I wish I'd told you. Before we…" Georgia bowed her head.

"Yes, you should have told me. I'll never get over Uly announcing your secret marriage at a family dinner, the very dinner my mother's engagement ring waited in my pocket for the perfect moment to…"

They stood in potent silence. After half a century, he still bore this grudge against her, against the rules that said cousins, first or second, shouldn't marry. Against his best friend, a man he'd been avoiding for decades because his first love chose him. Georgia held the pain of hurting him until his generous laugh exploded again. "Has that illiterate husband of yours ever figured out why I got so busy after you two got hitched?"

"Webster…"

He shook his head. "You might as well know. You're the only person in my life that caused me to do something I am truly ashamed of. I married Moira because I couldn't have you. That poor woman, she had to find her satisfaction in things. That's why she was so house-proud. It didn't take her very long to figure out she was second choice."

Stumbling away from him, Georgia turned to the woods. Webster caught her in a ferocious embrace. When he let her go, an unexpected peace leapt between them. Georgia swallowed tears. "I have to be getting back. Clytemnestra is with us."

"For the wedding?"

"Yes. I know Lola invited you, but I want you to promise you'll come."

"Uly really wants me there?"

"We all do. You're family."

Webster whistled under his breath. "I've got to hand it to him. He can still make me feel like a worm."

"I guess we both know how important worms are." She started back down the path, then turned to him after a few steps. "If there are so many people like me, why is the world in this terrible state?"

Webster brushed a mosquito from her hair. "You don't know about each other yet. It's people like me and my kids that make the news. Hell, we own the newspapers and TV stations. We decide which stories get told. Media ownership, that's where the power is." He felt her distress. "Don't you worry. Those fifty million, they just keep doing what they're doing, the way you do. Making change a little bit at a time."

Georgia closed her eyes, felt waves of grief passing up through her feet and into her heart. "What about you, Webby?" she asked. "Do you really want to sell just to please your kids? Doesn't the land talk to you anymore?"

If Webster felt the earth's grief, he made no sign. "Want to sell? Hell, no. It's been my one and only ambition to die right here. You know, just lie down in the woods and let the crows pick away, right down to my bones. Before Moira died and all this blew up with the kids, I was thinking of putting it into my will that they had to build a platform in the trees near our rock, like the First Peoples used to do."

Georgia did her best to hold onto the present with both hands. Webster stepped close, whispering, his hand light and warm on her shoulder. As they embraced again, she felt the dance of their early life together, a slow rhythmic waltz of love and pain. They stepped apart. She turned to the stream. He backed away and was gone.

1

Lola stood on the shoulder of the Essex Bypass holding a MAR-RY ME sign scrawled in lurid red paint. Cars stopped at regular intervals, but before Lola could speak with the drivers, Lila rushed out from the roadside scrub and smashed their car hoods with her chain. Georgia whimpered. Uly nudged her. Confounded by sleep and terror, she rose up on one elbow, frantic. "Is it Thursday?"

Uly threw off their top sheet. "Not yet." In spite of the ongoing tension between them, his familiar voice comforted her. "Don't tell me. Wedding dreams."

"Wedding nightmares."

"What did you find out? Does Webster plan to sell to TriChem?" Her husband's voice conveyed the usual mix of emotions whenever he mentioned Webster Jones.

Georgia ignored his question. "You're wearing your Saturday work clothes."

Uly snapped his suspenders. "Rain date. I told Max I'd help him with whatever we didn't get to Saturday. He's off all week." He looked away to hide his pleasure in thwarting her expectations that he would drive to Detroit for Tess Vaughan. "I thought I'd talk to him about the men from the plant, about our plans. He might be interested."

Looking to score another point for your team, Georgia thought, her anger toward him building again. She considered her plan to have her mother buy Web's farm, not for Georgia, she believed, self-righteous, but for their daughters. Webster's kids would get their money and the farms would be protected, not only from

TriChem, but from the ineptitude of Uly's city friends. Webster would remain on the land. Grow his alfalfa. Watch his TV shows. Fantasize about dying on his platform in the trees. Playing the grand lady, her mother would extend Webster's children an open invitation to the farm because, after all, many people cultivated an interest in their roots as they matured. Georgia imagined this unlikely future knowing Webster's children's return to the family farm would not happen, that years ago they'd converted to the Church of Toronto and Big-City Life. This meant the two farms would belong entirely to…

She shook her head to rid herself of adolescent revenge fantasies. With a gut punch, she realized Uly and the men intended to establish permanent logging and sand-and-gravel businesses even after the mortgage had been paid off, because these businesses provided alternative work to the car factories. For a moment she counted on Max's sensitivity to the land to resist Uly's invitation to join this madness. Then it dawned on her. Max would take part in any business that made it possible to spend more time near Lila. Accepting Uly's invitation to join the men would ensure daily contact. Stewing, Georgia brought up her promise to Alice Maude. "It's Tuesday. Tess is flying in. How long will you be with Max?"

Uly strived for an off-hand tone. "No worries about that. I've asked Max to pick me up. You can take the truck. I know how you love to drive in Detroit."

"How will I ever explain all your bumper stickers to customs officers?" She fell back on her pillow, appalled at the thought of driving to Detroit in what was sure to be blistering heat. "They're cracking down on crackpots. Your truck shouts crackpot to the skies."

Uly didn't answer. She went to the door, heard him running water in the bathroom sink. When he turned off the water, he began to whistle 'You are My Sunshine' loud enough for Georgia to hear.

2

Smiling a tight, smug smile, Uly looked in on Georgia before heading downstairs. "I forgot to tell you. I asked Max to the wedding."

She tried for lightness. "If you're near the bank, invite Harold and his wife as well. Goodness knows we'll have enough food." She added this last comment with muted bitterness not wanting to wake Clytemnestra.

After more stewing, she dressed quickly. On her way to the kitchen, she glanced into Lola's room. Willy, a satin eye masque dangling from his horns, had curled himself into a neat circle at the centre of the bed. "You look happy," Georgia whispered. Willy maaed his happy song.

Downstairs, Georgia watched the fine red line of heat expand on the eastern horizon. Wedding duties pressed in on her. She turned to Uly and his food preparations. "When are Spring and Jason arriving? I can't remember whether they said today or tomorrow. If it's today, Clytie will have to play hostess while you're with Max and I'm with Alice Maude and Tess." She searched for signs of guilt on his face. Found none.

"Mother said Wednesday, Father, Thursday," Uly said. He poured his barley water into a mason jar and secured the lid. "We'll have to wait to see who got it right." The elder Buttes were coming in from a New York City-New England tour and required nothing in the way of special preparation. Georgia looked up from these preoccupations to see Wayne and Lila jogging to the house.

"Good morning, Ma," Lila called. "We're going out for a run."

"I'm looking for horse ribs."

Scowling at the thought of jogging in building, humid heat, Georgia offered a brief wave of acknowledgment. She turned to Uly, ambushed by the longing to express a little kindness before the day spun them into their separate worlds. The phone rang before she could reach out to him. Listening to his easy conversation, she envied his time with Max as much as she dreaded Detroit's heat, its traffic, its speed. She touched his arm lightly, whispered, "I'd better remind Alice Maude about Tess." He pulled his arm away.

Crossing the road to her neighbour's farm, Georgia wept bitter tears. She hoped Alice Maude wasn't watching her turbulent approach. If her skittish neighbour saw her distress, it would send her deeper into her own. Drying her tears, Georgia rapped on the screen door. At that moment, Alice Maude's Grandmother clock chimed seven. Her neighbour would have been up for hours.

"That demon has her down there." Georgia turned to find the younger woman standing behind her, her hands empty of sharp objects. "When I've made everything clean, she'll come up again." Alice Maude, looking as prim as a porcelain doll, wore a freshly ironed summer dress, white ankle socks, and bear claw ice navigators. Georgia was about to ask if she meant Persephone when her neighbour waved her to follow her down the drive.

"Erie's young one. George's young one. That child will come up from all the darkness when I've done my job for Tess. They're connected. But you know that. I want Erie's young one back, too, for Tess, for Lila, but especially for Erie. She's her mother after all." She grabbed Georgia's hand.

Georgia shivered. "Has something happened?"

Without answering, Alice Maude let go of Georgia's hand and rushed into the dilapidated barn. Georgia followed, oppressed by the scent of rotting hay, and beneath this, fear, human and animal. She did her best to focus. "You remember, Tess is flying in later this morning?" Alice Maude stared into the darkness.

Georgia tried again. "Tess is flying in today. You asked if Uly would drive you to the airport. He's busy with Max Love this morning, but he's left the truck for us. Tess gets in at noon. We won't leave until about nine, so we won't have to rush."

Alice Maude escaped whatever led her to enter the barn. Stepping from hot darkness into warm morning light she finally answered Georgia. "You bring her home. If she's going to live here, I have to clean the place. I have to get everything ready for Tess and the other young one." In this moment, it seemed to Georgia they were two ordinary women talking about their everyday chores.

"Are you sure you won't come with me? We can make it an adventure. Have lunch in the Big Smoke."

"No. I have to do my job. You have to do yours."

"Shall I stay to help you? We can tell Tess to use a car service."

"No," Alice Maude cried. "You have to meet her. If you don't, she won't have the courage to come back."

Unnerved, Georgia walked with her neighbour toward the road. "If you change your mind…"

"I won't change my mind." Alice Maude's tone left no room for argument. "I have to take care of things here so they can come home."

"They? Is Tess bringing friends?" Georgia thought of the truck's countless bumper stickers, its bench seat, its three seatbelts. She thought of international travelers' all-too-frequent difficulties with Canadian customs officers.

At the mouth of the driveway the women stopped. "No. I have to clean the place." As if they'd just solved all their problems, Alice Maude embraced her friend. "Tess always loved you, Georgia. You're her second mother, not my sister, Grace. You always make her feel safe." She kissed Georgia's cheek. "I'll make sure everything here is perfect for her." She sounded like any ordinary woman preparing to welcome a beloved child home.

3

In the time before making her preparations for the trip to Detroit, Georgia showed Sadra and the girls how to wash and spin dry the young greens, weigh them, and fix the labels on bags. Kim made a game of it, adding nasturtium blossoms to the bags her mother filled with salad greens. Karen closed each bag with a twist tie, her mouth working to help complete this important task. Later in the day, with Wayne as their interpreter, they would read *Charlotte's Web* with Lila. As they did the day before, the girls and Wayne would draw pictures and tell Lila stories of their lives before they arrived in Canada.

An abundance of sugar snap peas compelled Georgia to fill a few pint baskets for the roadside stand before dressing for the drive into town. She looked up from this harvesting when a voice called to her from the front gate. It was a young man, a stranger, whose features slowly arranged themselves into the person she'd found in the drainage ditch two days before. "Good morning," she called. "I'd know you anywhere."

"You must be Mrs. Butte."

"Call me Georgia," she said, standing. "We've spoken on the phone, but I still don't know your name." Pushing aside her outstretched hand, the lanky stranger gathered Georgia into a full-bodied embrace.

When he released her, Georgia stepped back to get a good look at him. Tall, at least a couple of inches over six feet, he wore his long sun-bleached hair in a pony tail. His eyes were dark brown, his skin ruddy from sun and wind. He made her laugh out loud when he lifted her off the ground, this second time squeezing the breath out of her.

Laughing, she said, "Are you from around here, Mr. Mysterious?"

"I'm renting the old Beam place next to the Miner Sanctuary. Just for the summer."

"I didn't hear your car."

The young man made himself entirely at home, folding himself onto the platform swing. She had the sudden knowing that he too would become part of their family. "I don't drive," he told her. She detected a mild defensiveness when he expanded his confession. "I don't believe in cars. I've discovered this is a somewhat radical and unpopular view here in car culture."

Georgia felt she'd always known him. "How very nice for the environment."

When Clytemnestra opened the kitchen door, the young man leapt to his feet. Watching him prepare to meet Uly's sister, Georgia thought of the carved wooden men whose dancing legs beat out wild rhythms on thin paddles at French Canadian soirées in Belle River and La Salle. She introduced Clytemnestra, thinking the young man would say his own name. When he didn't, she prompted him. Seeming not to hear, he wandered into the garden.

Watching him closely, Georgia marveled when he began communicating with Sadra through a combination of sign language, English, and an unfamiliar tongue. Ending their conversation with a kiss to both the young mother's cheeks, he bent low over the closest garden bed as if in prayer. Clytemnestra nudged her. "Whoever he is, keep him. He's as adorable as Willy."

"Speaking of Willy, you gave him an eye masque."

"I did. He was feeling so blue. We have to keep up his spirits while that awful haircut grows in. How's Mae doing with his suit?"

Georgia glanced at the sun to calculate the time. "While I'm fetching Tess Vaughan from Detroit, you can take Willy down to Mae's to visit. I know she'd love to see you."

When the young man joined them, Georgia took his arm. "Son, I want to know your name."

"It's Pete," he answered offhandedly. "What can I do for you, Mrs. Butte? Georgia." He offered her a radiant smile. "I am at your service for the rest of my life."

Georgia's heart lifted. "I have to go to the airport in Detroit in a little while, but when I get back, we'll go over some possibilities."

She slipped into the house to make more tea and to spy on her visitor from the window. An iridescent chartreuse and gold aura fanned around him. "Pete," she whispered, savouring the name… "Peat."

4

Georgia filled her water bottle, packed a container with dried apple slices and sunflower seeds, and loaded the truck with salad greens and peas for the Windsor Farmers' Market. As she packed the crates, Karen and Kim made a game of reading the bumper stickers on Uly's truck. Finding her ID and American money under the truck's front seat, she slid behind the wheel. Pete surprised her when he opened the passenger door. "I told you. I've come to help you."

"But you don't believe in cars. Or ancient trucks, I presume?"

"It's true I don't drive them," he agreed. "And I think they're very bad for the environment and the people who drive them, but when I have to, I can get into one." One of his brown eyes looked directly at her. The other appeared to be studying the rear-view mirror. He blushed when this happened. "It's from painting so much," he said. "I have a lazy eye. But only now and again. It's happening now because of, you know," he smiled, sheepish. "It's from getting loaded the other night."

"Do you have your birth certificate for the border?" To her astonishment, he retrieved his passport from a back pocket in his trousers. "Not many people wander around with their passports at the ready, Peter. Did you just return from the states?" He seemed reluctant to answer. For a brief moment, the demons of doubt urged her to order him out of the truck. She didn't know him. How wise was it to cross an international boundary with a stranger? He could be one of the infamous Windsor drug lords, for all she knew, never mind the ax murderer Lola conjured, a sly criminal disguised as peat.

Punctuality won over fear. "Shut your door, Pete. We have to get a move on." The young man buckled his seatbelt before crossing himself several times. Georgia eased out of neutral and into first. "Are you Catholic?" she asked. He turned a puzzled face to her. "You crossed yourself."

"Oh, the crossing thing. I learned that from a couple of guys in my keyboard class in high school. They always crossed themselves before they took a test. They swore the Virgin Mary helped out anybody in a tight spot. If they asked Her to intervene."

Delighted to forget the perils of Detroit freeways for a time, Georgia picked up speed then glanced at the young man. "The papers said your parents reported you missing. How did they know you were in trouble if you're living at the Beam place? Are they there as well?"

"My parents live in Windsor. When I didn't answer the phone on Friday, they checked with my friends. On Saturday, they reported me missing. Everybody knows how I get when I've had a few too many and insist on walking home." He clutched the arm rest and hit imaginary brakes with his large right foot. "Sorry," he said. "I'll try not to take over."

"If you don't drive," Georgia said, "that's probably best."

To distract himself, Pete concentrated on the bumper stickers covering the truck's hood. "You said this is your husband's truck?" Georgia nodded. "Is he political?"

"Oh my, yes."

"Just what does 'Support your right to arm bears' mean? Politically?"

Georgia smiled at the mobile dictionary, an ongoing source of support Uly invented to disguise his dyslexia. The sticker Pete referred to was one from Uly's Grateful Dead collection. It sat under 'Give Us This Day Our Daily Dead' and 'Thanks Jerry.' Although he found reading difficult, Uly could memorize relationships. As soon as he saw the little Jerry Bears, he remembered that Give and Bears and Thanks could be found on his hood. "We're pacifists," she answered, "with a sense of humour."

"I get it," Pete said, delighted. "What about 'Visualize Whirled Peas'? What's the political thrust of that one?"

"Oh, that one's very important. It goes with 'Think Locally, Act Neighbourly' and 'Dance a Farmer Home.'"

"Where does he find them?"

Georgia wondered if one day she would confide in this young man. For now, she told him a half truth. "He travels some now that he's retired from the engine plant at Chryslers. He's a dowser and a builder, as well as a farmer. Whenever he hits a new place, as a crew member or on a dowsing job, he finds the local bumper-sticker emporium and adds to his collection."

"He's running out of room."

"Oh, no. He works in layers. And the epoxy he paints over them means this old truck will never rust." She was glad to speak well of Uly instead of nursing her anger at his willingness to decimate Webster's farm.

The young man nodded appreciatively. "I look forward to meeting the old dude."

Georgia smiled at 'old dude' and the hipster it conjured. "So, Peter, what are you doing at the Beam place?"

"I'm a painter. I've got a commission from the Miner Foundation to paint the geese and ducks. While I'm out here, I'm doing habitat sketches for some botanists at the University of Windsor."

His shimmering aura flashed in Georgia's imagination. Instantly, the car filled with swirling widgeon and mallard energy. "Did you study at the University of Windsor?" She was curious to know if he'd met Lila.

"I did a year in the BFA program before they threw me out. I'd already discovered my line. They wanted me to thicken it. And make it red." He laughed at his own bleak joke. "They need to leave people alone who've already developed a style. Independent studies work best for working artists like me. Other disciplines have them. It's just a matter of time before the institutionalized art types catch on." He jerked his hands out as if to save himself from falling.

"What is it?" Georgia cried, braking.

"Nothing. I just hate hurtling along like this. It is so unnatural. At least to me. My last name's Stone. I'm a Capricorn. I've got a Virgo moon and Taurus rising. Peter means rock. I don't think anyone is more attached to the ground than I am."

"Do you study astrology?"

"Hell no." He shot her a quick look. "Excuse me, Mrs. Butte. Georgia. I'm used to coarser company. I'll watch my language." Phantom feathers glowed pink and green in Georgia's peripheral vision. "Girl friends have been into this stuff. You know girls. They love to explain things. They have to figure out why I can't fly to Florida or drive to Montreal. I mean, I can do it, but I'd have to swallow a bus load of tranqs to be in a moving vehicle for that long."

Georgia wondered how Peter Stone would survive the journey to the Detroit airport and back. "If you change your mind about making this trip, let me know. After I deliver the greens to the market, I can drop you off at your parents' place." She was sincere in her offer but hoped he'd make the journey with her.

"I've got a theory," Peter Stone went on. "Fate brought us together, and now fate is telling me it's time I pushed the envelope of vehicular travel." He turned to her with an endearing smile and both eyes. "We're entangled now, Mrs.… Georgia. Saving a life is a very big deal."

Shivers crept over Georgia's forearms as she merged onto the Essex Bypass. Highway 401 and its four lanes of speeding traffic beckoned, but taking the major highway meant traversing the stretch of road where so many people died in a killer fog two years earlier. Feeling the agony of the people and the place, Georgia's stomach tightened. Given her new friend's palpable sensitivities, she decided the slower, less emotional route into Windsor would be better for both of them. "May I ask how you got your commission? It sounds like an important one. Someone must think very well of your talents."

"One of my professors recommended me. When he heard they were looking for a wildlife artist, he told them there wasn't anyone better."

"You're a realist."

"I love what I see when I look…at birds… at animals…at insects. Nature's designs are exquisite. Most people think, oh, yeah, peacock, shiny blue feathers tipped with round circles like eyes. They don't stop to marvel at the iridescence, the symmetry. And the asymmetry. We miss the essence of life when we don't look. Really look."

"My daughter's a carver."

Peter Stone's excitement exploded. "Oh, I know about Lila Butte. One of my friends has a chain trail on his hood. He stopped to ask if he could help her with a log she was dragging, then, out of nowhere… clunk. Everybody in the art world around here knows about Lila Butte. This guy with the chain trail, he's working up the courage to have her sign it."

Surprised to feel something other than anxiety about her daughter's habit of belting cars with her heavy-duty steel, Georgia permitted a small exhalation of pride. "Were you at school together?"

"My first and only year overlapped her last. I saw her in the life drawing studio a few times but was told to avoid eye contact. She had those chains on. I value my hands and arms too much to risk direct assault."

"I don't think she's ever attacked a person, has she?"

"You know how rumours are. Does she still wear the chains? She belted my buddy's car more than a year ago."

"Chain. A fairly long one. Yes, she still wears it."

Peter Stone put his hands on the dash, bracing as Georgia stopped for the light at Walker Road. "I don't like to pry, Mrs. Butte, but can you tell me why she wears it? I've heard so many different stories. You have to know. Lila Butte is already a legend in BFA circles. Hell, throughout the university."

"She's certainly a legend around our farm. All of Kingsville and Leamington know about her chain wielding habits."

"And nobody's pressed charges? That tells you what a great artist she is." Georgia took a quick look at Peter Stone. He was starry eyed, a true admirer. "If she weren't Lila Butte, nobody'd talk about her. Or she'd be in jail. But she's got stuff in the National Gallery already. I saw the owls she did for the Windsor Gallery. They're spectacular. I swear I can smell them when I get close."

Georgia prayed Peter Stone had begun the vital journey from his head to his heart. "Lila wears the chain because she was raped," she said. "She was very young at the time, not yet twelve. There were four of them, the youngest nineteen, the oldest twenty-four. She'd been feeding horses for a friend's family and was walking home for a swim. She was at that age when boys weren't even a blip on her radar. They did a great deal of physical damage and even more that's emotional and spiritual. It changed the world for Lila, for all of us. She went from being open and trusting to…" A muffled sound made Georgia glance at her companion. Beside her, Peter Stone sat weeping.

5

During her deliveries to friends who sold her greens at the market, Georgia's time with Peter Stone shifted between thoughtful silence and easy conversation. But after the last crate had been unloaded and she headed to the bridge entrance, her companion fidgeted. "What is it, Peter?" He pointed to the Ambassador Bridge.

"Don't worry," Georgia assured him. "I've crossed this bridge thousands of times." She marveled at the way an everyday activity to some transformed into a terrifying test of courage for others, a difference suggesting, to her at least, the influence of past lives. Wanting to soothe his distress, she told him the story of George Three Feather 'learning things' from those who danced beneath the bridge. Peter listened with distracted interest.

At the halfway point, she pointed out a high riding freighter lowing its territorial warning to a ship thrumming down river from Lake St. Clair. The young man glanced down then pulled his feet onto the seat as if the bottle-green waters of the Detroit River might somehow leap into Uly's old truck. The sight of the river below proved too much for him, and for the remainder of the crossing Peter Stone closed his eyes, clutched his knees, and maintained a terrified silence.

When they reached the American shore, Georgia patted his knee. "We're on firm ground again, Pete." Peter remained rigid. She pulled into one of four snaking customs lines and prepared to show her documents and answer the usual questions. "You can open your eyes," she said, hoping he'd look a little calmer when they reached scrutinizing officials.

To calm him, she began to coax him into the present moment with stories about border crossings. "Just look at all these trucks," she said. His eyes remained closed. "I read an article in Maclean's that claimed an idling truck at a border crossing emits about as much pollution as someone driving for a hundred hours."

Peter peaked out at the world. "That was as bad as mumps at twenty-eight."

Georgia saved her mump questions for some time in the future should they turn out to have one that included this level of intimacy. The exhaust from the idling eighteen wheelers prompted Georgia to rummage in the drawer beneath her seat for an ancient bandana. She held this over her nose and mouth as they waited to be summoned forward.

Many of Uly's older bumper stickers urged protests against NAFTA, but these had been epoxied over with more current concerns like 'Common Decency – Better than Common Sense,' 'Remember Walkerton – Protect People and Water,' 'Pesticides are All-Purpose Killers,' and 'Say No to Genetically Modified Food.' Some, such as 'Love the Earth – Harness the Sun' and 'Live Simply, that Others May Simply Live' were unassailable, but those dealing with time-sensitive political issues were eventually replaced by evolving environmental and social concerns.

Lila's special gifts to her father adorned the driver's door. 'A Meat-Eating Feminist is a Contradiction in Terms' sat above 'Marilyn Waring is a Global Visionary.' Beneath these stickers, in letters formed out of the tiny agile bodies of human and non-human beings, read Lila's special message to the world:

> LISTEN.
> EARTH IS CALLING.
> WE HAVE WORK TO DO.
> LISTEN.

At this border crossing, as at others, Georgia felt the incoherence at the heart of most people's lives. To make matters worse, a mere thirty miles away, TriChem sniffed around the scented markings made by Webster's children's longing for money instead of home. With a heavy heart she wondered if young Frank and Viola understood that the cars, the electronic trinkets, the trips to Cancun and the Caymans for which they'd gladly trade the family farm were all manifestations of the eternal sellout. "Only the bribes change over time," she muttered.

"What?"

Before Georgia could respond to Peter, a trucker in the next lane called to her. "My brother has a biodynamic farm up on the Bruce. I help support it with my runs." Waving goodbye, he pulled ahead for his interview.

Their customs interrogations uneventful, Georgia followed signs to the I-75, tumbling the TriChem situation over in her mind and heart as she navigated road construction. Peter offered a few noisy exclamations to ward off imaginary crashes. In spite of emotional overload and heavy freeway traffic, the pair made good time, parking and finding Tess's gate fifteen minutes before her plane's arrival.

If they got back to the farm around two, Georgia speculated, she might be able to work in the garden for an hour or so before going back into town to pick up Lela and Fiona. It occurred to her Uly might be available to make the second run into to town, leaving her to her knee pads and the emotional restoration of garden work. She prayed Tess wouldn't ask to shop in Detroit.

Peter led Georgia to a bench near Tess's arrival gate, folding onto it as he'd folded onto the garden swing earlier that morning. "Air conditioning," he said. "I don't like it much, but it beats sweltering. Who did you say we're picking up?"

"I don't think I told you. She's my neighbour's daughter, Tess Vaughan."

Peter whistled. "She's as famous as Lila Butte. You must have some magic ingredient in your water. I just read her West Bank report. Does she have a death wish?"

"My goodness! What makes you ask that?"

"Because she goes to places where she's likely to take a hit. They get to choose their assignments, you know. She was in Bosnia for years. Now she's mixing it up with the terrorists on both sides of the Israeli-Palestinian conflict. In those videos the networks run, you know, with the reporter's voice all crackly and guns and bombs going off in the background, she doesn't look much older than a kid."

"She's Lila's age. Thirty-five. You might know her father from the university. Chauncey Vaughan."

"Holy crap! That explains everything."

"What do you mean?"

"If that guy were my father, I'd have a death wish too." Peter Stone reddened. "I know I shouldn't speak ill of the dead, but he was a creep." He puzzled for a minute. "That was his place, across from your farm? How did you manage to keep your daughters safe?"

Georgia winced, glimpsing Lila's early shattering. She did her best to quell a sudden flare of guilt. "Most days, Tess played at our place. How do you know about the professor? Did you take an English course from him?"

"He taught first year English. He was disgusting. He hit on girls in the class."

"Oh, my," muttered Georgia. Overwhelmed by growing crowds, she took refuge in the contours of her sandaled feet. After a time, she said, "Out on the farm, he kept to himself, but when we did socialize, it was pretty clear he felt we weren't up to his standards. My husband used to fix what broke and Tess's mother,

Alice Maude, did all kinds of projects with me. You know, canning, drying, pickling. She is an excellent weaver but she stopped keeping sheep years ago. When Tess was fifteen or so, she moved to Toronto to live with an aunt. She finished high school there before attending U of T." Before Georgia could change the subject, Peter took up the theme.

"When I heard he fell and broke his neck while in a drunken stupor, I actually cheered, and I'm not by nature a vindictive guy." Georgia shifted uncomfortably. Swept up by strong feeling, Peter Stone continued his litany of complaints against Chauncey Vaughan. "He was such a woman-hater even adolescent chauvinists disliked him. Every year, in his very first lecture, he told students all great writing had been done by men and that women were capable of nothing more than inspiring them. Oh, and of cooking and cleaning, and servicing them, you know, sexually."

Georgia sat forward. "Inspiring men? What did women inspire him to do?"

"That's the thing. He hated the university's celebrity writers, trashed them in his classes. Subtly of course. But he didn't have the courage to write anything himself. For a while he told certain "special" students that he wrote under a pseudonym. But after he died and nothing surfaced, we figured it was more of his bull." Peter reflected for a moment. "It's nice his daughter puts that literary talent to good use. He was an awesome scholar, but power without love… Hey! There she is."

6

In crisp khakis and tailored shirt, Tess Vaughan looked more like she'd stepped from the pages of Vogue than a war zone in the Middle East. Georgia realized she didn't need to worry about requests to shop on the way home. Every inch of her polished, from her glossy hennaed hair to her Italian-booted feet, Tess Vaughan radiated professionalism. With only carry-on luggage, the international reporter was a member of the privileged few waved through customs without having to answer a single question. Her expression was hard to read behind her sunglasses. Then she spotted Georgia and grinned her kid's grin. "You came!" She dropped her bag and enveloped Georgia in a long, swaying hug.

First Erie, then Wayne, then Clytie, and now you, Georgia thought. Another of our Beloveds home. Holding Tess at arm's length, she shook her head. "I expected mud-caked boots and barbed-wire scratches on your hands and arms, but here you are, pristine and whole."

Tess laughed. "In my business, the real danger is during bar fights with other reporters." She nodded to Peter Stone. "Who's this?"

"I'm Pete," he said. "Mrs. Butte saved my life."

"Mine, too," Tess said, "several times." She looked around. "Where's Mom?" Georgia wondered where to begin. "What's up, Georgia? Is she bad again? Shit," the younger woman muttered. "Can't I have at least twenty-four hours of normalcy?"

Aware of the flow of people around them, Georgia wished for a quieter place for revelations. "I wouldn't call her bad, Tess. In fact, she's more engaged than she's been in a very long time."

Skeptical, Tess checked her watch. "I've been home less than an hour and I've got that old feeling." She rotated her shoulders before taking Georgia's arm. "You won't believe it, but when I'm away, I forget all about this place, my crazy mother, my dead father, my scared little-girl life. I'm somebody else. I'm good at what I do. I love my work. I'm well paid. I even get along with my colleagues. But as soon as I'm home, bam! I'm back in the Essex County Fugue State."

"I'm sorry, Tess," Georgia said.

"Was Mom very upset when I didn't come home for the funeral last year? Is this about that?" Defensive, she added, "I had flu like I've never had it before. They had to IV me. It was some new virulent strain. And I knew you and Uly would help her get through it." Tess dropped her voice, leaned into Georgia with a conspirator's glee. "To be honest, I thought if I came home, I might dance on his coffin. Did they bury him or did they say he'd defile the ground and toss him on the rubbish heap for the crows?"

"The crows wouldn't want him," Peter Stone said.

"You knew the bastard, too?"

"First-year English. Torment after torment. We were terrified of him."

Tess stopped to rummage in her bag for her cigarettes. "You probably have a smoke-free zone starting at the Arner Townline. I'd better get this in while I can."

Without warning, a few feet in front of them, uniformed officers converged on a Muslim family. "No!" whispered Tess.

"What is it, Tess? What's happening?" Georgia asked.

"Another great wave of insanity."

Peter Stone weighed in. "Another great wave of hate." The look Tess flashed him said he wouldn't get an argument from her. Peter nodded, appreciative of this sister in outrage.

Outside the terminal everything was business-as-usual, with travelers claiming waiting cabs and limos or the welcoming arms of family members. The detainment of the young, frightened family disoriented Georgia, as did the outdoor heat and noise. With take-charge energy, Peter held up his free hand to traffic, took Georgia's arm, and led her across the busy roadway.

"How's Lila?" Tess asked when they reached the cooler temperatures of the parking garage.

"Still chained, Tess."

Tess stared off into some distant battle scene. "Aren't we all?" Her resignation troubled Georgia. "I managed to talk my bureau chief into a month's vacation. They owe me six weeks, but I'm content with four. Do you think Lila will have time for me?"

"Of course." Georgia took Tess's arm, seeing not the hardened reporter but the early Tess, the young, entirely innocent girl.

"Who on earth is Lola marrying, anyway? I can't imagine anyone passing muster. Does she still crack her little gold-handled whip?"

"Her whip is considerably larger now."

"Who's Lola?" Peter asked.

Georgia was about to tell him about her youngest daughter when Tess began the litany of Lola's virtues. "She's the only person in all of Essex County to get one hundred percent in every subject she ever studied in elementary and high school. She was invited to train for Canada's synchronized swimming team but passed it up to study Education with an ESL major at the University of Michigan. For which she got a thirty-thousand-dollar-per-year scholarship, in US funds no less, so she could join the ranks of humanity's literacy evangelists. She's built like Marilyn Monroe, looks like Bernadette Peters, and quotes Joseph Campbell. Let's see, did I leave anything out? Oh, yeah. She's the only person I know who can make Lila Butte cry." She turned to Georgia. "How'd I do?"

"Quotes Joseph Campbell?" echoed Peter Stone.

"I kid you not. If she lived in the states, she'd be an icon by now. Tess tossed her cigarette on the ground, stepped on it, and then stooped to pocket the butt. "I swear by all the Gods and Goddesses you taught us about as kids, all my growing up life I believed she'd been transported into this galaxy from way, way out there."

"Mae calls Lola my changeling child," Georgia mused. "She has some truly wonderful qualities, Peter. But you have to spend time looking for them."

Tess leaned close. "So, who's the groom?"

Georgia's heart felt battered by the turmoil at the centre of Lola's drama. "Juan Elias, an El Salvadoran from a small farming community. Lola met him a couple of years ago, in one of her New Canadian classes." She edited out her opinion of this match. "During the war, his family and neighbours were helped by missionaries. Canadian Lutherans, I believe, helped them escape. His older brothers and uncles found their way to Leamington farms. When Juan joined them, his uncles encouraged him to learn English, so he signed up to take Lola's ESL class in Windsor. He's just let us know he wants Lola to move to El Salvador with him, to teach English and be a force for good."

Tess tossed her bag in the back of the truck before climbing into the passenger side and wrestling up the arm rest to make room in the centre of the bench seat. Impatient, she buckled Peter's seatbelt to end his fumbling. Cinching him in she said, "I wonder if Lola knows about Oscar Romero. It's great Juan wants to go back. Too many people are trading their cultures for this god-awful monster we've created in North America. Forget English. She should learn Spanish. Let others insist we learn a few languages besides the one associated with dollars and…" Embarrassed, Tess stopped.

Georgia wondered if she should mention the possibility of a non-wedding event. Instead, she gave herself over to another unfolding story. "Do you remember Persephone Woodburn?"

Tess turned to her. "Of course." A sudden flood of information, Tess, reporters, Erie's interviews with Lawson, crashed into Georgia's awareness. Before Tess answered, the older woman knew that as well as her middle east reporting, Tess had been investigating Persephone Woodburn's disappearance for decades. Tess's voice carried Georgia's grief as well as her own. "I'd been trying to ignore what happened to Lila for years." The reporter stopped when Georgia paid the parking fee.

When they were on the move again, Tess picked up her story. "When Persephone and the others went missing, I finally understood how dangerous it was for all of us. I escaped to Aunt Grace in Toronto. From the day Persey's story broke I knew I had to escape if I wanted to survive."

Peter swore as Georgia merged onto the busy freeway.

Tess took charge. "Close your eyes and count to six as you breathe in through your nose. Breathe out through your mouth in the same slow way, but for longer. I count to ten on the exhale." Peter followed her instructions.

After a minute or so, Peter brought his hands to his heart. "I feel calm. I really do." He pointed to Tess's nicotine-stained fingers. "So why do you smoke when you know this breathing trick?"

Tess shook her head. "You don't want to know. So, what's your story, Peter?"

"I'm a walker."

"That's it?"

"Pretty much." Peter rotated his shoulders as Tess had done in the airport.

"What's a walker?"

"It means driving and flying and even cycling and skate

boarding aren't desirable activities."

"You've got to be kidding. I'd fly without a plane if I could."

"When's your birthday?"

"August thirty-first." She glanced at Georgia. "Three weeks before Lila's."

"Well, there goes my theory."

"What theory?"

"That all Earth signs are reluctant travelers. You must have a moon in Aquarius. Or Libra."

"I have a moon in the sky, right where it belongs," Tess said. "You should have been in Saturday School with us. We had a great time. Georgia took us over the hills wearing sheets and told us to imagine how the fairies felt when they saw us dancing by. She had us jump off the bunkhouse roof so we'd know how great it is to trust gravity. And we spent hours in the Kingsville library, lying on our bellies in the stacks, reading whatever we pleased."

Tess turned to Georgia. "You're why I'm a journalist, Georgia. You let me read Adela Rogers St. John when I was eight or nine." She turned to Peter. "She never said anything was too difficult. She encouraged us to trust ourselves so we'd know what we needed when we needed it."

"Adela Rogers St. John?"

"An American journalist. I didn't get a lot out of her memoir, but I'll never forget her description of a family who died from accidently eating poisonous mushrooms. I said to myself there and then, I want to learn how to help people feel and see just through words. So, Peter, Georgia Butte not only saved my life, she changed it for the better."

Embarrassed, Georgia steered the conversation to Alice Maude's preoccupations with Erie and George. "How well did you know Persephone, Tess?"

Tess paused for a few moments. In the silence, Georgia felt the young woman searching for a way to protect her from something. When Tess began to speak, Georgia understood. It was Lila, the rape, the aftermath that prompted her reticence. At that moment, she sensed that Lila's story had somehow gained power over the years. She wanted to weep, for Lila, for Persephone, for Tess.

After a couple of false starts, Tess said, "After Lila stopped wanting to play, Dad took me in to town every weekend for swimming lessons. I first met Persephone at your farm, when she came with her grandmothers to buy vegetables. In town, on those Saturdays, I met her at the community centre. I'd swim there while my father was screwing young girls in his office. Persephone took swimming lessons, too. We hung out together while I waited for him. I missed Lila. Persey knew the story, so we had that… Then, when we were about fourteen, she arranged for her band to practice in one of the community rooms. She was the epitome of cool." The wistfulness in Tess's voice prompted Georgia to glance at her. In place of the worldly reporter, she saw the young, innocent girl Tess had been.

After a time, Tess risked the truth. "Lila kept to herself after that summer. I was lonely. During our first fall of swimming together, Persey and I became best friends. If she wasn't going to be at the pool when I visited Windsor, I called her after my lessons and we'd meet by the river. To smoke, to complain about our parents." With pantomimed curses, the interstate's crowd of trucks and cars passed increasingly harsh judgment on Georgia's one-hundred-kilometer speed. She responded with smiles and head nods. Because of Tess's story, she wanted to pull to the shoulder of the road to howl her grief like a dog.

7

Tess Vaughan stared out the window for a time. Then she closed her eyes, searched for how to continue. "For years I believed David Daniel Lawson killed Persey, killed all twelve of the missing kids, although he only ever confessed to killing the six young children whose bodies he'd led police to exhume. When I started work in Toronto, I met several journalists who'd been reporting on the case for years. Conversations with them changed my mind. Their theories were only speculative, but the consensus was that the older kids weren't Lawson victims."

Georgia acknowledged this information with a slight nod. "Nobody knows for sure, but it's a good guess for a number of reasons, these kids were ripe for recruitment into Toronto's underground. Lawson had no reason to lie about the murders. Nothing would have changed for him if he confessed to killing twelve kids instead of six. In fact, the police were so desperate to solve the last six cases they would have given him almost anything for information about more graves. But to the very end, Lawson said nothing about the older six, not that he had or hadn't killed them. He knew the media would remain interested in him only as long as he kept silent. He was playing reporters right up until the moment somebody slit his throat."

For a minute, Georgia couldn't think clearly. Then, insight struck. "Are you saying you believe Persephone might still be alive?"

Tess Vaughan looked down at her hands resting palms up in her lap, her hair falling forward, curtaining her profile. "Even if Lawson didn't kill her, supporting herself as a sex worker or drug dealer isn't exactly the key to longevity. And back then the AIDs epidemic and any number of STDs could have done her in, if heroin didn't. She wasn't on it when I knew her, but she'd have to graduate to opiates to endure the life. Almost everybody does who stays in it. And if drugs didn't get her, some psycho could have. Given the dangers of life on the streets, Persey's chances of being alive are slim." She paused, added, "Still, there is a chance."

"I remember those missing kids," Peter said. "I was in middle school when all that happened. It was all we talked about. Everybody was afraid to walk down the street alone, even in broad daylight. After that guy was arrested and confessed to killing six of the missing kids, they plastered the pictures of the rest all over the place. The woman you're talking about, Persephone, she was the Native kid, right?"

"Her father was a Temagami First Nation person," Georgia told him. "When I was young and living in Windsor, a neighbour adopted him. He was a doctor and he meant well. He wanted to save someone else's child, because he couldn't save his own."

Tess turned to Georgia. "That's right. You knew Persey's grandfather. I always forget you're the daughter of the big-money Scratches."

Georgia changed lanes to avoid a bottleneck at an exit ramp. Peter whistled his awe. "No kidding? A Scratch saved my life? We're practically neighbours when I live at home."

"Officially, I haven't been a Scratch for more than fifty years. Unofficially, I never really was one. Lola wasn't the first changeling child."

"Did you know Persephone's father when he was growing up?" Tess asked.

All at once, Georgia heard the young man's voice calling out from the midst of the geese feeding in the Miner cornfield. "We used to meet at Jack Miner's. Dr. Abernathy brought George down from the north in nineteen forty-five when he was a newborn. The first time I met him, he was a scrawny three-month-old. Once I finished university, Uly and I eloped and moved to the farm. It was nineteen fifty, so I was long gone by the time little George was wandering around Walkerville under his own steam. I saw him occasionally when I visited my family. Later, I met him many times, at Point Pelee and Oxley, but mostly at the Miner Sanctuary. He and Horace loved to explore the county together."

"Why do you suppose they visited the Miner place?"

Georgia hesitated, reluctant to speak of George's mystery or her own experiences with Alice Maude and the land. "I guess they were like the rest of us. They were drawn to the geese."

"That dude! The one who died on the Miner Road in sixty-four!" Peter could hardly contain his excitement. "I heard about him the first day I moved to the Beam place to complete my commission. Miner's caretaker, Walt, told me all about that crash. He was driving the tractor that night, taking combustibles to a cement warehouse because of the drought. He said the Abernathy kid turned off his lights when he was about a quarter of a mile behind him. Then Walt heard the car accelerating. He drove the wagon off the road, but the tractor got stuck in the drainage ditch."

"The drainage ditch I found you in, Peter."

Peter Stone took a moment to absorb this coincidence. "Wow," he said, feeling drawn into a mystery he couldn't begin to understand. "Walt said he tried to jump to safety before the car hit the wagon broadside but while he was in midair the fire blast singed every bit of hair off his head and body. He showed me his scars. He spent months in the hospital."

"What do you suppose George Abernathy was doing driving without lights at night on an unlit country road?" Tess asked.

Peter nudged her. "You want to hear something else that's weird? Walt said the rain started at the moment the car hit the wagon. Walt told me folks around Kingsville believe that kid somehow ended the drought."

An electrifying jolt passed through Georgia. "That's right," she said, her eyes wide with the shock of remembering a long-forgotten detail. "As Uly and I watched, it did rain, hard. And for hours." She had replayed that night in her imagination at least a thousand times, yet until this moment, she'd forgotten the drenching rain following the crash.

"Your mother and Erie have become friends, Tess. Erie and your mother began talking years ago. Just this past Friday, Erie visited…"

Tess turned to Georgia. "What?"

"Your mother sees Persephone's father dancing in the Miner cornfield. She hears him singing, too."

Tess brushed away tears. "And all this time I thought she was just plain crazy."

8

As she navigated the streets leading to the Ambassador Bridge entrance, Georgia meditated on the lingering scars of the late sixties' riots. It always chastened her to drive through this part of Detroit, her species' inability to live peacefully in community calling out from broken windows, charred porches, derelict lawns and gardens. Her work at the farm seemed inconsequential in the face of persistent North American injustices.

"I can't believe it," Tess said of the bleak landscape. "Nothing's changed. It's been years since I've been through here, decades since the riots and the military crackdown, but this landscape looks like all that horror happened a few months ago."

The three travelers felt in different ways the privilege afforded by their white skin. Finally, Peter broke the silence. "How do you usually get to your mother's?"

"The last time I visited, I flew into Windsor from Toronto." She turned to Georgia. "You and Uly met me at the Windsor airport." Georgia didn't hear, feeling again the explosive protests after the political assassinations intended to end the movements for change. Her heart raced with the escalation of policing and imprisonment, with the fury silenced by tanks, soldiers, lies. At this moment, everyday ordinariness felt absurd. It was not that nothing had changed after those sixties' dreams of equality. It was that the changes were so much worse.

Feeling impotent to change anything beyond her own commitments to live lightly and responsibly, Tess's answer penetrated her awareness. She replayed that earlier car ride, the reporter's commentary on the familiar, flat landscape of home vivid and astute. Barns in every state of repair announced the main source of income in the county. Daredevil chickens trusted to roam free skirted the roadway. Farm stands offered Essex County fecundity in myriad shades of yellow and green, orange and red, blue and purple. In spite of this bounty, the downtown Detroit neighbourhood they'd just driven through blotted out her optimism.

On the trip home, Peter Stone's feet remained on the floor as they crossed the bridge. His slow breathing and quiet conversation with Tess about the Detroit tragedies made the return journey nothing like their first crossing. Catching sight of a low riding freighter headed for Hamilton, Georgia was about to point it out.

At that very moment, Tess changed her light hearted mood, opening her neighbour's private Pandora's Box. "Did you know Georgia is a seer?"

Peter leaned forward to stare at Georgia's profile. "You mean like Tiresias?"

"She communicates with nature spirits. They help her garden."

Peter was more than ready to leave for a time the ongoing tragedies caused by human fear and stupidity during the sixties riots to enter Georgia's secret world. "Wow. What's that like? Do you see auras?"

A prickle of annoyance ran up Georgia's spine. Revealing her way of being in the world was something she shied away from, the word clairvoyant triggering a host of glamorous expectations that overshadowed the horrors she carried but could not address. For a moment, she thought of setting them both straight, but then she checked the sun. It was well past noon. She deflected Peter's interest in her other worldly knowledge with suggestions for lunch and a picnic by the river.

9

A handful of people stood on the platform to greet the two diesel engines and their complement of VIA cars arriving from Chatham and points north and east. As the train slowed, Georgia scanned the car windows for a glimpse of Lela. This daughter was forty-one now, she reminded herself, not twenty-one. She'd long ago assumed her share of rights and responsibilities in the adult world. There was no need to inspect her for signs of malnutrition, spiritual or physical, when she arrived home for Lola's wedding, an event this second daughter considered a sign of her youngest sister's poor judgment.

Small metal stools materialized up and down the platform. Georgia scrutinized passengers until everyone disappeared in the shadow cast by Lela Butte. "Le!" she called, waving. Lela rushed to her mother, spun her silly in a reckless, twirling hug.

"It's been too long. Too long," Georgia whispered into her daughter's cool, sun-browned neck.

Lela set her mother on the ground and drew back to have a better look. "You look wonderful, Mama."

Georgia laughed. "You sound surprised."

Lela scanned the landscape, pointed to a billboard advertising Scratch Single Malt Whiskey. "You live in the midst of ravening commerce. I was afraid you'd be a shrivelled little pea."

Fiona Rankin, the New Englander Lela met during her mime studies in Paris, gathered mother and daughter into a communal hug. When the women could finally make their relationship legal the year before, Jason, Spring, Uly, Georgia, Lola, Lala, and Clytemnestra traveled to Vermont to celebrate the couple's civil union. Lila stayed home, as she always did, to fight with Willy, oversee the farm, and work on her carving.

Tall, with dark eyes and silvering dark hair that bounced against her back in a single braid, Fiona was, like Lela, a proud 'Dirt Worshiper.' She wore her long skirts and silver jewelry as evidence of her membership in Goddess Culture, a benign belief system spreading farming know how, social justice, and joy. On this day, her spiritual mode of dress included a dark green tank top proclaiming 'Take Vermont Forward' in stylized sandy coloured letters, a long multi-coloured patchwork skirt, silver earrings, an amber necklace, and an assortment of wrist bangles, all of these items chosen carefully from their farm's permanent clothing exchange. "Hey, Gee," she said, assessing Georgia's appearance. "Life's been agreeing with you."

"And with you," Georgia said, taking Fiona's face in her hands and kissing first one cheek then the other. "You are a lavender and eucalyptus-scented goddess." She hugged this new daughter a second time then picked up one of their bags.

"So, Lola's actually going through with this craziness." Lela made this pronouncement then wove her way through clusters of people on the platform. Breaking through the crowd, she searched the parking lot for her father's notorious truck. "Wow!" she said, nodding at the ancient sticker-covered relic. "You've got Tess Vaughan in there."

"The reporter?" Fiona followed Lela's gaze. "Oh, my. She lives up to her reputation and then some."

Lela let go of her mother to put an arm around Fiona. "My very first crush. She's the person who convinced me I was destined to love women. Every time she walked into a room when we were young, I wanted to play with her hair."

"You were very good, as I recall," said Georgia, "restraining yourself."

"Well, yeah. She was just a kid."

"Le told you how she felt?"

Georgia smiled her proud-mama smile. "Lela has always been very open about her sexual orientation." For the briefest of moments, she allowed herself to believe she might have done at least one or two things right as a mother.

"My mother sent me to a shrink," Fiona said. "And when that didn't work, she encouraged me to make my home in Europe where 'that sort of thing' is considered normal."

"Is that what took you to Paris?"

"Yup. Socially aware women and unorthodox career choices. Who could ask for anything more?"

"Lucky me, huh," Lela said. She kissed Fiona's shoulder.

More returning children, Georgia mused, studying the pair.

She bowed her head, some new and unfamiliar knowing stirring at the edges of her consciousness. As she walked to Uly's truck, the knowledge burst upon her. The farm itself was changing, gathering energy, increasing its power to attract whatever might be needed to thwart the TriChems of the world. She vibrated with this knowledge for a moment, and then, the knowing was gone.

Despite protests from Tess and Peter, Fiona and Lela climbed into the back of the pickup. "I haven't seen this landscape for ages," Lela said. "I want to memorize the deforestation and Zug Island stench so that when we're back in Vermont and I get that homesick feeling, I can shake it off."

Georgia glanced at the rear-view mirror as Lela tied a kerchief over her mouth and nose, the receding Detroit skyline shimmering in cement-generated heat her backdrop. Opening to the green of growing things, Georgia did her best to replace all her worries with the delights of Essex County fecundity. Relieved to be so close to home, to problems she could solve, to connections she could foster, she relaxed into the final leg of her journey.

"So, let me get this straight," Peter said as follow-up to Tess's description of Willy. "This goat does his business in a compost pile, because he knows the garden's manure requirements. He wanders around the house whenever he feels like it. And he understands what everyone says. Did he go to university, too?"

"No," Georgia said. "Willy was home-schooled, as were my daughters, Lola excepted." She pulled onto the Essex Bypass, the Canadian and American cities now not much more than a diminishing amber haze. Already she could smell and taste the difference in the air.

"Jeez, Mrs. Butte. What else should I know about you?"

Georgia opted for truth. "The day I found you, I was called

to do it. It was hot. I was in a terrible mood. I'm a farmer. I had lots of things to do. In spite of everything, the Universe said walk, walk in blistering heat, walk to the Miner field. I wanted to cut through my neighbour's property. That route would have been hard enough, but so much better than taking the long way, walking on the dusty shoulders beside heat radiating asphalt. Still, I paid attention to that little voice that asked me to do the hard thing. That's why I found you, Peter. If I'd taken the shortcut, I wouldn't have discovered you in the ditch. The universe wanted you saved."

"Really," Tess said. Curious, she glanced at Peter. "I wonder why?"

Used to defending his art choices, Peter said, "I'm a great painter. Really. As good as…"

"Oh, no. Look at that." Georgia braked suddenly. In the distance, smoke billowed. "It's a fire, a big one." She scanned the horizon. "Near our house."

A sultry wind carried the ghostly remnant of thick black smoke in their direction. Alice Maude's cleaning plans flitted through Georgia's mind. "Oh, dear," she muttered. "I hope everyone's all right." She prayed Clytemnestra had taken Willy to Mae's. The thought of Willy in a burning barn made her accelerate. Lela pounded on the back window, pointed at the heavy smoke.

"It's my mother." Tess's certainty startled Georgia.

Georgia took in a breath. "Your mother knows your father hurt you in the barn."

"What?"

"She knows all about him, Tess."

"Oh, my God. And all this time, I've been protecting her. My therapist told me to write her a letter, but I couldn't do it. I said she was too fragile, that she was yet another woman driven crazy by… what? With all my words, I don't know how to describe what goes on between a person like my father and the rest of us."

10

Alice Maude's barn, in full blaze by the time Georgia parked near Mae Simpson's house, required several of the county's emergency response teams to put out the fire. Georgia counted three fire trucks in the Vaughan driveway and at least ten volunteer fire fighters flanking an Ontario Provincial Police cruiser. Willy was nowhere in sight.

Georgia parked Uly's truck on the shoulder of the road to search for the family goat on foot, but when she attempted to cross to the Vaughan property, a zealous OPP officer stopped her. "I'm a neighbour," she shouted over the din. She knew they were worried about the wind. If they didn't get the fire extinguished quickly, it could travel across the back meadow and destroy the Vaughan sugar bush. If that happened, the Miner property on the next road would be in peril. In that moment, Georgia felt the beneficence of their cold, hard, Saturday morning rain.

Lila ran to her from the farm logging road. "Ma, I can't find Wayne. I've looked everywhere. He was supposed to be out looking for horse parts." She pulled her mother close, whispered, "My acetylene torch is missing."

Georgia took Lila's hand. Together they wove through the crowd to Lela, Tess, and Fiona. The sisters embraced, then pulled Fiona and Tess into their hug. Georgia backed away. "I have to find Willy," she said, wondering about Peter. She spotted this newest family member weaving his way through the crowd to the fire site. "I'm going to check with Mae." No one heard.

Mae stood sentry on her front porch, Willy safely tucked between her and Clytemnestra. "I called it in," Mae said. "I was fitting Willy's wig right here on the porch when I saw the smoke." Willy tossed his head and pawed the porch boards to welcome Georgia.

Clytemnestra held on to the red chiffon scarf she'd tied around the goat's neck. "We don't want our Will running amok and getting singed," she said. She looked more the farm girl than ever.

Georgia climbed the first step to stroke Willy's snout. "Thank you for keeping him safe. Have you seen Uly?" Darker thoughts intruded. "Or Wayne?"

Mae pointed to the trucks in front of Alice Maude's house. "I saw Uly pull up in the first fire truck with Max Love. They're around the back. A police officer told us they were drenching the yard and the drive to keep the Vaughan house safe. I haven't seen Wayne since this morning. Do you think he might be in danger?"

"I haven't seen Wayne, either," Clytemnestra said, "but I left his mother and sisters at the pond. Sadra told me when a grass fire threatens a village back home, the safest place is in the waterhole. I went over to check on everything after the trucks arrived and tried to coax them out of the water, but they wouldn't budge. To be honest, I think they're having fun. What about Lila? I couldn't find her anywhere."

"I just talked to her," Georgia said, searching the crowd for her daughter's buzzed head. "I'm going to look for Wayne and Alice Maude. Keep Willy here until the fire's out and the trucks have left. I don't want him any more frightened than he is now."

"Come up here for supper," Mae called after her. "Bring everybody. I've got red lentil soup simmering, and Clytie and I will make cornbread." She thought for a moment. "We'll whip up a salad, and maple syrup sweet potato pudding for dessert. Before you go, give us a word about Lela and Fiona. And Tess."

Georgia smiled then. "They're all glad to be home."

11

Relieved to see her daughters heading to Mae's with Peter Stone in tow, Georgia drove to the Miner feeding fields on a hunch. If Wayne and Alice Maude set the fire together, she'd likely find them hiding in the Vaughan back woods. As she passed the old Beam place, she thought again of Peter Stone and his sudden addition to her growing family. The memory of the night George Three Feather died returned so strongly she felt the old dove-grey Imperial keeping pace with Uly's truck on the two-lane blacktop. She looked to her left, sure she'd see the car's ghostly presence, but the lane beside her was empty. She slowed, sensing she'd reached the place where young George turned off his headlights. It came to her then, why he'd driven in the dark. That night sky had been full of brilliant stars. And then, through some trick of time and space, he was beside her, a young boy driving fast, rained on by starlight.

She remembered how, on that long-ago night, the hellish heat had driven the Buttes out of doors in search of a cool breeze. Georgia replayed Peter Stone's story about Walt, witnessed on the road ahead the young farm hand's frantic attempt to get the wagon off the road as George raced toward him. Whether or not George brought the rain that ended the drought or changed the course of events because of his connection to land's mysterious power she would never know. What she did know perplexed her. Out of a cloudless night sky, rain fell. It was the first good rain to fall in weeks.

Georgia parked on the shoulder of the road, the vision of George Abernathy's young, half-naked form behind the wheel of his father's car unleashing sudden fury. Why this Indigenous child should have to sacrifice himself for the progeny of white people who not only displaced but murdered his people, who deforested what was, in truth, his land, his paradise, she could not fathom.

"Did you mean to die?" she cried, raging. "George. George. Did you know about the wagon?" She listened for his answer. None came. Aware now of Horace Abernathy, she recalled how the old man died, broken by drink, a few years after his granddaughter went missing. "Horace?" she said. "Are you here, too?"

"Who are you talking to, Gee?"

The passenger window framed Wayne's dusty, tear-streaked face. "Wayne! You're all right. We've been so worried."

He got in the truck, Lila's acetylene torch clutched in his hands. "I don't think you're gonna be too glad you found me. I burned down that barn. Well, me and Alice Maude, we did it together. Will the police take me away?"

"No!" Georgia's word was a command. She searched the trees at the edge of the cornfield. "Where is Alice Maude?"

"She's in the woods. I was hiding with her until I saw you park the truck. Are you sure they won't be taking me away?"

Georgia put her hand on his arm. "No one's going to take you anywhere," she said. "What happened with the barn? Was it an accident?"

"Heck no. She axed me to burn it. She said we needed to water the ground all around that rickety place to make sure the fire wouldn't spread, so we did that. Then I went in and set fire to a heap of broken boards she put in that pen near the middle of the big room. I thought it'd burn right down in no time so nobody'd notice. She said we had to do it. She said I came back so's I could help get rid of the bad stuff that happened in there."

Georgia eased the truck into first and crept up the road while scanning the edge of the woods for Alice Maude. "There. There she is." She parked next to a car with Michigan plates whose owners were across the road reading the plaque about Jack Miner. "Stay here," she ordered Wayne. "Promise."

He nodded, too frightened to disobey.

Seeing his fear, she said, softly, "Nothing bad is going to happen to you, Wayne." She offered him an encouraging smile. "Promise me you'll wait right here."

The young boy nodded again.

Broken corn stalks left to hold the soil in place after the previous year's harvest scratched Georgia's shins raw. When she finally reached Alice Maude, her neighbour grinned a welcome. "Do you see the smoke, Georgia?" She pointed to the sky. "The professor is gone. He can't hurt us anymore." On their way to the truck, Alice Maude chatted as if nothing extraordinary had happened. "Do you think Ulysses and Maxwell and Wayne will build a new barn for me? I'd like to have lambs again. I'll set up my loom and my spinning wheel. It's time I got back to work." She kissed Georgia's cheek. "'Weave and mend,'" she sang. "'Weave and mend.' That's what the song says. 'Old woman, weave and mend.'" Georgia's eyes leaked healing tears. When they reached the truck, Alice Maude touched Wayne's cheek. "Thank you for helping me get rid of the professor once and for all."

"You mean there was a guy in that barn? They'll lock me up for life."

"Not an actual man, Wayne," Georgia assured him. "His ghost. His memory. His bad deeds."

"He hurt my daughter," Alice Maude said. "He hurt my lambs." She squeezed her eyes shut. "He hurt me."

Georgia drove from dazzling sunshine into the shade of nearby maple trees, then into sunlight again. At the spot where she'd discovered Peter Stone, she touched her heart, said a silent prayer of gratitude. When she reached their road, she stopped at the roadblock in front of her family's old farm.

From the edge of the crowd on the road's shoulder Webster waved to her. Her heart lurched. They were friends again. She parked and rushed to join him. He surprised her with a kiss to both cheeks.

12

The fire extinguished and reports filed, the Buttes and friends wandered in clutches of threes and fours down the road to Mae Simpson's farm. The evening air, pungent with creosote, cleared a little when a cleansing wind carried the acrid stench eastward to strangers, some recognizing the scent of the tragedy visiting others. Georgia looked out over the citronella candles lighting Mae's picnic tables, marveling yet again at their growing family.

She scanned the chattering crowd, noticing Clytemnestra and Webster, the pair laughing over some joke. Across the table from them, Mae and Sadra appeared to be comparing the clothes they wore using a Somali-Canadian-sign language when words failed them. Karen and Kim sat with Fiona and Lela, working hand puppets Fiona made from Mae's sewing scraps in the time it took for Lela to make and toss the salad. She turned her head, discovering Lila leaning into Tess, her arm draped around her friend's waist, both women's eyes fastened on Maxwell Love as he spoke with Alice Maude about the accident report. Georgia heard Max say he was citing the cause of the fire as a welding accident. Wayne, sandwiched between Alice Maude and Max, appeared on the brink of abandoning an art career for firefighting. Only Peter Stone sat silent and alone.

Georgia went to him. "Hasn't this been a day?" she said, sitting beside him, his goose and peacock colours leaping from his shoulders to hers.

"Is it always like this around here?"

"No. Most days, when I'm not planting or weeding or harvesting, I get to sit and watch my favourite spiders spinning their webs among the reeds surrounding the pond." Her direct gaze made him blush. "All this excitement began when I found you in the ditch, Peter. How are you feeling? You look like you might need a good long sleep."

Both Peter's eyes rested on Georgia's face until the right wandered off, perhaps, Georgia thought, in search of a bed. "I love your family, Georgia."

"Good," she said. "You're part of it now."

"Think maybe Lela will ditch Fiona and marry me?"

"Not a chance. What about Lila?"

"Are you kidding? She terrifies me."

Georgia thought of Uly with a pang of something like guilt. With effort, she stuffed her outrage over his desire to save her old farm with his city friends. "Tess?" she said, preoccupied. "She's family."

"Never. Too many years of hero worship. On my part, of course."

Georgia took his hand. "Maybe you'll find your own wonderful partner and bring her, or him, out here."

"Do you think I'm gay?"

"Do you?"

"I've wondered. Especially at the end of a love affair I thought was going to last forever. They all get cut short by my resistance to taking my feet off the ground."

"That might be a challenge for a lot of people." She took his hand. "Maybe you're meant to be a monk. Marry your art. Live the ascetic life. There's great nobility in that."

Peter laughed at this idea. "I know myself pretty well by now, Ms…Georgia. I don't think there's a bit of nobility in me. My toes are webbed."

"I had no idea webbed feet precluded a noble life."

Peter's eyebrows indicated surprise at her ignorance. "A guy who can't leave the ground without panicking, who has webbed toes, and whose main passion is painting wildlife? That's not the stuff of nobility. Or mobility." He leaned in close. "To tell you the truth, I think my parents are afraid I'm going to starve to death. I overheard them talking about creating a trust fund to take care of me, you know, the way people do for their developmentally challenged adult children."

Georgia squeezed his hand. "Ah, but that was before Tess taught you how to breathe."

"That's true," Peter said, brightening. Aware of after-supper cleanup activities, he gathered their plates and cups. "I'm going to wash dishes with Mrs. Simpson. In my opinion, you can never have too many older women in your life." As she watched him unfold from his place beside her, Georgia felt Peter Stone slip into a niche in her heart she hadn't realized was empty. She glimpsed future days when she would come upon him painting herons at odd times and in strange and secret places, this man whose life she'd saved.

13

Although it was well past nine, the sky had not yet given up the last remnants of late-spring light. Seeing Lila and Lela together, Georgia missed Lala and decided to call her. She found Mae, held her in a long embrace, and together the friends made plans to meet the next day. Then Georgia began the walk home, taking the woods path rather than the road. She stopped when Uly called to her.

"Where are you off to?"

"I'm missing Lala. I'm going to call."

Uly fell into step beside her. In spite of their ongoing rupture, they walked easily together. "Big day tomorrow," Uly said after a time.

"Jason and Spring?"

"Maybe tomorrow. Maybe Thursday. I was thinking of the marquee de wedding, and our first dinner with our soon-to-be extended family members."

Too exhausted to resume their argument, Georgia went along with his forced merriment. "I can't remember when the Eliases are due. I told Lola they could stay here tomorrow night, but she might want them in town. For Thursday's classes. A human show and tell."

"Our youngest." He spoke quietly, as if Lola were within earshot and not thirty miles away. "She's reminding me more and more of your mother."

Mother, Georgia thought. I must call her so she can begin liquidating the Grandmother Jones assets she inherited. "I hope Mother isn't too disappointed about not coming to the wedding."

Uly put his hand on her arm. "I meant to tell you. Marguerite called while you were in Detroit. She asked me not to tell Lola because she wants to surprise her, but she's coming to the wedding after all. She's engaged a private nurse to chauffeur her, so she'll be out and about with her oxygen tank."

"Goodness," Georgia said. "Four people over the age of ninety are coming to Lo's wedding. And in a heat wave." She counted on her fingers. "Spring and Jason, Gertrude Bradshaw, and my not so sainted mother. Let's hope it's not too hot. Or too…"

Uly laughed. To Georgia, it was a mean little sound. "Don't bother yourself on the elder Buttes' behalf. They plan to die with their boots on. I'm sure they'd rather drop dead here, and at a wedding, than any place else." Georgia nodded, convinced her mother had been summoned by farm desires and needs. Whether she knew it or not, in Georgia's mind Marguerite Scratch had become their designated rescuer. The irony pleased her.

"Is Gertrude really a hundred and one?" Uly asked.

"She is." He took his hand from her arm. She put her hand on his. "I forgot to tell you. Tess told me evidence suggests David Daniel Lawson didn't kill Persephone or the other five older children who went missing that summer. Tess said police suspect the missing teens were recruited by a Toronto sex trafficking operation that was notorious throughout the eighties and into the nineties." Uly took in a ragged breath.

They walked together, neither touching the other now, Georgia aware of Uly's guilt at not being able to stop Lawson, Uly resentful she'd brought up the subject. For a moment, she thought better of saying more, to spare him, but the words came on their own. "Once he was imprisoned, Erie believed she could find out if he killed Persephone. That's why she moved to Toronto. It wasn't a better job. That was her cover story. It was to be closer to Millhaven, so she could visit him there."

She peered at Uly, but before she could make out his expression, he turned away. "Now Erie's connecting with Lila and visiting Alice Maude because Maudey told her about hearing Persephone's father sing in the Miner field."

Uly stopped, stared in the direction of Alice Maude Vaughan's skeletal barn. "I've wondered all these years, Gee," he said, his voice barely a whisper. "What on earth made David Daniel the way he was?"

She touched his face then walked on, leaving him to his sorrows. At the edge of the garden, she stopped long enough to pass her hands over the edge of the closest raised bed. When he caught up with her, he said, "It's childish, I know, but I want to believe he's not finished. I want to believe he's graduated to another plane where he can, I don't know, somehow atone for what he's done." A wave of tenderness for his suffering broke over her, but she did not let him see it.

Walking ahead, she said only, "Hurry, Uly. I want to call Lala before she goes to bed."

1

Georgia woke to echoes of Lala's voice crossing impossible distances. Initially, they'd had a poor connection with the Colombian healing camp. After much static, Lala called her parents on a different line. When they finally connected, Uly and Georgia discovered their eldest daughter continued safe and happy in an alternative medicine course focused on addressing the physical, emotional, and spiritual issues of local women and girls. When Georgia said Lala's wedding gift hadn't arrived, Lala assured her that all UPS drivers were romantics at heart and that any number of them would be happy to track down the wedding gift she'd sent a month earlier. Georgia made a note to call the UPS Toronto office the next day.

On the wave of optimism created by her conversation with her eldest daughter, Georgia made up her mind it was going to be a wonderful feast, no matter bride-and-groom difficulties and TriChem terrors. She looked forward to meeting Juan's family. His roots, like Lola's, were rural, their families no doubt sharing drought remedies, companion planting wisdom, and composting tips. The farm would draw a loving circle around them, and within this circle all impending disasters would shrink to nothing.

Uly rolled over, opened his eyes, closed them again. "I'm glad I refused to milk cows all those years ago," he said, serene.

"All you have to do is put up a tent."

With slow, deliberate maneuvers, he rose from their bed. "You're behind the times. Lila has a much bigger job for me before I get to flirting with the royalty of garment architecture. She's created what sounds like a Goddess version of the Colossus of Rhodes for this shindig. I have to help get it through the woods in one piece."

"Good heavens," said Georgia, glad to talk about matters that did not risk flaring tempers. "Why not assemble it at the wedding site?"

"I'll suggest re-assemblage if the thing looks too big to transport."

Avoiding their customary morning embrace, Georgia made her way to the bathroom, noting in passing Clytemnestra's open door and unmade bed. "Uly, where's Clytie? In the barn with Lela and Fiona?"

Uly wandered down the hall and peered into his sister's room. "Oh."

"Oh?"

"I think my sister may be with your cousin." He studied her face for signs of distress, hid his disappointment when he didn't find any.

Georgia did feel something suspiciously like jealousy suck the air from her lungs, but she'd learned long ago to hide her feelings about her cousin. Aware of her pettiness, she vowed to change. On her way to the bathroom, she discovered the door to Lila's old room ajar. Willy, disobeying Lila's keep-out orders, had taken possession of her bed, languishing there beneath far too many covers. He opened his eyes, gave Georgia a sorrowful glance, burrowed deeper into forbidden quilts.

Georgia tisked. "Lila will have your hide if she catches you in here." Willy peaked out long enough for her to see pale liquid oozing from his nostrils. "Oh, Willy, you've got the sniffles," she crooned. "Some burdock and pulmonaria tea will fix you right up."

At that moment, Clytemnestra appeared at the top of the stairs. "Don't worry about our Will. He's just jealous. He wanted to come to Webster's with me but I said no." Willy huffed out of his nest, dragged a quilt to the doorway, dropped it to nip Clytemnestra's hand. "Willy!" she cried. Unrepentant, Willy bounded down the stairs, banged around in the kitchen, then slammed out the kitchen door.

Georgia eyed her sister-in-law. Clytemnestra stood in a pool of sunlight without a trace of her glittery, fashion-plate armour. She wore a pair of overalls and an ancient Grateful Dead t-shirt. "You're shocked," she said, unable to hide her delight.

Georgia laughed. "Because you spent the night with Webster? We go back a long way, Clytie. I don't think there's much left for either of us to do that would shock the other." She hugged her sister-in-law, relieved to discover her earlier Webster pangs, whatever their cause, entirely gone.

"Nikos gave me an ultimatum. I had to stay in Marseilles instead of coming here, or he'd end the marriage."

Georgia felt some inner tension in Clytemnestra relax with this admission. "Oh, Clytie, I am sorry." Protective, she added, "Are you sure you're not using Webster as some sort of revenge against Nikos?"

Linking arms, the women headed for the bathroom. "Nikos and I have been in trouble for a while, Gee. He...No, he's not the problem. The truth is, I haven't felt real since I left here."

Georgia studied her sister-in-law for a moment. "Real?"

"Real." Clytemnestra undressed while Georgia adjusted the water temperature in the shower. "I'm told it's an enviable life I live, pleasing myself. But I have this farm in my bones. I know what it's like to look out over those fields and see young boys and girls learning to love and respect Nature. Nikos is generous but he loves money, not people, and certainly not trees and fields. 'Nature' is just grist for his entrepreneurial exploits."

"Surely he loves you?"

"He loves having a woman, Georgia, but honestly, how can he love me? He doesn't have a clue who I really am."

Georgia shed her nightie and stepped into the shower. Clytemnestra followed. "He's like a shark, always moving forward, always working the angles," she said, soaping Georgia's back before handing the bar to Georgia and turning around. "He needs an attractive partner to grease the wheels of commerce. Don't get me wrong. I loved being that partner for years. How many times does a farm girl get to live a glamorous jetsetter's life?" She thought for a moment. "I've enjoyed myself, but I haven't been, I don't know, authentic with him. The real me, the farm girl in me, I've held back from Nikos since the beginning."

"Why?" Georgia soaped her hair then passed the shampoo.

"Maybe to see if Nikos could tell when I was and wasn't present." Clytemnestra soaped her hair. "Don't laugh, but it's taken me years to figure out that being called Clytemnestra doesn't mean I have to live in a Greek tragedy."

Georgia did laugh. "You know what Spring says, Clytie. Everybody's Greek… and tragic."

Clytemnestra traded places to rinse. "True. We all have our Fates, our Gods, our Helpers, our Furies…even our Quests – accepted or denied." She took the towel Georgia offered. "But we're not all meant to live on the Aegean with King Midas."

Georgia sounded her own depths before asking about her cousin. "What about Webster? Does he see the real you?"

"It's funny about Webby. I don't think he's been real either, but don't ask me where things went wrong for him. Maybe we can help each other. I've learned from this farm that I am capable of summoning my whole self when its required. Maybe if I stay awhile, I can learn how to do it all the time. The way I used to before I fell for Nikos and life in the fast lane."

In the kitchen, Georgia and Clytemnestra found Uly spooning strawberry jam onto toast. "Did Webster tell you about TriChem?"

"He did." Clytemnestra met her brother's glance. "You look surprised. We talked all night." When Uly looked doubtful, she laughed out loud. "We caught up with one another, Uly. I have to work out what's going to happen with Nikos before I stir things up with anyone else."

"I've been his neighbour for fifty years and he hasn't invited me over for late night tea, never mind a catch up. You've been here a couple of days and already you've been admitted to the inner sanctum."

Clytemnestra leaned against the counter. "I don't know about the inner sanctum. We sat in the living room the whole time. By-the-way, the house looks fine. He just kids about all that stuff. You know what Moira was like, and he was married to her longer than he was his parents' child. He's been housebroken for decades."

Listening to this simple exchange between her husband and his sister, Georgia felt quiet joy. She took down the phone book. "Let's forget Webster for the moment and remember our assigned tasks. We have to phone UPS for Lala. She's sent something to Juan and Lola that's gone missing. We have orders to track it down."

Uly caught her buoyant mood. "I heard someone predict severe storms for the end of the week." He bit into his toast, chewed thoughtfully. "It must have been Max. He's the one to know about the weather." He poured out tea. "I think he mentioned twisters."

"Stop it," Georgia said. "You're making it up."

"I'm not. Max said there was no point in putting up the Marquee de Wedding because gale-force winds will blow it down."

"Let the twisters come. We can always use the common space in the barn. It's so lovely in there since you sided it."

"What siding? Where?" Clytemnestra asked.

"Your brother's a genius," Georgia said, glad to be able to feel something about Uly other than outrage over his alliance with his city friends. "He's insulated the whole thing. The lower floor is sided in pine, except for the back rooms where he has his workshop and Willy has his…" she assumed a conspirator's tone, "stall. The downstairs has become a great meeting room. We've had a couple of dinners in there, when the weather was too blustery for the garden and the group too big for the house. Everyone is impressed with the greywater garden. And…" She rattled on, full of an enthusiasm she hadn't felt since hearing about TriChem, "…transformed the old hay loft into eight bedrooms, all with two sets of built in bunk beds. We can host a crowd of WOOFERS whenever we need them."

"Is there a bedroom for me?" Uly laughed. "I'm serious, Uly. I want to move back home while I'm figuring out details with Nikos."

"You never have to ask, Clytie. This farm is your home as much as ours."

Clytemnestra kissed her brother's cheek. "I'll let Nikos know what I want and see if he'll be part of it. He's got lots of money. He could easily buy Webster's farm." Georgia's stomach tightened at the possibility of more interference with her plans. Oblivious to her sister-in-law's distress, Clytemnestra went on. "I realized something last night during my visit with Web. I've tried to duplicate this farm every place I've ever lived. I work like crazy making gardens, growing things that need more rain and soil than Greece can provide. I've been modestly successful, but only because we can afford all the resources to artificially create a miniature garden like this one. I've learned the hard way. A garden without all of you isn't what I'm after. I want to eat real Essex County tomatoes. I want to breathe Lake Erie's fishy breath. I want the girls, Willy, the pond, the cedars. I felt so at home when we were at Mae's last night. I belong here."

2

Georgia opened her mouth to tell her sister-in-law the girls were all grown up with lives that took them away from home. A glimpse of Lela on the path to the house silenced her. In one of Lila's sarongs, her second daughter looked fifteen and very much as she had before community activism called her to study theatre in France. As if to prove her mother wrong, Lela burst into the kitchen. "Are you having a meeting in here?" She kissed Georgia, then her aunt. "May I put in my two cents, whatever its about?"

"Your Aunt Clytemnestra is moving back home," said her father.

Lela sat down. "You mean back to Canada?"

"To Essex County," Clytemnestra said. "To the farm."

"What about the Conservatives?" Lela cried. "Aren't you afraid they'll send you to clean up toxic waste like in *The Handmaid's Tale*? You're over sixty. Your ovaries are no longer viable. You won't have much of a future here."

Clytemnestra dismissed the Conservatives with an elegant wave of her hand. "We mustn't depend on governments for direction. Surely you know that by now, Lela." She didn't wait for Lela's answer. "I've lived through all kinds of political madness overseas. The best thing people can do is make something good in their own communities, in spite of governments."

"But how?" Lela's anguish arrested Georgia. She settled the phone in its cradle. "How do you do that and avoid tribalism?" Lela cried. "Or worse. How do you get governments to stop funding war instead of education and health care?"

"From what I hear," her father said, "our conservatives are no match for yours."

Lela fought back tears. "You don't have to sound so happy about it. We worked like crazy to elect Al Gore."

Where did this come from, Georgia wondered, this belief that your father would be happy about something that causes you misery? She thought of Lela's community, all colours and sexual orientations – their common ground a deep commitment to social and climate justice. She had a flash of insight. Lela assumed that all men – men privileged by their white skin – wished the vulnerable of the world harm. Lela's girlhood, oriented to girls and women by the time she was six or seven, rose spectrally. Georgia watched Uly's stricken face blaze pink. His eyes glittered with sudden tears. It was not the first time Lela had wounded him.

Sensing their need to talk alone, Clytemnestra left Uly and Lela for the garden. "I need time with my hands in the dirt. If you need me, I'll be in the garden."

"I'll join you," Georgia said, wanting to give whatever needed to happen between Uly and Lela time and space to work itself out. "After I call UPS." She picked up the phone and dialed.

Uly said, "So, we're here again, Le. I hoped we'd grown past this by now."

Lela stifled a sob. "How can we get past anything when just because of your genetic makeup you get to ruin the world?"

Her father did his best to calm his defensiveness before he answered. "Regardless of our gender differences, Le, I'd say we're both gentle souls. Easily hurt, good with our hands when we're confident we know what to do. We're not much interested in academic stuff. I think we're both a little afraid of being judged substandard because we learn differently than a lot of people. It makes us shy. Defensive."

Georgia turned from the phone and its on-hold music when someone knocked on the kitchen door. Tess stood in the doorway, backlit by the sky's pewter glow. "I hope I'm not interrupting," she began. "I…Lala called me last night."

"What?" At that moment the UPS operator came on the line to explain that Lala's package had been successfully traced to a home in Toronto's Annex. Georgia took down the address and joined Tess.

"Lala called me at Mum's, after she spoke with you last night. She got UPS to do a trace. Her package got delivered to friends who were to bring it to you on their way to Pelee Island. She mixed up the dates. They're away for the rest of the month, but they've left a key with a neighbour. This neighbour is going to let me in to pick up the package."

"Why didn't she send the package directly to us?"

"Lala didn't say. I know this is a busy time for you, but could one of you drive me into town to pick up a rental? I've got a couple of quick work inquiries to make in Toronto that have to be done in person, so it's no trouble getting Lala's package while I'm there."

It was Uly who answered her. "Take the truck, Tess. We can do without it. Max volunteered as go-fer. I'll spend the day here, anyway, getting the place spiffy."

Tess turned to Georgia. "Are you sure you don't need the truck?"

"If we do, Webster's right next door." Georgia's heart lifted with uncomplicated affection for her cousin. "Jason and Spring are being dropped off today or tomorrow. If Max is available, and Webster as well, we're all set."

Uly told Tess where to find the truck's keys then turned back to Lela. "I'm going to help Clytie with the greens," Georgia said, linking arms with Tess. "If your mother doesn't want to go, she's welcome here, Tess. Or I can send Lila and Wayne over to keep her company."

"Thanks, Georgia. Believe it or not, she wants to come with me."

My, my, my, thought Georgia, anticipating soothing garden work. Imagine Alice Maude wanting to go to Toronto. "Thank you for picking up Lala's gift." She embraced Tess, and as she did, felt more of Persephone Woodburn's story interwoven with the journalist's life. Best friends, she knew from long experience, carry one another's stories in the same way that family members do. Whether they know it or not.

3

Working in the garden, her ungloved hands harvesting Georgia's microgreens, a flood of memories ambushed Clytemnestra Butte. In the years before she married, she'd been an industrial diamond buyer for a Windsor-Detroit supplier. After long flights to Amsterdam and the pressures of her work, she decompressed on the farm, helping Georgia with the children and the garden. Her life felt perfectly balanced, with the challenges of city work as satisfying as time with family and friends in the county.

Because of her parents' immersion in ancient Greek tragedy, the family regularly attended plays in Detroit at the Hilberry Theater. During a performance of *Seven Against Thebes*, she found herself sitting next to a real live Greek god. Nikos Patmos had been equally smitten. Not only was Clytemnestra Butte an easy conversationalist, her ardent suitor knew few families who would risk naming a daughter after the bloody Queen of Mycenae. Conversation with her parents charmed him as well, especially when he learned they were working actors in the ancient Greek tradition. At the play's end, Nikos invited parents and daughter to share enthusiasms over Retsina and spanikopita in Detroit's Greek Town. He listened to descriptions of the Butte farm amphitheatre with genuine delight, inviting them to visit his Athens home at festival time to attend the ancient theatre where Aeschylus, Sophocles, Euripides, and Aristophanes continued to instruct Greeks in the terrors of hubris and resisting one's fate. When he returned to Greece after closing a business deal with Ford Automotive, he promised to call Clytemnestra every day.

True to his word, she found herself falling in love with the exotic man who appeared to have been sent by the same Fates who laid claim to her odd family for almost a century. For her first visit to Athens, she bought a return ticket, to guard against impetuosity. She stayed a month, just long enough to fall in love with Greece as well as Nikos.

After that month, she returned to the farm, handed in her resignation, and gave her industrial diamonds family time to find a suitable replacement. Most evenings, she walked the farm, searching for support for her momentous decision to settle in Greece. After countless inner struggles, she came to realize that in Greece she'd be standing on the same Earth beneath the same sun, moon, and stars, a place different from home only in climate and culture. Once she'd settled in Athens, the Butte daughters, most frequently Lila, began their visits. With her nieces, Clytemnestra Butte discovered the magic folded into the myths, the art, and the ruins that dominated her new home.

Greece didn't feel like a "foreign" country, perhaps because Clytemnestra's Fields-Butte grandparents met over their shared passion for the Greek tragedians in the Kingsville library long before her birth. And there was this other, larger-than-life connection to the ancient world. As in Greece, Essex County's anomalous, meteor-created amphitheatre proclaimed the workings of the Fates to the world. Because of her life on the farm, Clytemnestra's meeting with Nikos felt pre-ordained. Nostalgic about those early days, Uly's younger sister sat back on her heels. She looked around, wondering if she had to leave the farm all those years ago to feel once again the unbreakable bond with the place that birthed her.

And then there was Willy. Clytemnestra recalled returning to the farm to help Uly and Georgia through the birth of their stillborn son in the early seventies. They'd named their fifth child Wendel, buried him in the Kingsville Cemetery, then settled into mourning the loss of their tiny, perfect boy. To help soothe their grief, Clytemnestra asked the Farm Fates for spiritual medicine. On the day before her return to Athens, she found Willy, only a couple of weeks old, at Colosanti's petting zoo. Remembering the tiny kid's instant attachment to her, Clytemnestra looked around, expecting to see Willy trotting toward her. Instead, she discovered Georgia heading her way.

Engulfed by memories of young, wild Willy, she laughed out loud. Willy had become the family's unofficial grief counsellor and brilliant at his work. She smiled at Georgia, glad to know Willy offered Georgia solace during this challenging time. "How is it in there, Georgeous?"

"The air's not blue, but they are."

The younger woman squinted up at her sister-in-law. "You must have seen this coming. Lela's always had a hard time with Uly. He's so…"

"Male?"

Clytemnestra stood, led Georgia to the swing. "Not male, perfect, Gee, just like my dad. Dads like Uly and Jason give us nothing to push against. It's up to us to create reasons for rebellion. When our dads are perfect, we have to manufacture quarrels if we're to separate psychologically."

Georgia laughed. "If you pushed against Jason, I certainly never noticed. He adored you. He still does."

"Oh, I pushed all right. I bought diamonds instead of farming full time. I chose Nikos over my life here. The final injury was refusing to have children of my own. Once I moved to Greece, there were always questions in Dad's letters. I don't know if he meant them to be taken this way, but I interpreted his interrogations about my fertility as not-so-subtle suggestions to begin my own brood."

"Wow. It's hard to believe that of Jason, Clytie."

"Believe it. Other people's parents might seem perfect, but our own? They can't be. How can we figure out who we are if we don't resist who they expect us to be?" Clytemnestra inhaled a deep, voluptuous breath, held it, exhaled dramatically. "We both know your expectations of her are Lila's problem."

This unsolicited observation infuriated Georgia. "You think I've tied her to me on purpose? You think I want it this way?"

"No." Clytemnestra kissed Georgia's hand and held on tightly when the older woman resisted. "We both know it's too safe for her here. That's why she's out looking for trouble every day, that's why she's smacking cars, that's why she has to leave. She won't grow if she doesn't. And I'm not talking about artistic growth. I'm talking about her growth beyond the rape."

Georgia's defensiveness bloomed. "Why should she leave here if she doesn't want to? Adventure is all well and good for the adventurous, but some of us bond with a place, a way of life."

"And some of us are stuck in traumas we have to heal if we are to live full adult lives."

Georgia turned away, ambushed by guilt. She stared out at Webster's field. It was alfalfa this morning and made no sign of the experiments that would turn it to ash.

"Don't be angry, Georgeous," Clytemnestra whispered. "I'm on your side. And Lila's. You know it would do her the world of good to move away from the farm."

Georgia's eyes flooded. "That's so easy for you, for us, to say. But how can she leave with that damned chain wrapped around her body, and an even bigger one we can't see wrapped around her heart? Here she can do what she needs to do to heal, but out there?" Shocked by the fear she felt when she thought of Lila leaving the farm, she cried, "What about what Lila wants, Clytie? What about that?"

"Remember what Mama always says. 'You can't let a baby suck on a bristle just because she wants to.'"

"Lila's no baby," Georgia snapped. "If you're such a damn expert, just tell me what to do. I'll get out my notepad."

"Wouldn't it be nice if it were that easy, Gee. We both know I don't have any answers, only questions. I've asked them. The rest is up to you." She smiled. "Oh, yes, and those Fates who trick us into thinking we know what we're doing when we don't have a clue." To break the tension between them, she added, laughing, "Just look at my mess with Nikos if you want to hear the Fates laughing. I screwed up my life royally. For years. For decades." She looked out over a landscape she loved with an ardour that terrified her. "And yet here I am, feeling the generosity of yet another chance to make things right." She kissed Georgia before returning to the work of harvesting, of remembering.

For a few moments Georgia swallowed sobs. Then, a vision of Lila's future wrapped around her. Lila chainless. Lila with Max. Lila pregnant. Calm settled over her. Like her sister-in-law, she went to work.

4

Georgia looked up from her weeding to see Lela, Lila, and Uly emerge from the kitchen. As they drew closer, she heard them talking about ways to bring Lila's completed project from the back woods to the meadow. Well, she thought, grateful to see Lela and Uly a little more friendly toward one another, shared ingenuity is a good start. She sat back on her haunches to survey the garden. In the curve of the spiral closest to the barn, Clytemnestra hummed as she weeded. Willy, a coarse stubble shading his mottled hide, his nose pulmonaria dry, pranced about as he had before the great shearing and Clytemnestra abandonment. Georgia whispered a prayer of thanks for Willy's short memory and forgiving nature.

She was startled out of this meditation by the unmistakable sounds of a greyhound bus navigating the shoulder of the road beyond their cedar hedge. Expecting tourists, she found her best welcoming smile as she pushed through the front gate. Instead of strangers, her mother-in-law stood on the Greyhound's lowest step, a backpack slung over her left shoulder, a rakish fedora hiding most of her close-cropped, bright red hair. "Spring!" Georgia cried.

"Take good care of our storyteller," the bus driver called over a chorus of goodbyes.

In mid-embrace Georgia asked, "Where's Jason?" Spring jerked her thumb toward the bus interior. Georgia boarded and called his name.

"Here," Jason answered, his small frame hidden by a group exchanging addresses. He emerged from this crowd to lurch down the aisle toward her.

"No other luggage?" Georgia asked pointing to his backpack.

"Nope. We've given away everything. Masques, boots, the whole shebang." Waving his goodbyes, he teetered down the aisle to her. Spring, Georgia noted, had stepped from the bus under her own steam. Following Jason, she saw he was far less sure on his feet, taking the stairs slowly, hanging on to the railing with both hands, inching down crabwise. At the bottom stair, Georgia squeezed past him. When she stood before him, he launched himself into her arms. "You look a picture," he said, patting her cheek. "Where's my boy?"

"In the back woods, helping Lila." Georgia took his backpack. "Great hats."

Spring touched the brim of her fedora. "Gifts from 'The Touring Travelers,' a Roma band we met in Massachusetts last winter. We danced and sang together after one of their shows. They loved your Syrtos improvisations. They are so kind to old hips." Her mother-in-law took hold of Georgia's shoulders, kissed her on each cheek.

After numerous goodbyes, the bus resumed its journey. The three Buttes negotiated the gate through the cedars together, unwilling to let go of one another. Finally, laughing, they turned sideways, forming a craggy chorus-line. On the far side of the garden, Clytemnestra leapt to her feet, whooped, and bounded toward them.

At first Jason pretended not to recognize his only daughter. "What a sight for sore eyes this garden is. Look at that romaine and those nasturtiums. It's visual ambrosia, Gee, especially after our time in the great cities of the world." Clytemnestra stopped a few feet in front of him. Ending the tease, her father grinned at her with undisguised parental pride. "Oh, my! Clytie, you really are a queen. Come here and let me pinch your cheek."

After their reunion, Georgia walked Jason to the swing, aware of Spring and Clytemnestra whispering secrets as they followed. "Pops," Clytemnestra called. "You look good, considering the miles you've got on your chassis."

Spring took a moment to brush away tears. When she'd composed herself, she gestured to the crowd assembling in the garden. "Gee, introduce us to the newest members of the family."

Georgia called Karen, Kim, and Sadra to meet the farm's elders. Although Jason and Spring were obviously delighted to meet the family of the illustrious Wayne, his sisters were too shy to return their welcoming smiles. As quickly as they could, they escaped to the orchard, their mother on their heels, scolding.

"I'll get Willy," Georgia offered. "I know he'd love to take you to Lila's studio. Uly's there. And Wayne. And a little surprise," she added, knowing they'd be tickled to see Lela and Fiona. "Maybe you'd like something to eat first?"

"We had a very late breakfast in Milton," Spring said. "A truck stop that served the best French toast. Local eggs, homemade bread, and real Ontario maple syrup."

"I'll have a glass of our well water, Gee," said Jason, raising a large boney hand as if Georgia were wait staff. She returned with water as Willy made his entrance, towing his cart.

"Your summer cut, William. How sensible," said Spring. Willy pranced about showing off Alice Maude's shearing skills. Spring turned to Georgia. "I have to say I can hardly wait to see the amphitheatre," she said. "I've been dreaming about it. Have you been using it?"

"We danced to it last Friday night, after our regular dance," Georgia said. "I visit pretty regularly, but we haven't used it formally since your big finale last year." Georgia smiled, recalling how they'd danced an ancient Greek dance, Issos, through the woods, their procession made more magical by torches. After their annual Welcome-to-Spring Ceremony in the Dance Temple, with votives lighting their way the sinuous line of dancers held baby fingers and sang to music played by young musicians Jason and Spring recruited from the Hilberry.

"That was a wonderful night," said Jason. He looked at Georgia with serene practicality. "I have to confess, Gee. I haven't got a long-dance procession left in me."

"That's all right," Spring assured him. "When we do it again, Willy will take us in his cart." Hearing his name, Willy dropped the cart handle to bleat a welcome. "Look, Jason. What a love you are, William." Willy offered a snort of pride before resuming his quarrel with his cart. Georgia came to his aid by harnessing him in place.

"How long will you be staying this time?" she asked, doing her best to calm Willy's excitement. "Uly mentioned you might have an engagement at the Hilberry in the fall."

"We've officially retired," Jason said.

Spring smiled. "Unofficially, we're going to help out with the students' new production of *Medea*."

Georgia looked from Spring to Jason sensing revelations to come. "Any plans to do something here?"

"Oh, well, yes, here. That's different." Jason said. "The kids from the Harlem classical theatre couldn't believe we'd played the Dodona. They treated us like gods." Basking in remembered accolades, Jason finished his water in tiny, savouring sips.

5

You've become a bird, Georgia thought, an ancient, craggy ibis. Spring, by comparison, was positively hardy. As if to prove Georgia's assessment, her mother-in-law climbed into the cart unassisted after Georgia settled Jason on the seat. Delighted to have passengers, Willy bolted. Georgia struggled to keep up with him.

"What are your plans now?" she asked, her breath returning when Willy slowed to crest their modest hill.

"We've come home to make plans with you," Jason said. "How would you feel about hosting us in the barn?"

For a moment, Willy's surge demanded all of her attention. When the goat slowed a second time, it struck her. Jason and Spring had come home. To live. She swallowed tears of gratitude, sure the farm had arranged this, had called home allies to join her in the fight to save the farms. "We'd absolutely love to have you here, but not in the barn. You can have whatever rooms you want in the house."

"Absolutely not," said Spring. "We want you young folks to have your privacy. We remember how it is. You can't have a really good scrap when you know somebody on the other side of the wall is worrying about you." As if stung, Willy bucked and darted forward. Spring held on to her fedora with both hands. Georgia did her best to hang on to Willy's harness and keep up.

Untroubled by Willy's mischief, Jason grew philosophical. "I never thought I'd say it, but *Oedipus* has lost its thrill. Not for others, of course, but for me. My own land is plagued. I plan to devote the time I have left to its healing." Georgia swallowed more tears. "Of course, the Greek plays are wonderful jumping off points into morality, especially for young people," Jason went on. "When we start out, we need an exotic landscape in which to set the great battles between creation and destruction, individuality and collectivity. But our young folks need to learn that our time holds the same great truths."

Spring patted his knee. "We've been thinking we might get Uly's city friends to write something for us, Gee. Set in one of the factories. You know. Use our ancient dramatic conventions for a contemporary drama."

"Willy!" Georgia cried, the possibility of a greater presence of city men unnerving her. "You must behave. Do you hear me?" If he did, Willy made no sign. Instead of slowing, he quickened his pace. Just as she considered throwing her leg over his back to stop him, Willy surprised her with a toss of his head and an abrupt halt. He glanced at Georgia for approval.

"That's better, Beauty." Georgia took in a great gulp of air. They were at the place on the path where the meadow beyond the trees transformed into a massive square-cut emerald winking through a lattice of leaves. "We're almost there," she said, aware of her resentment at being saddled with the responsibility for keeping everyone in her life safe.

Willy leaned against her. Georgia patted his neck and was bending to kiss his ear when he escaped her grasp. "Willy!" With horror, she watched Jason's precarious tilt to port on the way to Lila's studio. Spring grabbed his shirt to keep him in the cart. The old man bounced upward as the wagon veered right before disappearing around the front of the studio.

"Oh, oh, oh," Georgia moaned, overwhelmed by her own ineffectualness. "It's just too damned Greek to have a funeral and a wedding on the same day. Please, please, whatever Gods care for the old and infirm, protect Jason and Spring from all mortal blows, especially those delivered by truculent, sneaky, sadistic goats." She rushed down the path to the studio, relieved to find the wagon intact – its passengers laughing. "Willy!" Georgia said, breathless. "You are very, very naughty."

Jason waved at her. "What a ride. The old boy still has lots of spunk. Like me."

"Don't look so pleased," Georgia muttered. "I'm pretty sure he was doing his damnedest to launch you into the Underworld."

"Hey!" Lila emerged from the woods beyond the meadow. "Grandma! Grandpa!" She rushed toward them, light-footed despite her chain.

"She's fine," Georgia muttered, studying Lila. "She'll leave this farm when she's ready. I can't very well kick her off the place when..." And there it was again, the guilt she felt for not preventing Lila's rape.

"You look so good," Lila cried, helping first Spring then Jason out of the cart. "You have to sit for me in those hats."

Back on firm ground, Jason tipped his fedora. "Just say it. I'm shrinking. It happens to everybody over ninety I'm told – bone erosion due to big, internal winds." He patted Lila's face and chain. "Still armed for war? The Athena Response. We need a women's army ready to end the strangle hold the crazy patriarchs have on our world." Uly arrived, interrupting Jason's call-to-arms with a hug that triggered a coughing fit in the old man.

You and Willy both, Georgia thought. Your father will be lucky if he lives to see the wedding. Just then, Lela, Fiona, and Wayne stepped from the woods.

"Jason, look. It's Le! And Fiona! And Fling! Oh, this is fine!" Spring cried.

After waiting his turn to embrace Fiona and Lela, Jason turned to Wayne. "And who's this great big strong healthy lad?" he asked, tapping Wayne's chest. "I do believe I see wings folded inside your shirt. You must be Fling." He might have been six the way Wayne kissed and hugged these adopted grandparents.

"Lila, tell us about what you're working on for Lola's wedding," Spring said. Willy nudged Jason toward the cart. Georgia removed his harness.

"You'll see. They're in the woods." With Uly's help, Jason made his way up the slight incline leading to Lila's most recent creation.

"We've got the big garden cart up there," Uly assured his mother and father. "You can ride back to the house with Lila's…"

"Lila's what?"

"They're very hard to describe, Gramps," said Lela. "In fact, they kind of defy description. What do you say, Wayne?"

"I never seen anything like 'em. If I hadn't helped make 'em, I'd say they couldn't exist."

6

On the way to Lila's surprise, Spring linked arms with Georgia and Fiona. "I can smell the lake," she said. "Do you think we could take a quick trip to the Point before the festivities tonight?"

Georgia thought of Tess's Toronto trip. Four hours each way added to however long it might take to find Lala's package and conduct her own business. "We're without wheels for a bit."

"Willy could take us," Spring said.

"Absolutely not." Spring's laugh reminded Georgia of the porcelain gull wind chimes that used to hang on the Jones farmhouse porch. "Promise you won't even think of letting Willy take you on busy roads in that cart."

"It's too late to keep that promise," Spring said. "If our time has come, all the caution in the world can't stop it."

Georgia suppressed the urge to snarl. Instead, she said, "I'm not worried about you. It's Willy. Clytie would never forgive me if an eighteen-wheeler did him in. You know how busy all the highways are these days." Fiona, who'd been silent during this discussion, kissed Spring and Georgia before sprinting to catch up to Lila and Wayne.

When she was out of earshot, Spring nodded at Jason, as if he'd been the topic of conversation all along. "His mind's going, too." Georgia took in her father-in-law's unsteady gait. "We were doing *Antigone* to fundraise for the kids in Harlem, when he walked off stage to go to the bathroom. Right in the middle of one of Creon's speeches. I found him dozing in the wings when it was over. When I asked him what was going on, he said he couldn't remember walking off stage."

Georgia blinked back tears. "I'm so glad you're home. Does he know?"

"He's blissfully unaware, at least so far." Spring smiled. "Isn't that great? I wouldn't want him to feel embarrassed. He's always played his parts so well."

Walking with Spring, Georgia felt drugged by sunshine and the aftermath of her race through the woods. She stopped, stooped to pick a few wild Marguerites bobbing amongst the grasses, hoping Spring might be an ally in her efforts to stop TriChem. "I'm beginning to think the real purpose of Lola's wedding is to bring everyone home to the farm."

"Really?" Spring took a moment to assess Georgia's mood. "What's up?"

"Webster's kids want him to sell, to a big chemical company."

Spring snorted disbelief. "Why would a big company want a little farm in Essex County when they can ruin thousands of acres in Saskatchewan?"

"Our growing conditions are similar to Northern California so…"

Spring sputtered impotent fury. "We've already got enough people working this beautiful Earth to death. We need to plant trees, stop erosion, close down the damn industries that are poisoning the air and water and giving so many people cancer."

Georgia took her moment. "Uly's come up with an idea," she said. "He and some of the men from town want to buy Web's place. They're thinking of logging," she said. "When the land's clear, they'll start a sand and gravel operation to pay off the mortgage."

Spring frowned, but didn't say why. "I'm glad he's not taking this lying down. Why haven't the men made Web an offer?"

Distressed by Spring's reaction to Uly's plan, Georgia couldn't answer. She was alone, she realized, in her vision for the farms.

"You know we've never worried about money. How much is Web…"

"Harold Shuttleworth says farms are going for thirteen thousand an acre when they're fully productive."

Spring stopped. "He's got more than two hundred acres over there. That's…"

"Small change to this chemical outfit." Georgia couldn't hide her bitterness. "The research they conduct on two hundred acres will yield billions once they convince farmers they can't live without whatever poisons they create. They've got markets for this stuff all over the world now, markets that are growing because people like us are forced to sell to agri-businesses cannibalizing small and medium sized farm." As they approached the woods, Georgia did her best to shift mental gears. Once she saw Lila, Lela, Fiona, and Wayne standing on scaffolding attached to two huge effigies, wonder replaced her TriChem anxieties.

Georgia's hands fluttered to her face. When the wave of wonder receded, she looked around. From their vantage point on the ground, Uly and Jason were advising placement of various items. "Who do we have here, Lila?" It was Spring who asked.

"We have the Green Man and his Lady, Summer." Sensing her mother's intuitive understanding, Lila smiled and nodded at Georgia. Nothing needed to be spoken between mother and daughter. In this moment, they shared the same Universe, the same profound connection, to the farm, to the Mystery.

"They need black-eyed Susan crowns," said Jason. "Aren't they majestic, Springtime?"

The sculptures, woven from small pliant birch and beech branches, stood some seven feet tall. Beautiful and impossible,

Georgia thought. How do we have an ordinary human wedding in the presence of such Beings? "They're wonderful, Lila. Have you figured out how to get them to the orchard?"

Lila jumped down from her makeshift perch to view the Lord and Lady from Georgia's perspective. "I thought you could just ask them to walk down there by themselves, Ma."

Spring turned to her daughter-in-law. "Can you do that, Georgia?"

"No, Spring." She looked at Lila, relieved to see her laughing.

"We can take them down one at a time," Jason suggested. "In the big cart."

"No Grampa," Lila said. "They can't be separated." She turned hopeful eyes on her father. "I thought maybe you could ask Max to come over with his flat bed. We could lever them on and ride down to the orchard on the old logging road."

Georgia, spellbound by blooming images of Lila and Max, said, "Max told your dad he'd help out all day. Shall I call him, or would you like…"

Lila suppressed a burst of giddiness. "You do it, Ma. I have…"

"Shall I invite Max for lunch?"

"Sure." Although she tried to sound indifferent, Georgia sensed undercurrents of excitement deep in Lila's Soul. Closing her eyes, she became privy to more of the secret life Lila and Max had been weaving together, through Lila's requests to help with logs, and through dreams as inseparable as Lila's massive Green Man and Summer Goddess. After a few startled moments, Georgia turned from these windows into her daughter's hidden meetings with Max Love to observe the real, flesh-and-blood Lila standing before her. Chained, defensive, she appeared as wounded as ever.

After kissing her most unpredictable child, Georgia began to walk back to the studio. Willy walked by her side, bumping her hip and pestering her to put on the halter he held between his teeth. "Only if you behave yourself," she said, slowing to eavesdrop on Uly and his parents walking behind.

"Georgia tells me you're looking to buy the Jones' farm, Ulysses," Spring said. "We've got some money put by. Let us help."

"What do you want with that old place?" said Jason. "You've got more than enough land to feed this family right here."

Uly filled them in on the threat to the farm. "Webster's kids want him to sell to an outfit called TriChem. If he does, everything would be poisoned in three months."

"Oh, those bastards," cried Jason. "Still trying to beat Mother Nature into submission. Did you hear that, Springtime? Webster's kids want him to sell to the enemy. Now there's a subject for a play."

"Shush," Spring said. "Remember how sound carries. Web could be out working this minute."

Georgia slowed to join them. "I don't think he wants to sell. He's just trying to keep his kids happy." She thought of the inevitable hurt and anger acquisitiveness inspired when it was a substitute for happiness. With sudden, devastating clarity, she knew Webster wouldn't live out the year if he sold the farm to TriChem. She stopped, let the others go on without her.

7

Spring turned from her husband to her son as they walked in slow, pleasurable companionship on their way to the house. Georgia watched them, touched when Uly bent low to hear something his father was saying. Then resentment flooded her heart.

She stood for a moment, nursing her disappointment with her mother-in-law's acceptance of Uly's scheme. As quickly as her anger flashed, tears came. "They're all home," she whispered to the trees, "and I am utterly alone."

At that moment, Clytemnestra's words replayed in her viscera. The suggestion that instinctive, motherly protectiveness had crippled Lila took Georgia's breath away. She closed her eyes, searched for times when she encouraged Lila to take a step toward independence. There were many, she insisted. It was far better for Lila to be guided by her own wisdom. She dealt in symbols, experienced intuitive leaps during and after her carving process, talked things out with her therapist. Lila could be trusted to know when she could handle the outside world's pressures, its cacophonous, rioting sounds, its random and calculated violence.

Georgia quickened her pace, raging against Clytemnestra's unfair judgment. She was Lila's mother, after all. This daughter's childhood violently ended when she was still a vulnerable child. For a moment she wondered if Marguerite would similarly respect her healing process. She stopped, said aloud, "My mother?"

With considerable pain she acknowledged that Marguerite Scratch was nothing like the intuitive person she herself had become through the birthing and mothering of her four daughters. Her first experiences of authenticity in childhood and adolescence had been on the Jones farm, and then, in her maturity, through her years of learning at university. What no one understood was how her schooling continued on the Butte farm, not only about growing food, but about the nature of the land's life, its voices, its stories. Feeling the fundamental difference between her mother and herself made her sad beyond words.

Without warning, a worrisome possibility occurred to her. If she asked her mother to buy the Jones farm, she might inadvertently encourage more of Lila's dependence. She looked in the direction of Webster's place, its geography so much like the Butte farm's it was impossible for a stranger to tell where one farm ended and the other began. There were no fences between them. There had never been any artificial boundaries. There were fields and woods and a single meandering stream. There were the farms' massive stones, boulders that for her had become the land's large, quartz-studded, all-seeing eyes. And there was its massive amphitheatre mouth, that oracle where Mystery proclaimed its Presence.

"Damn you, Clytie," Georgia said. "Independence isn't what we're after here. It's interdependence. That other notion is just the lingering influence of those Ayn Rand books you read when you were a girl." She walked on, her eyes leaking tears from some newly discovered territory in her heart.

8

By the time the Butte extended family gathered for lunch, the sun rode high in the western sky. Max Love, the hero of the hour, sat next to Lila, leaning over from time to time to drop some quiet word into her upturned ear. Georgia took in Lila's flushed face and felt again the presence of her daughter's secret life with Maxwell Love, their shared hopes and plans now obvious, at least to her.

Before lunch, Mae, Sadra, and Clytemnestra carried wedding clothes from Mae's sewing studio to the upstairs bedrooms. Now the women sat together sharing dress making techniques. When words failed to convey their meaning, they pantomimed information, delighting in mutual expanding understanding. Nearby, Wayne, Kim, and Karen encouraged Willy to perform, placing food on his snout and clapping when he tossed his head to catch the delicacy in his mouth. When Fiona joined Mae, Clytemnestra, and Sadra, talk turned to solar ovens and outdoor earthen ovens, the latter using dung as a fuel. Fiona sat rapt, nodding, understanding everything.

Accepting Georgia's invitation, Webster sat between Spring and Jason for the afternoon meal. No one spoke of TriChem, but the threat ribboned around them whenever talk turned to his children in Toronto. Webster took Jason's hand at one point, marveling at its smoothness then displaying his own calloused, working hands, each man's beautifully expressive in different ways.

Lela and Uly sat together, silent and a little dour, their forearms not quite touching, but their faces open now, and a little hopeful. They'd accomplished the impossible when delivering Lila's Lord and Lady to the meadow. During their problem solving, they'd forgotten their quarrels and worked well together.

Although absent from their conversations, the chemical threat spoke in their silences. Witnessing her family members' shared enthusiasms, Georgia's heart ached, for the farms, for all their inhabitants. To shake off her grief, she turned to the early afternoon's store of harmony. The trees all around them, infused with brilliant light, appeared to incline toward the human diners. Surrounding their gathering, she caught glimpses of otherworldly beings drawn by the joys of food sharing, storytelling, skills swapping, and through everything, the peace that came with work in the garden.

Feeling called, she rose from the table, walked to her spiraling beds, passed from one to another of their unearthly visitors until she stood in the shadow of Lila's great Lady and Lord of Summer. For minutes or hours, they held her in thrall. Then, from a very long way off, the phone rang. Georgia turned in time to see Lela rise to answer it.

"Ah, yes, there is an outside world," she whispered, "where life is lived as if there are no forests to soothe our spirits, no ponds to wash away our weariness. How terrible to live imprisoned by cement and steel, by greed and speed, how tragic to be separated from the perfumed scents of lake and forest."

"It was Tess," Lela called. She was so engrossed in delivering her message she missed her mother's quiet anguish.

"Tess," Georgia echoed.

"She can't get Lala's package until late tonight, so she'll start back early tomorrow morning. She promises to be here by ten or so. She and Alice Maude are staying with friends." Georgia smiled, nodded, these changes of little consequence given the larger stories playing out around her.

9

Lola's marquee arrived much later than expected. Her father, always able to see the humour generated by his youngest daughter's military preciseness, observed it was a good thing the bride was not present to assign detentions to the delivery crew for their tardiness. The meadow site chosen, people gathered to watch the unloading and offer help and advice that was, in most instances, graciously declined or ignored altogether. As the centre post slid into the hole created by two crew members and a post-hole digging machine, everyone cheered.

During hole filling and pole straightening, Georgia heard Maxwell Love ask if he might be Lila's date for the wedding. She heard his question clearly although the pair were well out of earshot. She looked around, finally seeing the couple on the far side of the marquee. As she watched, Lila nodded. Then, to her astonishment, Lila took the end of her chain and placed it in Max's hands. With amazing clarity, Georgia heard Max ask, "Are you finished with this for now?"

With a casualness that belied her decades of post-rape terror, Lila unwound the chain, looping it over Max's forearms as she did. "Maybe you can keep it in your truck, in case I need it for tree hauling." Georgia understood. In this ordinary moment of wedding preparations, Lila's chained existence ended. Georgia bowed her head feeling overwhelming gratitude.

In the bliss that followed Lila's unchaining, Georgia wandered into the garden. After lunch, Jason had retired to the swing for a nap. "Something wonderful is happening," she whispered in his ear. He responded with a contented chirp. She went to the house for pillows. After settling him into a more comfortable position, she returned to the meadow.

There, Lila organized a group to move her Lady and Lord, now secure on a low dolly, into their places for the wedding. She'd woven the pair together, their arms around one another's shoulders. Beneath this weaving, she'd created an archway between their lower bodies. Once she fixed their final position, she demonstrated how people would pass through the arch then walk through the meadow to the marquee. From the marquee, they'd follow a second path to the circle of chairs where the wedding would take place. She asked volunteers to gather cedar boughs, some to surround the base of the couple, some to edge the path to the marquee, some to mark the path from the marquee to the wedding site.

People scattered, leaving Georgia alone with the Lord and Lady. Leaking tears, she saw how they would stand all through this bright day and the next, blessing the farm's visitors with renewal on the eve of Spring's transformation into Summer. She saw, too, how, after the wedding, beneath a pashmina of stars, the pair would slowly disappear into the farm's unfolding Mystery, their work of blessing the farm with rebirth and fecundity complete.

She wanted to believe that Lila's intuition led her to create the magic they needed to protect the farms from TriChem, that her Lord and Lady would charm Marguerite Scratch into buying Webster's farm, for her, for all of them. She stood for a moment feeling boundless gratitude. And then the garden called her to weed.

10

Lola arrived at five-thirty, Juanless. Georgia wondered again how she might tell guests there was to be no wedding. Perhaps it would be as simple as "El Salvador has called to Juan's heart, Windsor to Lola's." It really was as simple as that. She could suggest their celebration be about endings and beginnings. Seeing Lola's determined face, she realized her youngest wasn't feeling at all philosophical. As her mother looked on, Lola embraced Lela, her Aunt Clytemnestra, and her grandparents with manic force. Then she called for attention. As if delivering a message on her school's PA system, she informed the crowd that Juan's family had been detained at the Canadian border and wouldn't arrive until much later. At the conclusion of this impersonal speech, she headed to her mother.

"To be frank, Georgia," Lola said, leading her mother to the orchard, "I'm relieved Juan isn't here." Her voice quivered with irritation. "I really don't know what to think. He's still insisting on going to El Salvador." She paused to wave away gnats. "I agree that teaching there is a worthy endeavour. Inspiring people to know themselves and the world is always worthy work. But I can't see myself going all the way down there to get a job that's not as stable as my current position. If I left Windsor now, I'd lose my benefits. I've already invested eleven years in my pension, money that's locked-in. We need to strategize, Georgia. I'm counting on you to persuade Juan to stay."

Georgia did her best to swallow heaving waves of grief. She wanted to believe that telling any of the girls what they should do had never been her parenting style, but after her conversation with Clytemnestra, doubt flooded her mind and bullied her heart. Even now she had to stifle the urge to tell Lola to set Juan free.

Unexpectedly, Grandmother Jones's housekeeping advice popped into Georgia's head. "Perhaps you've come upon a time in your life when you're being offered something more than monetary security?" Georgia suggested, intending this as a segue into her grandmother's middle-way philosophy – not as obsessive as her own mother, nor as relaxed as Webster's parents.

"Like what?" Lola asked, her voice ice cold. Georgia sensed her youngest daughter's impulse to make a break for the Kingsville Hotel to get rip roaring drunk.

"Well, like adventure, Lola. Like love."

"Love." Lola snorted her disdain. Anxious, she passed her half empty coffee cup from hand to hand. Georgia felt the wisdom of the middle way go down for the count.

"You're getting married tomorrow. At least I think there's still a possibility you might be." She gestured to the tent where Wayne and his mother set up warming stands on the buffet table as Lela and Fiona arranged Jones silver with the linen napkins Georgia had embroidered on winter evenings too long ago to remember. "Just look how everyone is helping to create your wedding,

Lola. There's quite a bit of love here already, and it's all for you." Lola stared into the tent's interior, her eyes misting over with a look Georgia couldn't read. "Perhaps you don't love Juan? Perhaps the need to get married got in the way of how you feel about this particular person?"

Lola scoffed. "I haven't had the luxury of feeling for a very long time."

The words slammed against Georgia's heart. "What?" she cried. "Feeling, living from our hearts, this is what our family has always been about. How can you say you haven't been feeling? What on Earth have you been doing all this time? And don't tell me you've been thinking, Lola Butte, because you know very well you can't really think, not clearly, not wisely, until you've listened to your heart." Georgia's own feelings eclipsed the prudence her intellect called for. "You know the heart, Lola. Your heart. It's where you feel, where you discern, where you choose to love, to marry. Or choose some other path." She ignored her daughter's scornful glance. "How can we be on the brink of your wedding if you haven't been feeling – and loving – with your whole heart?" Lola teetered on the brink of tears but refused to give in to them. Instead, she sipped coffee.

After a potent silence, Lola said, "Stop saying 'love,' Mother. I don't even know what the word means."

Open mouthed, Georgia watched her youngest daughter rush into the marquee to attack the flowers on the closest table, smothering the more delicate daisies with a bullying peony. She followed, did her best to keep pace with Lola's sprint from floral arrangement to arrangement, massacring bouquets as she went. Violating the last of the centrepieces, she turned to Georgia.

"Stop looking at me like that, Mother. You know I do what I have to do – to get the prizes, to earn my salary, to get married, to have a family. If my heart were the guide of my life, I wouldn't have left this farm. Ever." Her face contorted with a swallowed sob. "You made it perfect for us here." Her voice rose to a furious pitch. "That's why Lala and Lela and Lila wanted to be home-schooled. How could any place be as magical as this farm?"

Georgia whispered, "Lola." Lola ignored her.

Lola's continued in her high-pitched wail. "I saw how they struggled to get away from you and Ulysses. That's why I decided I'd leave early. To avoid future entanglements." She took a shallow breath. "Please don't talk to me about my heart, Georgia Butte. It hasn't got a thing to do with my marriage to Juan."

Georgia's hands fluttered, protective, to that region in her body where her own heart surprised her with its steadiness. Standing before her raging daughter, she pushed first one foot, then the other, into the ground. It was all she knew to do. Ground yourself, she thought, ground yourself and stay present.

11

As she stood in deathly silence with Lola, Georgia noticed an approaching figure with relief. Before she could say a word, Peter Stone broke the spell rooting Georgia to the spot. "You must be the remarkable Lola Butte. I've heard so much about you." Ignoring the obvious tension locking the women in emotional combat, he smiled at Georgia then turned to Lola, kissing her on the mouth. He ended the kiss with a full-bodied embrace. Georgia looked on, shocked to see Lola slide her arms around Peter's waist.

After at least a minute, Peter released the bride-to-be. Lola grabbed the closest chair to steady herself. Peter turned to Georgia. "I slept most of today to recover from our trip yesterday. I feel so much better. My father brought out soup and mail. I've got another commission in town, so I'm pretty much a new man. It's all thanks to you, Mrs.... Georgia, and to Tess's breathing technique. What can I do for you besides mend your youngest daughter's broken heart?"

Before Georgia could answer, Lola rushed to the house. Peter nodded at Georgia then took off after her. Georgia stared at the pair. "Oh, my," she said, dazzled by the colours shuttling between them. She held her breath when Lola turned to face Peter.

"You must be the man my mother rescued from the ditch." Lola said.

Peter Stone bowed low. "I am that very man, Lola Butte. Because your mother followed a hunch – in spite of considerable personal discomfort – I am here at your service and not in a mahogany box at Kelly's Funeral Home. I owe her a life and am following my own hunches on how to repay her." He bowed a second time, his warm brown eyes fastened upon Lola's delighted, blushing face.

Georgia joined them. "Lola's distressed because her groom has decided to move back to El Salvador."

"Your groom," Peter repeated. Georgia watched as he made the necessary internal adjustments. "You feel tricked. Betrayed."

"Yes." Indignant, she said, "There was no talk of El Salvador until this week. It's a life-changing move. I have family here. A profession I love. And I do literacy volunteer work that means everything to me." She smiled shyly at Peter Stone, then looked away, a blush spreading over her face and neck. "Oh..." she began, the pink flush deepening to rose. "I need time to think."

Peter studied the wedding tent. "More time than a day."

Lola looked up at him. She did her best to rein in her lust but it was a losing battle. "I'm certain Juan will come to his senses. I have no intention of calling off the wedding." Lola turned to her mother in an ineffectual attempt to dismiss Peter Stone. "Moving to El Salvador doesn't feel like an adventure, Georgia."

"Well, then," Peter said, taking Lola's arm. "You won't go. You'll take the time to work through your feelings. Summer arrives tomorrow. You can think and feel to your heart's content right here on this wonderful farm." Furtive, Georgia looked about for Clytemnestra. "And you'll be able to visit me at the Beam place. I'll introduce you to the peafowl. I'll show you my mating studies."

Lola's arm swept out to indicate the wedding preparations. "But look at all this. Look at my marquee." She turned away to hide her silly grin. "Tomorrow is the most auspicious day for a wedding for decades to come. And Mae's been sewing for weeks. Georgia and Ulysses even learned an Epithalamion for the occasion."

Georgia recalled Willy's gleeful mischief. "You needn't worry about your wedding poem, Lo. Willy ate it before your father and I had a chance to learn it." She could barely see Lola through the colours binding together her youngest daughter and Peter Stone. "As for Mae's clothes, there's always the dance. And this tent can be… Well, let's wait and see." More to herself she added, "We have food and company and a lovely place to celebrate Summer's arrival. I don't think people will be too distressed if you don't get married."

"But I want to get married, Mother. Don't you remember Juan's public display of love? You know perfectly well everyone at school is expecting me to return a married woman for the promotion meetings and IPRCs on Friday. They've ordered a special lunch from the Mini. And lemon cream cake, to match my Mustang, from Just Desserts."

Peter leapt in. "Perhaps I can help," he said. "If your former groom wouldn't be upset, that is. I'd be happy to marry you. I plan on staying right here in Essex County. Forever."

Tempted, Lola forced herself to back away from him. "We can't do that. We don't even know each other. What would people think?" She started for the house again. Peter followed.

Dazzled by the colours ricocheting between them, Georgia made a low, awed whistle. "I'm a very good painter," she heard Peter say. "I currently have a commission to paint the geese and other fowl at the Miner Sanctuary. After that, I'm doing a nature mural on the side of the University Avenue fire station in Windsor. There's a movement afoot to make city people more aware of the diversity of the Carolinian forest. It's a migration mural, so people can see how many species depend on our…" The pair disappeared into the house before Georgia could hear Peter's final words. With surprising joy, she sensed Lola's dilating pupils and rising passion.

12

Webster Jones, his wheelbarrow laden with mock orange blossoms from the shrubs surrounding his barn, made his way toward Lola's marquee. Georgia caught their scent before she saw her cousin and his load of beauty. "For little Lola," he called, shy.

Georgia hugged him. "Let's find something to put them in."

Webster hesitated a moment. "Actually, Gee, I was hoping Clytie was around. She suggested I bring the flowers. I think she's got something in mind."

To hide her disappointment, Georgia pretended to search for her sister-in-law, staring into the meadow, empty now except for

Karen and Kim playing on the swing. "I think Clytie may be at the studio with Lila. I saw them head into the woods a while ago."

"Maybe I should just stick these in water and wait until tomorrow."

"Oh," Georgia said. "They'll make the rehearsal supper far more festive…" Sensing his reluctance to let her take the flowers, she said, "Juan's relatives have been detained at customs. I'm sure Clytie won't mind if we fill the time making wreathes."

With a slow smile, he agreed. "I'll go change for the party."

Georgia stood still a moment, sorting her feelings until Sadra rushed from the barn, clapping her hands at the wheelbarrow full of flowers. "Fordatent?"

Georgia nodded, smiling, before giving in to the mild irritation Webster's preference for her sister-in-law's artistic talents provoked. She welcomed Clytemnestra home, but she was not going to surrender this particular wedding to her managerial talents. She unloaded the boughs, passing them to Sadra and pointing to the tent's cool interior. "We'll make wreathes. Do you know wreathes?" She shaped a bough into a circle.

Sadra nodded. "I know wreathes."

On their return from the pond, Fiona and Lela joined the flower arranging festivities, glad of the shade the marquee provided. Kim and Karen were quick studies and their mother needed no instruction at all. Buzzing wisdom about flower magic zipped among them, Georgia inhaling and exhaling their chatter with the flowers' potent fragrance. After several breaths, she felt invisible hands turn her toward the meadow. A hum, barely audible over talking and laughter, vibrated up from some secret farm source, shivered into the trees, and leaped from the leafy canopy into the clear, still air.

Georgia's gaze drifted back to the marquee's shadowed interior. Beyond the marquee, Clytemnestra emerged from the woods, her head wrapped in a bright red scarf. Behind her, in a small wooden garden cart, a Herma stood looking skyward, its oversized phallus pointing directly at her sister-in-law's back. Georgia turned to see Sadra, her eyes growing large at this sight of the Herma, call to her daughters and point. The two young girls giggled. Karen dashed to meet Clytemnestra and slip her first wreath over the Herma's proud erection.

Uly appeared behind his sister pulling several Hermae, all gazing skyward, in the largest garden cart. "They really are very beautiful," Fiona said. "Phalluses looking to Spirit. Lila's a marvel."

Lela tossed an oversized wreath at her father who immediately slipped it over his head. "After we're finished decorating the tent," Lela said, "do you have time to show me your design for the new type of yurt? Fiona and I are going to build one when we get home. Mama said you and Max and Lila designed one that uses a cable instead of a centre beam? Out near the pond?" Her father bowed with exaggerated graciousness.

Georgia felt the peace of bridged divides. She glanced westward. It was close to six already. Willy trotted into her mind. "Has anybody seen Willy?"

"He and Wayne are looking for horse head materials at the studio," Uly said. Georgia was about to ask him to bring them both to the house when a man in a white uniform opened the front gate then disappeared. Georgia added a wreath to the pile growing in the centre of their circle then headed to the gate, her heart racing with knowledge her mind did not yet know.

As she walked through the garden, the mysterious hum she'd heard earlier now pulsed beneath her feet. She looked around expecting others to remark on the throaty sound but no one appeared to notice. "So," she whispered, "you're a little song for me alone."

By the time she reached the foot bridge, the man in white reappeared, this time pushing a wheel chair. In opulent summer finery, Marguerite Scratch perched on this moving throne. Over her head, an oxygen tank dangled from the steel pole attached to the chair. "Mother," Georgia whispered, knowing she would not hear. "I will forgive you every last thing when you buy Webster's farm for me, for us." Forcing a smile, she said, "I can't quite believe you're here, Mother. You look lovely."

Fluffed to a glossy perfection, Marguerite Jones Scratch sat in a lavender chiffon cloud a shade deeper than her wispy hair. "I wanted to surprise my girl," Marguerite said in her thin, airy voice. "Lola thought I'd have to stay in bed, but look, Nurse made me mobile."

"Call when I'm needed. I'll be right outside," the young man said.

"No, no," said Georgia. "Please, come in. Take off your jacket. Make yourself at home. We're glad to have you join us,…"

"Hero Lafontaine. I'm Mrs. Scratch's private nurse until next Monday." He smiled a hero's smile.

"Hero. What a remarkable name," said Georgia.

The young man coloured. "I know. A boy named for a virgin priestess who drowns herself for love. What were my parents thinking?" He paused then added, as if this explained everything, "It was the sixties…"

Georgia was about to tell him about Ulysses and Clytemnestra when memories of Lila's grief and the other sixties children seeped into her consciousness. She did her best to welcome him and her mother. "Here is Grandmother Scratch," she called to the wreathe-makers. "And Hero."

Lela rushed to greet her grandmother and her nurse. "Grandma," she cried, bending to kiss the old woman. "Welcome, and welcome to you, Hero. We're so glad you're here."

"Are you the perverse one who married a girl?"

For a second, Georgia wished she could ask Hero to take her mother back to the city. "I don't know how perverse I am, but yes, I'm the one who married a woman," Lela said. "It's time you met Fiona." She hailed her partner.

Marguerite studied Fiona for a moment before asking, "How will you have children? I suppose you'll adopt from some country overseas?"

Unruffled by this intrusion into their private lives, Lela said, casual, "Oh, we've already adopted lots of kids."

Georgia's mother frowned. "Where's Lola? I want to surprise her. I brought her my trousseau." She fixed Georgia with a cold stare. "I had all my lovely satins and silks ready for you, but you ran off with that Butte boy." She said this as if she hadn't seen Ulysses Butte since the summer night when he and Georgia eloped and made their pilgrimage to the State of Georgia. "You know," she said to Lela, "your mother is like you, always trying to shock people. The first time I visited her on this farm she was wearing overalls and digging in the dirt. I thought she was a man."

"Grandma!" Lola, her hair tousled and her face radiant, rushed from the house. She stopped in mid-flight, aware suddenly of the significance of her grandmother's presence. "You've come for the wedding."

"Where's the groom? I want to get a good look at him before I bestow my blessing." As if on cue, Peter Stone, as disheveled and radiant as Lola, emerged from the house. Lola offered Georgia a quick apologetic smile.

"You must be he," said Marguerite, signaling Peter Stone to pay court with a wave of her gloved hand. Georgia looked on, her heart beat slowing to its usual rhythms.

"You look presentable enough," Marguerite said to Peter. "My granddaughter tells me you're quite the artist." She extended her hand.

Peter basked in unexpected fame. "She did? Wow. I had no idea she knew about my work."

Before Lola could explain to her grandmother that Peter Stone was not the groom and that Juan Elias's artwork adorned her Windsor home, Spring called out from the back door. "Has Willy been in Lola's old room? The place is an awful mess." Guileless, she added, "Lola, be a good girl and clean it up for your mother. With all these people coming, she's going to need to have it ready for your guests."

Crimsoning to the roots of her tousled curls, Lola tried to suppress a gorgeous smile revealing everything. She rushed back to the house. "Why don't you give her a hand, Peter," Georgia suggested. "There are fresh linens in the hall closet."

"You've saved my life a second time," he whispered.

13

It was almost eight when Juan Elias parked his employer's pickup in front of the Butte farm. Beside him on the bench seat were his mother, Esperanza, and his aunt, Juana. In the storage space behind the front seats were sandwiched his three younger brothers – Eduardo, Carlos, and Pablo – along with Jesus, his cousin. The boys were dressed in identical white shirts and black jeans, a tribute to their modest boy-band success back home. Georgia hovered on the periphery of the garden, watching their flurried arrival and invoking miracles.

"Who on earth are they?" Marguerite asked, her reedy voice barely audible over boisterous greetings. Everyone had an opinion about the newcomers' border crossing adventures. Rested after his afternoon doze in the swing, Jason squinted in the direction of Marguerite's hawk-like focus on Juan.

"Marguerite, that man in your sites is Juan, Lola's intended." He used his sonorous stage voice to make this pronouncement.

"No." Marguerite's contradiction did not invite argument. "You're in a muddle as usual, Jason. The groom is that tall young man…" She searched the crowd for Peter Stone.

Spring patted Jason's shoulder. "New plots developed while you were napping."

Initially distressed to find himself among so many strangers, Juan relaxed when he discovered Spring and Jason in the welcoming crowd. The elder Butte photographs were present at all the citizenship parties Lola threw for her graduating students. For Juan's party, Uly had delivered baklava from Greek Town and Georgia recited, as Jason's proxy, "Ulysses." Juan remembered this pivotal moment, whispering to the old man, "To rust unbur-neesed… Yes? Not to shine in the used."

"'Unburnish'd'," said Jason, leaning into Juan's enthusiastic embrace. He offered both his soft cheeks for the young man's kisses. "You remember the Tennyson." With sudden vigour, the old man stood and called for silence before reciting the poem's concluding lines:

> *Tho' much is taken, much abides; and tho'*
> *We are not now that strength which in old days*
> *Moved earth and heaven, that which we are, we are;*

One equal temper of heroic hearts,
Made weak by time and fate, but strong in will
To strive, to seek, to find, and not to yield.

He bowed low as the crowd erupted with applause.

When this burst of excitement calmed, Juan looked around, recognizing Lola's revered grandmother from the several photographs Lola had on her walls. He looked to Jason, then nodded at the old woman. Jason returned his nod with an encouraging smile. Juan presented himself to Marguerite. She did not respond. Thinking the old woman might be deaf and blind, he bent low to offer a gentle embrace. Marguerite raised both her gloved hands in protest. Bewildered, Juan moved on to greet Spring. "And so lovely are you, the Mrs. Spring. Prettiest than your photograph."

"But you are lovelier," Spring said. "You are the Green Man, Juan, Summer's Consort. You are the Great Impregnator. You are the Corn King."

"I do like these things you says to me." Juan's blush proved his delight. "You will journey to my native land with the Beautiful Miss Lola. She will learn from you these words. We will be happy in El Salvador."

Eavesdropping, Marguerite cried, "What about Peter?" Before anyone could answer, Jesus, older and more worldly wise, guided Juan to the marquee. Watching with suspicious scrutiny, Georgia's mother cried, "Spring! What is that they're babbling?"

"They're speaking Spanish, Marguerite. Juan comes from El Salvador."

"Oh, he must be one of Lola's little students. And those young boys and their mothers must be the Mexican Mennonites, come to cook and serve. Spring, push me to the tent, will you?

Hero has gone off to revel."

"Stay here, Darling," Spring ordered Jason. "I'll be back for you." Seeing Spring struggle with the wheelchair, Fiona came to her aid. In honour of the season, she'd changed into the gauzy green tunic Mae created for her that afternoon. On her unbound, flowing hair sat a wreath of black-eyed Susans. Around her ankles and toes, she'd wound crocheted metallic threads.

"Let me give you a hand, Spring. Grandmother Scratch, do you want to go to the tent?"

"No, no, no," said Marguerite, aghast at Fiona's outfit. "Please finish dressing."

"I'm as dressed as I'm going to be for the last night of Spring." Familiar with this Ancient's prudery, Fiona laughed. "Let me take off a little of what you've got on. You're positively entombed in all this fabric. Nylon doesn't breathe like natural fibers, you know. Clothing needs to breathe when the weather is muggy and hot."

"No!" Marguerite held on to her lavender chiffon hat and stole. "You may be unaware of this, young lady, but your dress is shockingly revealing."

"Mae made it." Fiona twirled her pride in Mae's artistry. "Isn't it gorgeous? And it's cool."

"I'm sure it's meant to be a slip. Underneath a nice slimming sheathe." Fiona pushed the chair with surprising speed along the path to the marquee. "Spring," Marguerite called. Pretending to be out of earshot, Spring walked Jason to the meadow. As a last resort, Marguerite summoned her daughter. "Georgia Scratch! Your mother needs you."

From across the garden, Georgia smiled and waved, deciding to ignore her mother's imperious cry for help. At that moment, Webster arrived at the Butte meadow. He wore a batik blue and green shirt, loose black trousers in the style of harem pants. On his feet he wore sandals without socks. Georgia smiled at the glaring whiteness of his skin.

"You look very handsome," Georgia said, joining him at the foot of Lila's Lady and her Green Man. "Very handsome and… Mediterranean."

"Thank you." He looked at her batik sarong approvingly. "I think we share the same tailor." They laughed together.

Uly called to Webster from the shade of the marquee. Webster smacked a kiss on Georgia's forehead before answering this summons. She had not expected Uly's kindness toward her cousin. "Oh my," she said seeing the men embrace. "Uly and Web, hugging after all this time." She looked around.

In the middle of the marquee, Lila fiddled with the sound system, shouting for people to dance when music blared from the speakers. Nearby, Juan's brothers quibbled over the best sites for speaker placement. Earlier, Uly had strung twinkle lights around the marquee centre pole and now Clytemnestra was weaving Webster's remaining mock orange blossoms into the tail end of the spiral at the pole's base. Kim and Karen appeared to be persuading Juan's youngest brother, Pablo, to teach them how to dance. Jesus came to his flustered cousin's rescue, swinging each of the young girls in wild swing dance moves before planting them on solid ground and demonstrating the jitterbug. Juan joined Uly and Webster at the punch bowl, glad to listen to their marquee structure discussion, including their reasons for preferring actual buildings over Lola's flimsy but glamorous 'garment architecture.' Clytemnestra completed her decoration duties and joined Juana and Esperanza.

Georgia's breath caught as she realized Peter and Lola were nowhere to be seen. Impatient with herself for expecting the evening to unfold in the manner of conventional rehearsal dinners, she did her best to accept the end of these foolish hopes. Looking around, she became aware of a building joy as people got to know one another. "I should know by now," she told the humid air. "Love is going to triumph, no matter what."

14

"Phone for you, Gee," Fiona called from the garden.

Georgia put aside planning how she might broach the subject of purchasing the Jones farm with her mother to walk to the house, the swish of her sarong as she walked the familiar path anchoring her in the sensuous present. 'Dancing, dancing, dancing,' the cool fabric whispered. She heard again the great hum she'd heard earlier that afternoon. As she approached the house, the hum traveled to her chest. When she answered the phone, she felt prepared for anything.

"It's Erie Woodburn, Georgia."

"Hello, Erie." With a magician's explosion of light, a young girl dressed in black materialized in Georgia's mind's eye. Persephone. "How are you, Erie?"

"When I heard Alice Maude's barn burned, I wondered if she'd be with you. I've been calling since noon, but I can't reach her. She invited me out tonight. To visit with Tess."

"She and Tess have gone to Toronto. She must have forgotten…"

"To Toronto? Do you know what time they'll be back?"

"I'm afraid she won't be back until tomorrow. They're picking up a gift Lala mailed from Colombia." Georgia felt the younger woman's disappointment in her own throat. "I'm sure Alice Maude meant to let you know. With the barn burning, and Tess home, I'm sure she was overwhelmed." She paused then added, "I don't know if Alice Maude told you. She and Tess haven't seen one another for almost two years."

"Tess didn't come home for her father's funeral last year?"

"No. She was sick with influenza." Unspoken speculations flowed between the women. Georgia remembered Tess's 'I was afraid I'd dance on his coffin' remark.

After a few more moments, Erie said, "They need time to catch up."

A strange conviction took hold of Georgia. "Come out as you planned. Alice Maude would want you to. Tess was glad to hear of her mother's friendship with you."

Through the kitchen window, Georgia watched ribbons of colour dancing through the garden. "Why don't you bring Lillie and Gert out tonight? We're having a very informal get together with Juan's family." Tempted as she was to admit there might be an uncoupling rather than a coupling, she refrained. "Come out tonight and stay over."

"Are you sure there's room?"

Georgia thought for a moment. "Does Gert need anything special in the way of sleeping arrangements?"

"She gets up in the night to use the bathroom."

Georgia mentally counted bedrooms. "She and Lillie can have the main floor bedroom in the barn. It has its own bathroom. Would you like a room to yourself?"

"I've already packed my tent. Alice Maude said I could pitch it out back, at the edge of her woods and the Miner cornfield."

"I know the spot." Georgia recalled her own experiences

with George Three Feather at the Miner place. As she opened her mouth to share these beautiful moments, the farm's great hum vibrated up through the kitchen floor and told her not to mention them. "We'll see you soon, Erie. Tell your mother and grandmother how much I'm looking forward to visiting with them."

So, Georgia thought, wandering to the back door. Erie may find George tonight. Noises from upstairs startled her. "Willy?" she called. "Is that you?" It was Lola who answered. Georgia's youngest daughter stood at the top of the stairs in blush muslin, Peter behind her, his long hair braided with greenery. The colours between them glowed water-iris blue, rose, and gold.

"Have you thought about what you're going to say to Juan?"

Lola and Peter floated down the stairs, then followed Georgia into the kitchen. Surprisingly pragmatic given her rosy glow, Lola said, "I think I have to marry him, because of the house and all he's done to convince everyone that he loves me." She turned to Peter. "But El Salvador is too far away. Juan is simply going to have to stay here." Peter put his arm around her.

"Peter," Georgia said. "You mustn't do this for me."

"This?"

"Whatever it is you're doing with my daughter."

"No, it's not for you. I hope that's okay." Leaving them to their unfolding story, Georgia headed out to their guests. Beyond the garden, the farm's great throbbing hum vibrated beneath her, traveling up through her body to join the hum in her chest.

15

Erie, Lillie, and Gertrude arrived to find guests mixing easily, talking, dancing, toasting new friendships, love, and the glorious evening. Now and again, someone called out a toast for Lola and Juan. The bride and groom came together in these moments, sharing awkward hugs and swift, stilted kisses.

Her TriChem terrors muted by the conviction that in a parallel universe her mother had already purchased the Jones farm and gifted it to her daughters, Georgia smiled upon the boisterous gathering. She was a little troubled when she saw Lola between Peter and Juan, her daughter's eyes raised to Peter's animated face, her smile suggesting she possessed some new and vital knowledge. Juan, open and friendly, looked from Lola to Peter with guileless curiosity.

Beyond them, Mae danced with Juana and Esperanza, this trio shimmying to Etta James's "You Can Leave Your Hat On." At a table near them, Webster and Clytemnestra, their heads together, leaned toward their inevitable coupling. Georgia looked away from their incubating fires to Hero, deep in conversation with Lela and Fiona, suddenly knowing he would find his way to their community in Vermont. In this vision, she felt again how greater-than-human powers were calling people together, here, at their farm, and all over the world. She felt again the great hum, beneath her feet and in her chest. So much of what had seemed random and chaotic now fell into a pattern of indescribable beauty and profound meaning.

Someone called her name. When she looked from her inward visions to her companions, she saw Uly with Spring and Jason, the three of them waving and laughing about something they might share with her later. She stepped out of the tent, gave her full attention to the darkening sky.

High above, brilliant stars brought to mind the night George Three Feather died. She wondered if Erie had set up her tent by now, was perhaps hearing George's song for the first time. And then Webster was beside her, his arm around her shoulders, his breath warm on her hair.

"Come back to the party, Gee. Everyone misses you."

She took his arm and walked a few steps. "Look at this," she said. "After all this time, we still have the same stride." She opened her mouth to ask if he felt the farm's hum, but invisible fingers pressed against her lips. As they walked together, Webster nodded at the young Elias boys where they sat practicing their English, but Georgia could see only Lila, chainless, sitting back-to-back with Lela on the ground as they had when they were children. Feeling her mother's eyes on her, Lila looked up.

"Ma, come sit with us."

Georgia looked to the meadow. "Your Lady and her Green Man are bringing something very special to our gathering." She peered at the giant Beings poised on the threshold of the meadow. "I don't know how you've done it, Beauty, but I half expect them to slip-step up the path to join us." Lila laughed. The sound thrilled her mother.

Jason banged the table and held up his hands. When the crowd stilled, he made his invitation. "In the spirit of the occasion, I propose we each take a candle and pay homage to the amphitheatre." After several minutes, the revelers organized themselves behind Willy's cart. In it, Jason and Spring sat like royalty.

Georgia kept to the sidelines, looking for Wayne. Earlier that evening, she'd watched him dance with Jesus and the other young men but had lost sight of him after the music stopped. She slipped through the trees into the garden, empty now except for swallows feeding on the insects attracted by the festive lights. She headed to Alice Maude's.

The barn had burned cleanly. Only a few charred boards remained where the northern wall had been. Georgia stared at the ruin, aware of the acrid smell of burnt, water-saturated wood. The Vaughan farm felt lighter. She turned from the ruin to find her neighbour's house in darkness. She felt bereft until she heard the unmistakable sounds of singing.

It was Wayne's chicken song. Georgia knew then. The young boy was helping Erie set up her tent. "Wayne," she called. "Erie. Shall I help, too?" Their silence told her everything. She turned back to their farm, catching sight of Lila's Lady and Green Man in the distance. For a moment, she felt sure she saw them move.

1

Sunshine. Georgia opened her eyes to brilliant light, whispered her gratitude for fine weather. No twisters. No black clouds. Not even the sign of a June shower. Summer in all her green glory and grace had taken possession of the farm. The previous night's revels in the amphitheatre washed over her. "Our Celebration has been so much better than doing *Oedipus*," Jason intoned during his final benediction. "No one died or went blind."

She felt for Uly, found his place empty. She felt relief and a little guilt. They'd been careful to avoid one another after the elder Buttes arrived, neither willing to bridge their TriChem rift. With effort, she put Uly out of her mind.

"I've overslept," she said to the fine summer morning. "I guess as mother of the bride I can loll around for a bit longer." She luxuriated in the sense of vanquished foes, sure her mother, tucked away in the barn with Gertrude and Lillie, her stony heart softened by Sadra, had been prepared by the Farm Fates to save them all.

Willy appeared in the doorway with a wooden spoon clenched between his teeth. Georgia patted the bed. "You may come in, Mr. Naughty." Willy dropped the spoon and trotted to her. "You almost killed Grandma and Grandpa yesterday." Willy shook his head. "Do you like your new suit? You looked very dashing in it." Willy smirked. "Good. You'll be even more beautiful today. Mae's made you something very special." Willy climbed on the bed to nuzzle Georgia's ear.

"Where's Uly?" Willy snorted ignorance. "You slept in too? Aren't we the lazy bones! I bet he's out there cleaning up all alone." Willy farted.

"I want none of that while we have company, Willy, at least not during the ceremony. If there is one." He farted once again, a long melodious tune pungent with the after effects of Mae's Humbugs, Juana's tortillas, and Esperanza's beans and spicey rice. Willy," she said, realizing the embarrassment he would cause wedding guests who did not share the Butte family's delight in four-legged relatives. "I want you to drink a bucket of water this morning. Let's clear you out before any more company arrives."

Woman and goat left the bed together, Georgia to dress for her wedding day tasks, Willy to evacuate his bowels in the compost heap. Clytemnestra appeared in the hallway outside Georgia's door. Willy maaed, picked up his spoon, and cut his yellow eyes in his aunt's direction. Clytemnestra followed him downstairs.

"You're wearing another scarf." Georgia joined her sister-in-law in the kitchen. "What's this? A new look?"

"Yes. New life. New look." Clytemnestra kissed and hugged Georgia. "Company," she said, pointing out the screen door.

Juan's mother and aunt, their arms full, headed to the house. "Huevos," said Esperanza, holding up a bowl filled with eggs. "We cook for you this morning."

"How lovely," said Georgia.

"Refried beans we make already. With jalapeños. We make papusas, also." With smiles of appreciation, Clytemnestra and Georgia introduced the women to the farmhouse kitchen. Outside, guests and family members began to set the table in the garden.

The meal prepared, everyone gathered. The Elias boys and Wayne's sisters took their food to the pond. Georgia watched them until Lila caught her attention. Chainless, her third daughter stood to address the crowd. "To the first day of Summer." She toasted the day with her grape juice.

"To Summer," repeated family members and friends.

Lila sat. Her father stood. "To the Solstice," Uly raised his glass as he spoke, "our longest day, our shortest night, and our most intense experience of physical enlightenment." Everyone toasted the Summer Solstice.

Georgia mulled the most recent miraculous happenings – Lila's unchaining, their renewed friendship with Webster, the Elias family members' safe arrival, her mother's redemption after years of foolish social snobbery. She listened, catching a few of the details trimming this story or that. People smiled, laughed, basked in the sunshine of their perfect day.

She turned to Webster's farm. No smoke, no stench, only alfalfa singing its green song, sweet and irrepressible. This sight made her search for her cousin in the gathering. And there he was, with Clytemnestra, their faces soft and radiating some new knowledge only they shared.

"Hey, Gee," Wayne said from the buffet table where he stood deciding on his next course. "You got everything you need?"

Georgia nodded. "I'm fine." She tossed him a reassuring smile.

Hearing her mother's voice, Lila looked up from a conversation with Lela and called to her. With wide-eyed happiness, she touched her heart, and, pointing at Georgia, mouthed 'I love you.' To Georgia, Lila's summer shirt and cut-off jeans seemed the loveliest clothes in all the world.

Willy pranced from person to person, cadging admiration

and breakfast delicacies. When he came to Clytemnestra, he head-bumped her back. She turned, stroked his bristled chin, then kissed him between the eyes. They were friends again.

2

It was almost noon by the time the farm's human guests cleared away their breakfast chaos and began preparations for the wedding ceremony and feast. Max delivered the rest of the casseroles from the Gordon Market Caterers along with a basket of Shasta daisies, a gift from Lydia Gordon. Her note read, "Some of Nature's Brides for your Lola."

Lila suggested a communal swim after the group completed various wedding-tent tasks. It pleased Georgia to see everyone head to the pond. As they drifted away, she suggested they lunch casually, when hunger brought them to the kitchen. Later, after play and rest, they would come together to prepare for what Georgia now thought of as their Mystery Event.

She returned to the kitchen to stand in the doorway, enchanted by the people Lola's desperation to marry had called to the farm. Gertrude and Lillie sat in the shade of the gazebo, the elder Persephone grandparent working a needlepoint chair cover, the younger holding a book and staring into the dream unfolding above its pages. Seeing these elders, she remembered her mother.

As if she'd summoned Marguerite simply by remembering, Hero emerged from the barn pushing Marguerite in her wheelchair. He parked the chair in the shade of the gazebo, set the chair's brake, then bent low to receive further instructions. When he returned to the barn, Georgia seized her moment.

Leaving the kitchen, her entire being merged with her dream of the two farms' shared future. On the short walk to her mother, she mulled the miracle of farm rescue. She halted in midstride when Webster called to her. Rattled by the unexpected, Georgia opened her mouth to beg a few minutes grace, but before she could speak, Hero opened the barn door and called to her cousin. Webster mouthed 'later.' She nodded. Then, without understanding why, she closed her eyes. A vision unfolded, the people gathering for Lola's wedding transformed into seeds borne to the farm by mystical winds. As suddenly as it came, the vision released her. She resumed her walk. When only a few feet separated them, she said, "How are you, Mother? I hope you had a good night."

3

"How lovely the garden looks, Georgia. Everything is splendid for our girl. If we can just get those young men to do a general tidying of petals and leaves…"

Georgia heard in her mother's voice the distant scream of a leaf blower. With that scream, all her strategizing evaporated. Anxiety flooded her mind and heart. She heard herself blurt, "A chemical company is interested in buying your old farm."

"Whose old farm?"

Georgia swallowed a tangle of emotions before she could speak. "Your old farm, Mother. The Jones's family farm."

"Webster's farm?"

"Yes, Webster's farm."

"Well," Marguerite said, patting her stiff artificial curls. "That's great news for Webster."

Georgia's anger leapt out. "No, Mother, it isn't. This company builds research plants that experiment with poisons. They poison the air, the land, the water. Our farm will…"

Her mother interrupted with her belittling, hospital-board Chair voice. "Surely, you aren't going to tell me you're against research." The old woman dabbed at the corners of her mouth with a lace handkerchief, a gesture that conveyed disdain to her daughter.

She couldn't keep the defensiveness from her voice. "Of course I'm not against research, as a general rule. But Mother, this kind of research poisons farms." Cunning transformed her mother's face. Georgia's heart missed several beats.

"What do you mean, 'this research poisons farms?'"

"They experiment with chemicals, to kill insects." But her mother wasn't listening, was, rather, strategizing the best way to win their current thrust and parry.

Cool, Marguerite said, "Of course, they'll want your farm, too. What a stroke of luck. I've been thinking about how to broach a subject I've had on my mind for some time."

When the hit came, Georgia fought to keep her footing. She shifted from foot to foot to ground herself. Her mother's actual response was so different from the one she'd been imagining that she couldn't quite believe what she said. Uly, if he were here, would whisper 'Lucy van Pelt,' and delight in Georgia's naiveté.

Sensing her advantage, Marguerite continued. "I've decided it's time for all of you to move to Windsor, to be close to Lola and her groom, and to me. Lola will begin her family. You'll be a grandmother, finally. And I'll live with you, in the Old Walkerville home you buy when you sell this farm to that chemical research outfit."

"Mother," Georgia said, drowning in waves of turbulence. "You know I can't move into town." Before Marguerite could contradict her, Georgia bent to the ground to hide her tears. "My life is here, Mother. I've never belonged in the city."

The old woman huffed with impatience. "As your father

told you a hundred times, Georgia Scratch, you are unrealistic. You can't avoid cities. The cities of the world are the great generators and protectors of modern civilization."

Her mother's use of her birth name felt like the coup de grâce. "Mother, I don't want to fight with you."

"We're not fighting," Marguerite said, dismissing the thought with a backhanded wave. "We are politely discussing the future. You have a golden opportunity to sell this farm to the researchers and move into town. You'll be lucky if they want it as well as Webster's. Besides, a woman your age and with your advantages should not be working. It's unseemly. I can't imagine what people think when they see a Scratch covered with dirt."

Georgia groped for her Grandmother Jones's middle way. "Maybe, one day," she said, these traitorous, appeasing words almost choking her. "Maybe one day we could move to town, but at present, I'm still a farmer." She closed her eyes. "I was hoping you'd consider buying the old farm for the girls. So, they'll have what we've had."

Her mother straightened in her wheelchair. "You have a very short memory, my girl, if you think I'll spend a cent of your father's money after you…"

"Not father's money, Mother. I'm asking you to spend Grandma Jones's money to save the Jones farm."

Marguerite raised an eyebrow. "When did you get so interested in my mother's money? As I recall, you've been pretty high and mighty about accepting any money from me for a very long time."

Georgia shifted her attention to the garden and its harmonies, taking in the beauty she'd helped to create. A fresh spaciousness allowed her to see Spring and Jason navigating the slight hill that led to this standoff with her mother. Her mother's mild voice brought her back to their argument. "You are being pig-headed, as usual, Georgia. Research drives progress." She might have been commenting on the weather and not the potential death of all Georgia loved and cherished.

Calmer, Georgia said, "This kind of research will ruin everything you see."

"Ruin? Oh, Georgia, just because people don't do what you think they should, you can't accuse them of ruining everything." Seeing the elder Buttes, she said, "Ah, here are Jason and Spring. No unpleasantness in front of them, please. No scenes. We don't want to spoil Lola's day."

Smiling with artificial conviviality, she added in a voice only Georgia could hear, "I thought you knew. The Jones money is long gone. It was your grandfather's wish that I contribute my share of the family estate monies to the Liberal war chest and as soon as mother died, I made sure they got every cent. Young Paul Martin, a Windsor boy, is going to be the saviour of this country once we get rid of that bumbling Frenchman. You'll be able to take a great deal of pride in your family's contributions to his election." She turned from Georgia's stricken face to the elder Buttes. "Spring! Jason!"

"Are you all right, Gee?" Spring closed the space between them, cupping Georgia's face in hands far too large for her delicate, old-woman's body. "You've taken a turn." Georgia made a feeble gesture, mumbled wedding excuses, and fled to the kitchen's cool stillness. There she wept, muttered, shed more tears. When she heard the rattle of Uly's truck, she felt she'd been mourning her murdered dreams for days. Without knowing where the strength came from, she splashed water on her face, and with her best welcome-home smile, left the house to greet Tess and Alice Maude.

"Oh, Georgia, I'm so sorry," Tess said.

Glad to see Tess and Alice Maude, Georgia began her assurances. "We were fine." As if her own grief were catching, she saw in Tess's face some new circumstance. "What is it, Tess?"

Before Tess could answer, Lala Butte appeared on the gate's threshold. "Hi, Mom. How do you like that UPS service!" The eldest Butte daughter held out the parcel that had been Tess's ruse for the Toronto trip. Georgia gaped at this tanned and windblown apparition. Laughing, Lala wrapped her mother in a tender embrace.

"How can this…you were in…Lola will be…your father…your father…your sisters…"

"I was on my way when you called. I had a hunch you'd call before the wedding, so I left instructions to fake a bad connection and forward the call to my hotel in New Jersey. When we talked, I was just about to leave for JFK and the red-eye to Toronto. As soon as you told me Tess was home, I called her to see if we could finish some business in Toronto that we began before I left for Colombia." Lala hugged her mother again. "I'll tell you all about me later. Right now, Tess needs to talk to you. And I have to surprise Dad and the other Ls. Is Lo here yet?"

"No, not until after four," Georgia said, breathless with happiness. "She insisted on working today."

Lala grinned. "It figures. Is she still our Barbie with a briefcase?"

"No," said Georgia, stroking her eldest daughter's hair. "It turns out our Lola is full of surprises, too." She turned to Tess. "You were so, so good to do this."

Tess took Georgia's hand. "I'm afraid the excitement isn't over." Beside her daughter, Alice Maude stood smiling at Georgia, a normal, happy smile. "We've got news, about Persephone."

With Tess's words, the pale, beckoning arm Georgia had seen earlier in the week flashed in her imagination. "What news?"

"Lala will tell you everything." Tess took Alice Maude's hand and turned to the front gate.

"At least tell me if she's alive, Tess."

Tess shook her head. "We don't know for certain. Lala treated a woman with a Persey tattoo on her arm at her St. James Town Clinic a week before she left for Colombia. She let me know, and I sent word to my contacts in the city, other reporters who share deep background on the Lawson case. Last month, one of them tracked this woman down. Last night, Mom and I met her. We want Erie to meet her as soon as she can."

"What can I do to help?"

"Could you call Erie and the grandmothers?"

Georgia briefly bowed her head, acknowledging the farm's mysterious powers of attraction. "They're here. They came out last night." She felt the lightest touch, as if the arm she's seen in her mind's eye had become a flesh-and-blood arm, its owner beside her. "Tell me, Tess. Tell me what you can about the woman Lala treated."

Tess squinted into the sun. "I know the timing is wrong, but could you bring Erie and her mother and her grandmother over so I can tell you together?"

"The timing is perfect," Georgia said, surprised by this truth. Hearing a great joyous yelp, she turned as Uly lifted Lala off the ground. She hadn't known how much she'd been missing her eldest daughter until she felt Lala's arms around her. "My very first song," she whispered. "Lala. All my daughters, home, and on the first day of Summer."

4

After Tess shared what she'd learned about the young woman with the Persey tattoo, Alice Maude made tea. In the wake of these potent discoveries, Georgia was glad to slip away from the intense hope Tess's story inspired. Outside, she studied the space filled by the Vaughan barn's ghost, speaking to this emptiness what she hadn't said to her human companions. "Isn't it amazing what we can survive?" On her slow walk home, Georgia acknowledged Webster's alfalfa field with a reverent nod, feeling its lambent green reality respond to her with a subtle wave and rustling song. At the threshold of the cedar gate, she put out her hand, stroking its bird handle for the first time in a week, this gift Uly carved for her when they'd first become the farm's caretakers, the bird's belly fitting snugly into the hollow of her hand. As she opened the gate, the farm's great hum took possession of her once again, a comforting vibration looping from her feet to her heart to her mind and down again.

With careful attention, she stepped onto the path leading to the first of her spiral growing beds, her breathing attuned to the rhythms of this abundant life. Just beyond the squash pyramids, Esperanza and Juana were helping Sadra put wedding clothes together for Kim and Karen. Observing this unfolding scene, the wedding with all its prickles returned to her consciousness. "If only I knew what to say to you," she muttered, addressing the absent Lola. "Marrying for pragmatic reasons is fine, as long as both parties create the terms."

Georgia's wedding worries dissolved when Lola's sisters caught her eye. The three women sat at the harvest table as they had when they were young. After a moment of daughter joy, she became aware of Uly and Webster fussing over the sound system, taping the wires skirting the periphery of the tent, listening to the speakers they'd positioned and repositioned for the tenth or hundredth time. In their voices she heard echoes of all the times they'd called out to one another as excited boys.

Clytemnestra, food overseer in Georgia's absence, looked up from organizing the buffet that would replace Lola's formal sit-down dinner now that most of the county had been invited to the Butte festivities. Seeing her sister-in-law's head covered in yet another scarf, Georgia wondered if perhaps Clytemnestra was undergoing some kind of hair transformation, replacing her dark tresses with platinum blonde for the big event. When her sister-in-law called out that they had bread enough to feed everyone in the town of Kingsville, Georgia whispered, "Let them come. Let everyone come."

Again, she felt enveloped in the spell cast by the farm's great weaving energies. In the midst of her private ecstasy, Jason's sweet tenor caught her attention. As she walked toward him, her mother's refusal to buy Webster's farm slammed against her heart. She looked around, praying she might avoid Marguerite at least until nightfall when shadows would hide her hurt.

Fiona fell into step beside her. "Want to talk about it?" Georgia managed a small smile before declining. "I'm getting safety pins for Clytie." The younger woman touched Georgia's arm, then backed away. "Find me if you change your mind."

"Safety pins," Georgia mused. "Yes, they can fix just about everything that might need fixing at a wedding. How clever you are, Clytemnestra. How very wise."

Returning her attention to the table where her daughters sat in animated conversation, she thought a miracle often looks so ordinary. With slow precision, and following an edict delivered by an irresistible power, she walked to the front gate. There she found

Mae climbing down from Maxwell Love's truck. Georgia smiled. "You are just the people I've been looking for."

"Max found me on the road," Mae said. "I was bringing this down to Willy." She held up Willy's silver lamé wedding costume. "Didn't he look great in his seersucker last night?"

"He did, thanks to you. Come see who Summer just delivered."

"Wow, the famous Lala Butte," Max said, embracing the eldest Butte daughter. He turned to Lila. "Do you have time for a swim before I help your dad with the chairs?" Her sisters released Lila with smiles.

"Doesn't that do your heart good?" Carefully holding Willy's outfit away from snagging shrubbery, Mae nodded in the direction of the pair passing through the Lady and her Lord on their way to the pond. "You must be walking on air. And look at Lala. Such a woman of the world." Mae leaned into the group to touch Lala's shoulder. "Welcome home, La. You and Le have given your Mama the best present." The sisters kissed Mae on both cheeks before asking about Darlene. Mae beamed with parental pride. "Dar's good. She's in Detroit right this very minute signing her new contract."

"Will she be out to the wedding?" Lala wanted to know. She and Darlene had bonded when they met in Toronto at health care conferences, Lala as presenter, Darlene as feature writer.

"She said she'd do her best."

Smiling her Black Madonna smile, Mae let Georgia lead her through the garden to the house. When they were alone, Mae said, "You're looking like you've got something more important than wedding clothes on your mind." With slow and painstaking precision, Georgia began her revelations about Tess's Toronto discoveries.

5

Lola arrived at the farm at five-thirty, her hair shellacked into meringue peaks by an invisible fixer, a testament to time spent as featured 'Bride-to-Be' in her local salon. In each hand she held an extra-large coffee cup. She looked around the garden, frantic. Seeing her mother, she cried, "Where's Juan?"

"Come to the barn, Lo." Restored by her time with Mae and an unusually long shower, Georgia wore her proscribed wedding garb confident of pleasing Lola. She took her daughter's arm. "I have a surprise for you."

"I'm expecting Reverend Tansy any time now," Lola said, gulping in the green-scented afternoon air. She assessed her mother frankly. "At least you and I will be presentable for the occasion. And Grandmother Scratch, of course."

Georgia heard the terror beneath Lola's officiousness. As they entered the barn's common room, Lola dissolved into tears. "Reverend Tansy wants to go over a point or two with Juan concerning his expectations about the Virgin Mary's participation in the ceremony." As if the two topics were equal and related, she added, "And I have to do something about this wretched hair."

"How about using some mosquito netting as a veil, Lo? I bet we could create quite a train for you." Laughing, Lala stepped out from kitchen shadows. "How's my baby sister on her wedding day?"

Lola handed her coffee to her mother and rushed to her favourite sister. "I'll leave you two to have a visit." Georgia deposited the cups on the counter trusting Lala to calm her baby sister.

Uly fell into step beside Georgia on her way to the house. Without a word, he steered her toward the swing. She bristled. When they sat, he studied her face in a way that unnerved her. "What's up?" he asked.

"You know very well what's up." She turned her face away from him. "You and your friends want to set up extraction businesses on Web's farm." Images of clear-cut land and gravel pits shimmered before her in late afternoon heat.

He passed a tanned hand over his mouth and throat. "We'll talk about new developments later. We've got enough to contend with." He gestured toward the tent.

She sensed an unfamiliar excitement around him. "You'd better tell me what's going on. You don't want me figuring it out during the wedding." With a playfulness she didn't feel she added, "It wouldn't do for the bride's mother to explode during their vows, and the way I'm feeling right now, explosions are a definite possibility."

"It's Web's place. I just heard something that will make you happy. The men took a vote about the fastest, least labour-intensive way to pay off a mortgage." He grinned, pleased with himself. "The logging and gravel are out. They've created a business plan for an indoor-outdoor paint-ball centre."

Georgia erupted with the anger she hadn't shown her mother. "This is madness, Uly. Pretending to kill one another? Promise me you'll discourage them. They'll listen to you."

Uly looked at Webster's alfalfa field and took her hand. She pulled away. "Just think about it for a minute, Gee. The indoor games are contained in a cinderblock building. It doesn't have to be heated. The only degradation, besides the building site, will be the driveway and parking lot. The devastation to the land was far greater when they were talking about logging and sand-and-gravel mining. The men who researched the project say the return on a paint-ball centre would be three times the logging and mining return, and without the major investment in extraction equipment.

The mortgage will be paid off three times as fast."

"By people paying to pretend to kill each other? This is as bad as Scratch whisky money. This is wrong, Uly. Wrong."

"It's not as wrong as TriChem."

"What kind of argument is that?"

He narrowed his eyes and dug in. "This is the best solution we've got."

"No. I don't believe that. I won't believe it." Music screamed from the marquee, making Georgia jump. She turned to him, her mind churning. "Lola is in the barn with Lala. You'd better get dressed. We can't sort this out right now. We'll talk later. After whatever this thing is going to be."

"Promise you'll think about the advantages."

"No. But I will try to understand why you'd go along with such a scheme when the world needs food, Uly. And peaceful Earthlings. Now more than ever." Willy maaed his way up the path. "I'd better get you dressed, too," she said, relieved by the simplicity of her relationship with the goat blinking his goat's code for everlasting love. Still hopeful he could persuade her to go along with the new plan, Uly touched first Georgia's ear, then Willy's.

"Get dressed," she said. "Go." Georgia watched Uly as he walked to the house, noticing how he listed slightly to the right. "My expectations about Mother were foolish, but you?" She felt utterly alone.

6

The younger, high-spirited Elias boys enjoyed ushering guests to the marquee for pre-wedding socializing. Witnessing their innocent, infectious joy, Georgia felt some small resurgence of tenderness toward the male sex generally. As she considered how best to work things out with Uly, she heard raised voices coming from inside the tent. There, Juan and an unknown woman were locked in heated dispute.

"The Blessed Virgin is important at the weddings with the brides and the grooms," Juan said, his voice raised to cri-de-coeur pitch.

"I simply don't have any statuary," the woman answered, equally frustrated. "As I said, Mr. Elias, I'm an Eco-Pagan. We believe in trees, grass, stars, not statues."

Juan frowned. "I have the beliefs in these things very well, but the Blessed Virgin is not the statue only. She is the Saint and must be also inco…pated in the weddings."

"Incopated?"

Georgia welcomed this opportunity for peacemaking. She admired the woman's swirling robe, its dusks and midnight blues, its spattering of golden stars. "Incorporated?" she suggested, joining them, offering her hand. "You must be Reverend Tansy."

"Incorporated," the woman repeated. "You mean you want the Virgin incorporated into the ceremony?" She bestowed on Georgia a grateful smile.

"Yes, yes, the incorporated," Juan repeated with growing heat. "Incorporated. She must be here…to bless our unions."

Exasperated, the woman said, "Surely everyone knows by now that the current de-sexed Catholic Virgin was given status by the early Christians in order to exploit the power of the Great Goddess of the Old Religion." Juan's mouth opened in protest. The Reverend Tansy held up a silencing hand. "You know, Mr. Elias, it was the Great Goddess who blessed all the sacred sites — the stone circles, the holy wells, the groves." Looking around, she softened. "Just like this one." She offered a reverent glance to the orchard before continuing. "The early church had to connect the old ways to their upstart religion in order to get people to believe in it, so the new priests created the idea of the Mother of God, a virgin no less, to discourage pagan revels, a sexless goddess only subliminally associated with the Divine Feminine of earlier times. Think about it, Mr. Elias. Priests – all of them male – wear dresses. Even the Pope."

Unimpressed by this history lesson, Juan said, "I am hoping the Blessed Virgin is sexless, Senora. She is the Virgin. You know what this means?"

Georgia placed a soothing hand on Juan's arm. "Might I make a suggestion? I'm the mother of the bride."

Hearing this news, Reverend Tansy offered a second smile and a passionate, "Blessed Be!"

"We have so many guests with us today," Georgia continued, "I'm wondering if we might invite one of the women to become a living Virgin Mary for the ceremony?"

"Oh, Mrs. Georgia. You will save these days." Juan hugged her. "The living Virgin will be so good. And she will wear the white and blue robes for the purity."

"Is this all right with you, Reverend?"

"I'd prefer a robust Demeter figure in terra cotta, or a Mexican Madonna clothed in blood red, but I welcome the Goddess in any form for our ceremony." The Reverend took in the general chaos beneath the marquee. "Actually, Mary's done some great work during the last few decades, thanks to the Beatles. Paul was writing about his own mother's appearance in a dream, of course, but every human mother is a stand-in for the Divine One we all share."

The woman's smile grew sunnier as she turned to Juan. "Will you ask your young musicians to play our bride into our circle of love?" She looked around. "I see you've set up our altar and circle out there, in all this gorgeous light."

"The living Virgin and the music. I do like these thoughts." Happy again, Juan followed the swift moving EcoPagan out of the marquee.

7

Casting about for a glimpse of the bride, Georgia turned to the house. For a moment, she imagined Lola's dress on its scented hanger fluttering out the upstairs bathroom window in an escape attempt. She fantasized her own escape until the farm's hum returned, traveling from the ground to her chest in a comforting whoosh. She closed her eyes, opened them to the clear sky arching over everything, a sky Virgin-Mary blue.

Laughter brought her gaze to Earth. After feeding the young men, Esperanza and Juana released them to resume their wedding duties. Georgia waved, again moved by their exuberance. "They look very grown up in those suits," Georgia called.

"Little mens," said Juana.

Yes, thought Georgia. We all begin our lives with such innocence. She thought of Uly, boisterous, brilliant, hungry for new experiences, and Webster, calm and steady, his capacity for joy expanding with farming's inexorable requirements. Then, Marguerite caught her eye.

You are shrinking, Georgia thought, at once aware of the nearness of her mother's death. You, and Jason, too, are disappearing before our eyes. Feeling a rush of tenderness, she closed the gap between them. "You look lovely, Mother. How is your room in the barn?"

Her mother offered her a devious grin. "It's a very nice room. I was just telling Lela that when I move into the barn, I'll have lots of Scrabble partners."

"Didn't you just tell me it was time we all moved to the city?"

"That was before I heard that Jason and Spring are moving into the barn. It's boring in the nursing home. People are only nice because they're afraid of me. If I'm not going to die this minute, I might as well enjoy living." She smiled at Lela who'd taken on wheelchair navigation duties. "And Hero likes it here. He's very handsome, don't you think?"

"Before you moved to the nursing home, I begged you to move in with us," Georgia said.

"You're not going to say 'I told you so' are you?"

Georgia laughed. "I think I am."

"Smirking is not what ladies, young or old, do in public, Georgia Scratch."

Lela patted her grandmother's hair into place. "I told Grandmother Scratch Fiona and I will come back to help Grandma and Grandpa with their plays."

Marguerite attempted humility. "The girls say I'll make a great crone. I might even learn to juggle those…what were those things we were playing with, Le?"

8

Overseeing several finishing touches to food and wedding finery, Georgia searched for Uly. Instead, she met Peter Stone, waving and rushing toward her from the meadow. "Mrs., Georgia. You can't let her do it."

Seeing him rush past her, Marguerite said, "It's the groom."

"I should be the groom," Peter said, stopping to clarify. "He's the groom." He pointed to Juan and his ongoing negotiations with the Reverend Tansy.

Georgia placed a hand on Peter's arm. "Steady," she said. "Lola will find herself. You have to trust her." Tears flooded her eyes. She turned to her mother with a fresh wave of tenderness. "This is the young man I found in the ditch on the Miner Road, Mother. Peter, this is my mother, Marguerite Scratch." She gestured to Lela. "You remember my second born, of course."

Peter made an impressive display of manners, bowing first to Marguerite and then to Lela. "How could I forget the Vermont sister? Graduate of the Marcel Marceau School in Paris. You're the only mime I know."

Lela smiled. "What a refreshing greeting. Lola usually introduces me as a daughter of Sappho." Lela left Georgia with Marguerite, linking arms with Peter and leading him to the marquee.

For a moment, Georgia listened to her mother complain about heat and abandonment. "You might ask me to push you, Mother. I'd be happy to help you if you asked."

"I shouldn't have to ask, but if you insist." With exaggerated politeness Marguerite said, "Take pity on an old woman. Push me into the shade."

Before they could start up the path, Uly called to them from the kitchen doorway, splendid in his Nehru jacket. "That young man's right," Marguerite said, ignoring Uly. "He should be the groom. Where did you say you found him?"

"In a ditch," Georgia said. "Down the road from the Miner Sanctuary. He was dehydrating in the sun." As Uly approached, she hoped to rekindle a little of the tenderness she felt for her mother for her partner of fifty years.

"Ah, the beautiful Scratch women," Uly said, joining them. He kissed Georgia's cheek before taking over wheelchair duties. "I think we're all just about ready. Juan is dressed, Carlos has the ring, and Lola is waiting for me to walk her from the house to the meadow the way I used to when she was little and wanted to see the stars at night."

Happy to put aside her anger about his paintball plans with the city men, she said, "Peter's here. I think he might speak up when the Reverend asks if anyone has any objections."

"Do Eco-Pagans do that?"

"What on earth's an Eco-Pagan?" Marguerite quivered with disapproval. "She's not one of those speaking-in-tongues, dancing-all-about ministers, is she?"

"Yes, that's exactly what she is." Georgia said.

It was Uly's turn to smile. "How does Reverend Tansy feel about Juan's insistence on the Virgin Mary's presence?"

"The Reverend is entirely flexible. It seems that as long as the ceremony is outside and she can invoke the seven directions, she's open to whatever wants to happen." Georgia scanned the house for a glimpse of their youngest daughter.

"What about Lola?" Uly asked, following her gaze. "Do you think she's all right now she's spent time with Lala?"

"Let's hope so." With a sudden rush of acrimony, Georgia thought to ask him if he'd come to his senses about the consequences of a paintball centre, but the Virgin Mary blue sky insisted on goodwill. "Lala or no, our youngest will do what she's moved to do. We have to trust her."

Uly's eyebrows expressed his surprise at Georgia's mellowness. He settled Marguerite beneath the marquee, turned to Georgia, and opened his arms. She gave him a playful push toward the house. "Get with it, father of the bride. If you need to tranquilize her, there's Rescue Remedy in the bathroom cabinet. We'll take up our positions and defend you if we have to. Although we both know you don't deserve defending."

"What are you talking about?" Marguerite demanded.

Uly planted a smacking kiss on Georgia's mouth. She pushed him away. "Nothing important, Mother. We're just having a little fun."

9

At the appointed time, the Reverend Tansy called the wedding guests to take their places around the cedar-and-wildflower bower Lela and Fiona created in the meadow. To arrive at the wedding circle, guests left the marquee, circled back through the meadow to the farm's gardens, then passed through the opening made by Lila's Lord and Lady. As the wedding guests formed their procession, the Reverend Tansy studied the sun. Her calculations complete, she told Jesus to remove four chairs in the eastern quadrant of the outer circle. She nodded her approval before summoning the young ushers to a conference. Eduardo and Carlos listened with eager politeness, but the youngest brother, Pablo, had a fit of giggles. "After the bride and her father have come into the circle, you'll close that gap and stand here," she said. Her accompanying pantomime dissolved all language barriers.

Somber, the older boys nodded their understanding. Pablo, his face increasingly pink, continued to giggle. "Stop fooling around, Pablito. Comportarse!" Jesus hissed. Pablo hung his head and did his best to stifle the urge to laugh outright.

Georgia watched the guests process into the circle, aware of building tension in her jaw and neck. Mae smiled and waved, knowing Georgia longed to kick off her shoes and head to the pond for a restorative swim. She touched her heart and smiled encouragement. Georgia returned their special signal. Then she turned to their wedding guests, absorbing compliments regarding the flowers, the meadow setting, the perfection of the day itself. In the end, the tension of not knowing what might happen during the ceremony proved too much for her. With apologies, she headed to the house.

In the cool, shadowed kitchen she stood for a moment wondering what she'd come for. Then she knew. On their honeymoon, Uly had given her a pendant, fossilized bone and onyx teardrops married in a perfect oval, each containing at its centre a dot of its opposite. He gave her this gift on the same day he told her he'd confused the State of Georgia with Georgia O'Keeffe, her namesake. Feeling his embarrassment over the mix-up his dyslexia had caused, she'd pointed out the colour of the soil and how it exactly matched her sandy red hair. "You knew without knowing you knew," she'd told him. "This Georgia is as important to me as the other. Maybe more so."

It was true. On their tour of the lower US states, they'd discovered countless sultry similarities to their part of marshy, humid Essex County. By the time they arrived home, her metamorphosis had completed itself. Georgia Scratch no longer existed. In her place, a vibrant Georgia Butte, her hair, Georgia-soil terracotta, began her new life.

She couldn't remember the last time she'd worn the pendant but sensed she needed it on this day, for her own balance, for Lola's, for the land. She rushed up to her room. In a black lacquer box embossed with a golden dragon, this box a wedding gift from Grandmother Jones, she found the pendant wrapped in a small circle of white silk.

Slipping the pendant over her head, Georgia startled at the sudden appearance of a stranger staring at her from the dresser's mirror. She would have stayed to visit with this tidy woman, but the sound of tuning instruments summoned her return to the garden. On her way, she bent to lightly brush her fingers through bordering clover plants, looking from their dusty green leaves to the clear blue sky. "Even when I'm confused and utterly lost, this beauty, this abundance, is always here to guide me." She touched the Lord and Lady as she passed through the space Lila created to bless the day's unfolding.

10

After she sat and settled herself, Georgia exchanged smiles with guests, now and again crossing and uncrossing her legs to release building tension. With one of these crossings, her body offered up a sense memory of her long-ago birth…a forceps-initiated yank from her mother's body into a coldly sterile hospital room. She'd birthed her own children at home, her wise flesh labouring with muscular intelligence, working with each of her babes until that fifth time when she had to labour alone. The memory of tiny Wendell's profound stillness brought tears to her eyes. She closed them quickly, wanting to stop the flood of emotion threatening to spill out into the glorious afternoon. When she opened her eyes, the sight of Mae, her Black Madonna face lifted to the sun, calmed her. She waited for Mae to feel her eyes on her, to open her eyes, to smile and touch her heart once more.

Drum beats, faint at first, grew louder. The crowd hushed. Beneath these rhythms, Georgia heard the delicate strains of a classical guitar, and beneath these reverberations, the subtle shaking of maracas. She suppressed a laugh. The young boys, not knowing any conventional wedding songs, were playing "Let It Be" with a Latin beat.

The Reverend Tansy called out the lyrics and encouraged the crowd to sing.

"That's an odd song for a wedding," someone whispered, not knowing of the groom's Virgin Mary requirements.

And then the crowd, in unison, gasped. Willy, spectacular in his silver lamé wedding costume, pranced up the path pulling their smallest garden cart. In it, a life-size Virgin Mary stood, dressed in tablecloths white and blue. The Virgin scattered orange-blossom petals as a sedate Willy drew her through the Lord and Lady, bypassed the marquee, and curved around to the eastern opening in the circle.

To complete Willy's ensemble, Mae had fashioned a silver lamé wreath studded with brilliant orange and yellow marigolds, this summer crown encircling his knobby horns. The lamé on his back undulated in sensuous pewter waves, conjuring for Georgia Lake Erie on a stormy day. As he entered the circle, Willy glanced at Georgia. She felt in that glance his promise to be on his best behaviour. The crowd continued to sing of Mother Mary and her help in difficult times for the wedding party.

Having birthed itself through the Lord and Lady's sacred aperture, the Elias Boy Band followed close on the heels of the Blessed Virgin's cart, their instruments humming and twanging. Following close behind, Lela and Fiona processed, Lela's hair decorated with Daisies and Susans and Marigolds, Fiona's tucked into Wayne's green Octoberfest hat, her braid dotted with orange blossoms. Georgia suppressed another laugh when she realized Lela wore the demure yellow eyelet Lola insisted Mae make for Lila. Fiona, at the bride's request, wore the same filmy green tunic that had scandalized the Scratch matriarch the day before.

Because of the time their processing took, the Reverend Tansy had the crowd launch into a second rendering of "Let it Be." Their timing allowed Lila to make her dramatic entrance as Maid of Honour in her unmaidenly red cape. She too wore a wreath of Shasta Daisies and black-eyed Susans on her head. From beneath the bright cape, peaked a matching red sheath dress. Georgia's eyes leaked. Guests whispered their approval.

And then time stopped.

11

A second great communal gasp arose from the crowd as Lola of the sculpted hair and ivory gown, on the arm of her handsome, smiling father, made her way through the opening created by the Lord and Lady of Summer. Georgia winced. Her youngest daughter's unsmiling, determined face and storm-cloud aura transmitted terrible pain.

"What a lovely bride," murmured those tricked by Lola's glamour. Georgia looked to the Virgin Mary for comfort. At that moment, their human stand-in's veil slipped. Lala Butte was home.

Upon entering the ceremonial circle and guiding her to the altar, Uly released Lola to her place beside Juan without receiving the usual affectionate-daughter kiss. Following the bride's instructions, her father took his seat beside her mother.

Georgia looked from Lala to the bride and groom. The Reverand Tansy lifted her arms to quiet the crowd. Lila, Lela, and Fiona took their cue to join the wedding party to the left of the bride and groom. Juan's brothers closed the outer circle and made their way to the right of the groom. Lala readjusted her Virgin Mary robe and veil before bringing hands to her heart. Willy nodded at admirers between nibbles of birch leaves Uly offered.

"I think we all agree," the Reverend Tansy began. "This beautiful meadow is the perfect setting for all the marriages that want to happen today." Georgia sat forward, intuition twitching. Reverend Tansy gestured to Lila's massive sculpture. "This, the longest day of the year, marks the marriage of Summer to her Consort, The Green Man, He who will be harvested in only a few short weeks, He who is willingly struck down with the dry husks to become fertilizer for yet another season." The Reverend's hands floated up and settled down in the imitation of Mother Nature's life, death, and rebirth dance. As Georgia listened, Webster's alfalfa appeared, tall and lush, in her mind's eye. She smiled at this bounty, then felt in her flesh TriChem's fiery presence. In an agony of grief, she focused on the ceremony. Protecting Webster's alfalfa would have to wait.

"From this pinnacle," Reverend Tansy intoned, "we watch the light begin its steady decline, reminding us we must prepare for that time when all this Summer sunshine will be but a glorious memory." She glanced around the circle, her gaze settling on the perspiring bride and her stiff-backed groom.

"Look, too, at Juan and Lola, standing here in the beauty and strength of adulthood." More melancholy seeped into Reverend Tansy's voice. "In a twinkling, this moment will be but a memory as Lola's wrinkled face and Juan's bent back replace this day's perfection." Guests muttered dismay. Georgia caught Pablo's giggles and did her best to suppress a nervous smile. "Yet, in spite of our temporality, indeed, because of it," the Reverend continued untroubled by protests, "we join hands and thank Mother Earth and Father Sky for our lives – brief though they may be – and for our place in the great, timeless cycles."

Guests uttered a few more protests. The Reverend Tansy ignored them. "At this, the high point of light in our Northern Hemisphere, we ask you to witness the coming together of two human souls who vow to love the pond and its fish and turtles and frogs as they love one another, to love the trees and all the creatures who live in and near them as they love one another, to love the meadow grasses and their insects and rodents as they love one another, and," she said, throwing her arms skyward, "to love the Planets, the Sun, the Moon, the Stars, the Galaxies, and the countless Universes as they love one another." The Reverend paused then, intending guests to soak up this abundance of love. She turned to Juan. "It is now time for Juan, our virile groom, to speak the story of his love and make his vows. Juan?"

12

Juan stepped forward, turned an awkward half circle, acknowledged guests with a stiff bow. "First," he said, his voice not much more than a hoarse whisper, "I want to make the thanks for my Madre and Tia and little brothers and cousin Jesus for coming on the long ways they come to be with us this fine day." Everyone smiled. "It was the long trip," he continued. "And the hard ones. They come by the buses and sometimes the legs feel the pains and the waters they drink boils in the bellies." His Aunt Juana, straining forward to hear every word, brushed away these inconveniences. Esperanza nodded, brought her hands together in prayer.

Juan turned to the band. "Very good playing and singing, Little Brothers. But you have the improvements made from when I hear the playing back home." The young men sent out splatters of sound to bless the groom. His own family members duly honoured, Juan turned, to Uly and Georgia. "And I do thank Miss Lola's the parents…" He offered Georgia a warm, innocent smile.

"Mrs. Georgia and Mr. Ulysses, I am thanking you and the sisters so much." He gestured to the setting. "You make this place so beautiful for us." He turned to Lola. "And now I must speak to the beautiful Miss Lola, Angel of the verbs and the nouns and the other parties of the speeches. The Virgin has heard my prayers as you walk with Mr. Uly to this holy of ceremonies. She tells me I have the hopes for the forgiveness." Lola beamed a triumphant smile. Seeing that smile, Juan said, "No. No. I am going to say some things here that I want to say before but I am not allowed by the pretty teacher." Lola's smile vanished.

Georgia closed her eyes amid uncomfortable throat clearings. Juan, without a trace of malice, explained the autocratic way Lola had conscripted him into marriage. Not understanding the stir his description caused, the young groom mopped his face with a handkerchief as startlingly white as his dress shirt. "All the times I am in Ontario, Canada, I am very lonely for my home. And I want the beautiful teacher to see the works of my hands, even without the English, so I make the carvings for her house. And the… you call it… harbour… for sitting inside with the vines growing all up and down on it. Like this one we have for our wedding. Some birds in the branches I carve around her porches, too." He took a gulp of air. "But I do not want the marriage because I must be returning to El Salvador." Murmurs grew louder. "Miss Lola can make the school there in my home, but she is my friend and teacher only." Feeling immense relief, Georgia looked up into the vast blue sky. A heron headed northward from the lake. She caught Webster's eye, nodded to the heron. He mouthed 'Great Blue Goddess.'

Juan turned to his bride. "I am marrying not you, the pretty teacher. I must go to my home. I am with the farmers back home my country's future." Lola dipped her head to hide her face. "Miss

Lola, Angel of the nouns and the verbs, the Blessed Virgin says I must tell you what I am understanding now. I make your house so beautiful so I will not miss my own home. I do not know you think my carvings says I wants the marriage with you. You make the mistake about that. Today we fix a mistake." People shifted in their chairs, coughed politely, stared at their knees. No one except Georgia dared look at the bride.

13

Georgia felt her own lungs breathe with, for, her daughter. Stunned by the unexpected turn in the proceedings, Reverend Tansy looked about for guidance. Lola's ivory satin murmured in response to a playful breeze. The Reverend turned to the bride. "Perhaps the bride may want to take some time…"

Lola held up her hand. "No," she said, taking charge. She gathered her dress in the careful way of brides the world over and turned to face her guests. With a pugilistic tilting of her chin, she began what sounded to the assembled crowd like a legal rebuttal.

"I too want to thank my mother and father for this beautiful setting and our families for creating the most spectacular wedding party ever." She turned, offering prayer hands to the Virgin Mary. Lala dipped her swaddled head. "Esperanza and Juana," she continued, the epitome of graciousness, "Thank you for traveling all this way and for bringing your wonderful sons through the hardships of truck stops and customs searches. You are all so very, very brave."

When Lola kissed her fingertips then launched an invisible dove in the direction of the Elias family, Georgia knew. Her youngest daughter would not pretend to be the heart-broken, jilted bride. She relaxed into a buoyant sea of trust, catching Mae's eye and mouthing 'beautiful dresses.' Mae raised her eyebrows to convey sympathy at the proceedings, temporarily blinding Georgia with glimmers of silver.

"About our marriage," Lola said, turning to her groom. Wedding guests strained forward, eager to hear her every word. "I have spent a long time holding myself aloof from marriage, Juan, but what you did for my house moved me more than I can say. I see now that I assumed you were proposing because I listened to your hands. Your carvings are so exquisite, I didn't see how I could refuse you." Lola took his hands in hers.

"I've proposed to all my students from the beginning of my career and usually we all have a good laugh about it. When I do this, newcomers learn about teasing and joking. And flirting, too." She smiled as she touched his cheek. "You are easy to love and admire, Juan. I am honoured by the beauty you created to adorn my home."

The youngest Butte daughter gestured to Lala in her guise as the Virgin Mary. "The Blessed Virgin has been guiding me as well. She tells me that just as you must go back to El Salvador, I need to stay right here. All our new students need to learn to narrate the big stories of their former countries as well as the stories they learn in their new ones. More than anything, newcomers need an advocate to support them through the challenges of resettlement."

Georgia looked from Lola to Uly. He watched their youngest daughter with something akin to awe. All around them, friends and neighbours listened to Lola with rapt attention, their surprise at this turn of events expressed in wide eyes and parted lips.

"And so," Lola said casting a tearful glance around the circle she had called, "I know you'll understand when I tell you that I reached the same conclusion as I walked up the path to this sacred moment. I cannot, must not marry you, Juan Elias, even though you are a good person who makes very beautiful carvings."

Peter Stone did not try to conceal his relief. With a joyful whoop, he flung his straw hat high into summer's first early evening sky. Lola held up her hands for quiet. "Please know, Juan, I will always, always care for you, as a teacher cares for her students. I have faith that effective communication skills will be well served in El Salvador because you are there." Lola's dimpled smile signaled the end of the drama.

Everyone erupted in applause. Fiona, caught up in the moment, began a jazzed-up rendering of "I'll Fly Away." Lela joined in, encouraging guests to dance. Flummoxed by this turn of events, Reverend Tansy held up her hands for attention.

"Dearly Beloved," she cried. "I remind you that we are gathered together today to join loving human partners and the natural world in the holiest of unions. I get paid whether anybody gets married or not, but this lovely setting, the food, the music, these fruiting trees… all beg for a wedding. Surely there is one couple in this splendid gathering ready to marry today?"

Georgia's heart stopped. She pinned Lola with a don't-you-dare-even-look-at-Peter-Stone stare. Peter, to his credit, stood statue still, his eyes on the ground. She looked for Max and Lila. Max had turned to Lila, prompting her to shift on her feet, ready to run. He grinned at her gullibility, bumped his hip against hers. When Lila laughed, Georgia breathed again. Then, invisible hands yanked her to her feet.

14

"I want to marry," Georgia said, shocked by her own proposal. She looked around, bewildered for a moment. Then she understood. "I want to marry this farm, and Web's, and Mae's, and Alice Maude's." She took a breath, waited for what came next, closed her eyes, opened them to take in the expectant faces all around her. "I want all of you to marry these farms with me. I want us to find a way – together – to save these farms from TriChem." Tears blurred her vision.

"Young men," she said to Uly's city friends, her voice carrying grief and joy and hope. Her tears fell. Her gaze cleared. "I know you think your dollars-and-cents approach may seem best, but paintball war games, or logging, or mining for sand…" She closed her eyes, listened for the farm's voice. "Amusements are not what we need now. For decades we've been amusing ourselves into states of destructive stupidity." She turned to Uly. He was staring at her with a look she hoped transmitted his willingness to support her. "Uly and I, we know this land, all land, is too precious to plough under for any more of the wrong things. We have to be visionaries. We have to create something new, and we can only do it together, with all of you."

Suddenly, Maxwell Love was on his feet, his voice full of excitement. "Like the mushroom growers in Spain who bought their company when owners wanted to sell it out from under them. They formed a cooperative to make sure each employee has a stake in the work of the company. This is what we can do. This is what we have to do." Georgia looked from Max to Lila to Uly.

Then, Gertrude Bradshaw spoke. "Food is what we need. Local food. Grown with awareness of soil and water health. Food grown on a small scale, to make it safe, to make it sustainable, not only for the land and water, but for the human beings who coax it into life. Food to feed people when…" she opened her arms, including everyone, "When we wake from our various nightmares."

Georgia knew Gertrude was thinking of Persephone when she spoke these words. Then Mae was speaking. "Georgia and I, we've been feeling a prowling, cynical energy sniffing around out here." She looked for Alice Maude and found her standing now, arm-in-arm with Tess. "Alice Maude has felt this at her place, too. For a good long while, we've managed to defend ourselves against the big companies that want to absorb small farms like ours, massive agribusiness outfits who want to grow corn and soybeans, to create cruel, disease-riddled feed lots for beef cattle and expand an unsustainable dairy industry." She took a breath. "What do you say to helping us protect this land?"

Georgia sought out Webster. He sat staring at his hands. "Web," she said, her voice quiet now. "You simply can't sell to TriChem. Give us time to create a fund to buy you out. Just give us time." She smiled at him. "This vision we're incubating can only succeed if…"

She felt again the farm's great humming life vibrating in her chest and beneath her feet. "We'll sell shares, get townspeople involved. Kingsville and Leamington are close enough to benefit from having a stake in wholesome food. And Windsor's not that far away."

She laughed then. "We already sell our apples in Chatham. All that's missing to save our farms is community. We can keep out the marauders of the world when we work together." She swayed a little, then righted herself. "Let's all marry this land today." The company erupted in cheers. Uly wrapped his arms around her.

15

Georgia held on tight to Maxwell Love as he spun her around the dance space magicked into existence by the twinkle-lit marquee. Although the Elias boys were playing "Jailhouse Rock," Max found a polka in its rhythms and was traveling around the tent's periphery at warp speed. Giddy with dancing, Pelee Island wine, and general happiness, Georgia shouted over the din. "Thank you, Max, for…" Max grinned stupidly. Suddenly Uly and Lila were beside them, Uly shouting, "Switch!" then dancing off with Max.

"I'm glad to get you alone," Georgia said, dancing her daughter out of the marquee. Under the stars, Georgia held Lila close then at arm's length. "I have a gift for you, Beauty, one I've been saving for a year now, for just the right moment." She laughed a little drunkenly, still in the thrall of the girlish pleasures stirred by her own surprise proposal to the entire gathering. "It was Willy who dispatched the professor."

"What?"

"Willy's been watching out for Alice Maude and Tess for years. Last spring, when he found the professor drunk at the edge of the stream bank, he took aim and let him have it." She looked up to the stars. "Alice Maude saw it all. She's sure Willy only meant to teach him a lesson. She guessed later that Chauncey was so drunk he couldn't lift his head out of the water. She found him dead after she'd walked Willy home. She said Willy pranced all the way, as if he understood he'd put an end to the terror she'd lived with for years." She studied Lila's startled expression. "She doesn't want word to get out, Lila, so this is a secret you must keep. Alice Maude has always been very protective of Willy."

"Willy's been protecting Alice Maude?" Lila repeated.

"He has. For years and years and years."

Lila scanned the crowd until she discovered Willy at the buffet table. She set off at a run, her red cape flying. Sensing her approach, Willy turned and lowered his head. When Lila dropped to her knees beside him, the goat smirked. Georgia watched this unfolding detente knowing their truce wouldn't last. The pair enjoyed their battles too much to abstain from them entirely, but on this auspicious evening, they made their fragile peace.

Georgia wandered around the marquee marveling at the gathering Lola's adventures in marriage proposals created. She paused when she noticed Peter Stone hovering at a discreet distance from her youngest daughter and the Elias boys, all of them earnestly responding with examples whenever Lola called out a part of speech. Their band had only just been replaced by Lela and Fiona, seasoned DJs, who rocked out with Buffy Sainte-Marie's "Starwalker."

"Noun," Georgia heard Lola cry.

"Egg! Hay! Barn! Chicken!" the young boys responded.

"Verb."

"Run! Jump! Swim! Play!"

Feeling her mother's eyes on her, Lola said, "Dance," and left them to join the gyrating crowd. She smiled giddily as she wove her way through well-wishing wedding guests. When she reached her mother, she grinned.

"I am so proud of you, Lola. You're incredibly brave to change course like this, and in public." Lola nodded, not quite believing she'd done what she'd done. "Proud is too small a word for what I've seen you do today." Tenderly, she brushed wispy curls from Lola's forehead. "You made me feel something so... big. I think it might be... cosmic joy."

Lola laughed at her mother's hyperbole. "Lala's been telling me about the coffee growers in Colombia, about the struggle they have to make a sustainable living once the big corporations move in. She suggested I start a unit with my students about working conditions, here and in their countries of origin. I'm already planning field trips for next September's students. We'll go out into the community to ask coffee shops to carry Fair Trade coffee, from Colombia and other countries, to support small farmers."

Georgia's eyes brimmed. She was remembering Ruth Welding's comment about Ontario's teachers being powered by the coffee industry. What better group than teachers to transform that industry's practices? What better Inspiratrix than Lola Butte?

"Lala thinks grocery stores are ready to carry fair-trade brands once they understand how they can raise consciousness about the connection between a fair wage, sustainable growing conditions, and the need to support small farmers. She says the fair-trade movement isn't the answer, that food sovereignty is. That's what folks were talking about during the ceremony. But fair-trade and sustainability movements provide ways to raise awareness about our need to support small farms, no matter where we live." She exuded the pleasures of her expanding mission. "This is the beginning of a new wave of food consciousness. My students and I will help to spread the word."

In her enthusiasm, Lola reminded Georgia of the eager girl who raced down the pathway shouting about tadpoles, sure she was the first person to ever witness these watery wonders. She kissed her daughter on both cheeks then nodded to Peter. "You know I found him just for you, don't you? He gave into stupidity and risked his life, just so you could find each other. He's yours, Lola, and you're his, in every possible way."

Lola didn't try to hide her dopey smile. "I felt it when I first saw him. He studies geese, peacocks, and peahens all day long, Mama. He's told me about his paint studies – iridescent blues and greens he experimented with to find peacock colours." She kissed her mother's hands. "In the fall, he…he might move into the city… with me. But not until he finishes his commission out here. His next one is in Windsor. He could walk to work from my house."

Just then a shout went out from the group. Georgia released Lola to join a swiftly forming conga line. As she watched Peter and her daughter find their way to one another, she felt the call of her own unfolding journey. Like them, she had to find her way forward, to feel her way into a future riddled with uncertainty.

16

After dancing for a time, Georgia stepped out of the tent to commune with the death throes of endings and the birth pangs of beginnings. She closed her eyes, savouring the joy and the pain of inevitable change. When she opened them again, she discovered Webster and Clytemnestra together at the fire Uly and Webster built in the meadow where their wedding circle had been. Clytemnestra was tossing something into the fire while Webster looked on. Feeling Georgia's eyes on them, they waved her over.

Smiling, Georgia stroked Clytemnestra's newly shaved head. "This is very striking, Clytie. Have you entered your Buddhist Nun phase?"

"Lila and I did a ritual early yesterday morning. I'll let her tell you what she released. I buzzed off my hair to symbolize my new, uncomplicated life." She kissed Georgia. "Just so you know. You inspired me with your amazing invitation to marry the farms in our neighbourhood. I'm ready to begin again. Here. With all of you." Georgia took in a great breath, tasting cedar and lake and fire all at once. Webster reached for her hand.

"I'm starting over again, too, Gee." In that moment, Georgia sensed they were all on the verge of a transformation that had begun with the call to save their neighbouring farms.

Clytemnestra slid her arm around Georgia's waist. "Web says he's going to make his place worker owned, like the mushroom farmers Max talked about. I'm buying a share for each of our girls, and for Sadra, Wayne, Kim, and Karen. And one for me."

Georgia struggled to hold back a great wail of gratitude. "What about your kids, Web?"

Webster grinned at her. "I guess how they feel doesn't matter as much as it did before you invited us to marry this land. We're the ones who live here. We're the ones this land has taken hold of. We're the ones who partner with it, who meet its needs and recognize and celebrate its gifts." He looked at Clytemnestra then at Georgia. "If enough people buy in, I could pay the grandkids' tuitions. I'd like to do that."

Georgia kissed first Webster, then Clytemnestra. "What a vision, Webby. Forest mushroom harvests. And Lela and Fiona know all about Permaculture gardens. Maybe we could start farm-life experiential workshops and farm-to-table food for local school cafeterias." Her eyes widened, recalling her own outrageous plans. "And hemp, hemp Webby, for building and clothing and food."

Staring into the flames, Georgia brought her hands to her heart. "But we can't forget Uly's friends from Windsor. They're looking for something meaningful to be involved in outside the city, something that will bring them satisfaction and maybe even joy. What we'll create and work for together will be so much better than anything that any of us might imagine alone."

"I guess growing good food's about as meaningful as we can get," Webster said. "At my place, we'll start with the forest-mushroom enterprise. Knowing this land like I do, it's just a matter of time before we diversify." He nodded at Georgia. "Like you."

Georgia searched her heart for a hard place regarding the city men but found only tenderness and wisps of a growing, greening love. They would invest in the farms, come to help, to learn, to get their hands in the soil, and she would welcome them. They would come and she would look into their eyes and see her own yearning for home, her own fierce determination to protect what they'd been part of for as long as she could remember. They would come and together they would meet the land's limits and discover the land's expanding visions. And these men, she knew, would remind her what life in the city had taught them. She would remember that Uly, her husband of fifty years, belonged to them as much as to her and to the farm. Arm in arm, they wandered back to join in the dancing.

After dancing with Webster and Clytemnestra, then with Uly, then with Alice Maude and Tess and Mae, the farm's vibration took hold of Georgia once again. She left the group to walk to the fire, looked from face to face to face as others joined her. Fiona let fade the last strains of the "Krishna Waltz" on her autoharp, and when the song ended, the remaining revelers joined the outsized version of the circle hug that ended all their Friday night dances. Georgia took in the firelit faces, seeing in her swaying companions the beauty, the mystery of the land's magic. She closed her eyes.

When she opened them, wonder flooded her senses. Across the circle, Alice Maude held on to Willy's undulating silver and black costume with one hand and to Tess's hand with the other. Georgia did her best to catch her eye, but Alice Maude's attention belonged in this moment to other kin. Beside Tess, Peter Stone whispered something to Mae that made her smile her best Black Madonna smile. Closer to Georgia in the circle, Sadra swayed, Kim asleep in her arms, Karen holding her skirt with one hand and Pablo's woven sash with the other. Beside Pablo, Wayne stood, almost asleep on his feet. Sensing Georgia's glance, he raised his chin to her, this small gesture their telepathic sharing of contentment.

Georgia shifted her gaze to the candle-lit table beneath the marquee. There Jason, Spring, Marguerite, and Gertrude sat deep in conversation. Lillie and Erie, their arms around one another's waists, stood behind them. A little behind mother and daughter, Georgia saw the shadowy form of a girl/woman longing to be found by her human kin as she'd been found by her father's spirit in dreams, in visions. These women would be making plans, Georgia knew. Lillie and Gert would be telling Marguerite and the elder Buttes about the miracle of finding their Persephone after all this time, and if not their Persephone, then another lost daughter who might find healing through knowing Erie, her mother, her grandmother, and the place that held her story, all their stories. Seeing them, Georgia took comfort beyond measure.

As her glance drifted from face to face to face, Lake Erie's pungent scent flooded her senses. She looked down, half expecting to see its waters baptizing them on this eve of transformations. But no, Lake Erie had not puddled around her feet. Only the scent of past joys and those to come, invisible yet potent, blessed them all.

Then, Lila was beside her. "Wayne's horse is ready to assemble, and he wants to get an early start. The Elias boys are helping him. I told them they could have a sleepover in the studio." Georgia took in Lila's flushed face and shining eyes. "Max and I are going to his place." As she moved away from her mother, Lila nodded to Willy across the circle. "I told Willy he could sleep out there with the boys, too, but just for tonight." She boomeranged back to kiss her mother, then she was gone.

Georgia shifted her attention to her circle companions swaying beneath the stars. As she did, Lela broke the circle to lead a spiral in to the centre, inviting dancers to bid goodnight to the great leaping flames and to answer the stars' call to shine in the vast darkness. Georgia danced the familiar pattern, forward, forward, forward, and a lilting, rocking back as she held tight to Clytemnestra, ahead of her as they moved closer to the fire, and to Uly, behind. When the last person had whispered words of gratitude for the new season, the spiral reformed into a swaying circle and then into hugs and plans and promises regarding future gatherings.

Georgia felt the onyx and bone pendant where it lay upon her breast. She searched for Uly, and when she found him saying goodnight to his city friends, she waved and called out. "Thank you so much for making this day so perfect." Smiles, waves, promises to come to the next dance drifted to her on the warm night air. She watched each turn, disappear into the darkness of their first summer night.

Then Uly was beside her, his scent as familiar as the lake's, his arm around her waist, his eyes open and clear, his face pensive. "I don't know how you did it, Georgia Butte, but somehow, you managed to make everything come out right."

"I didn't do a thing, Uly. It was the farm, the land that grows us."

A look of wonder came into his eyes. He raised his arm, pointed to the barn. "Is that…" Georgia followed his finger to Lady Jane where she stood in the lilac shadows beside the barn.

"Come here, Beauty," Georgia said. "Come say goodnight to Uly." The horse nickered and was gone.

ACKNOWLEDGEMENTS

The Buttes has been fed by countless streams of inspiration, the most recent of these generated by local and regional organic farmers in Vermont and New Hampshire. My earliest experiences of the relationships created by local farmers occurred in the fifties, in my birthplace, Essex County, Ontario. During the summers of my childhood, our family took weekly trips to farmstands, at times as stand-alone adventures, at other times on the homeward journey from Point Pelee. After having a walk through the park's Carolinian forest, a swim in Lake Erie, or a family picnic in one of the many park pavilions, my mother would stop at the farmstands dotting meandering two-lane highways to buy fruits and vegetables. Fresh tomatoes, fresh corn, fresh green beans, fresh peaches, fresh watermelon, this list was so long my mother dubbed Essex County the "breadbasket of Canada."

Visits with our local farmers were always part of these food adventures. We learned of challenging growing conditions for those who chose to stay small, and of planting, weeding, and picking done by hand — what has come to be described as labour-intensive, a term that fails to invite the images of people at work in the fields. We listened to stories about sore backs and sun burned shoulders, of weather catastrophes, of pests that decimate an entire crop in a single afternoon, and of children romanced away from farming by city life. These visits ensured that when we sat down to a meal of Essex County abundance, we blessed the farmers who grew the food because we heard first-hand of their trials and had the pleasure of eating their triumphs.

Learning from these farm families the rewards and challenges of growing foods sparked my imagination regarding the source of what I was eating no matter where I traveled. In the early nineteen nineties, I began visiting with local and regional Ontario farmers, who, along with firefighters, are the true heroes of contemporary life. My research first found a home in a non-fiction study, *Transformation in Canada's Deep South*, then leapt out of its factual descriptions of innovations into the imaginary farm belonging to the Butte family. This farm, loosely based on my childhood experiences and my adult research into Essex County's rural communities, gestated for a long time, constantly gathering energy.

When I began to visit Vermont in the late nineties, I saw a bumper sticker that thrilled me. Instead of the patriarchal "Who's Your Daddy?" this bumper sticker asked, "Who's Your Farmer?" Here was a state that valued its small, local and regional farmers. I owe an enormous debt of gratitude to these New England real-life Butte counterparts as I do the local organic farmers in Essex County, Ontario. I couldn't have imagined the evolution of this fictional family's farm over a century were it not for the visionaries who address climate change, human and animal health, and social justice by weathering tough times and continuing to produce nourishing, safe, and delicious fruits and vegetables. I am awed by their work in the world and hope what these farmers inspired in my imagination will strengthen the network of local and regional food systems everywhere.

ABOUT THE AUTHOR
AND THIS NOVEL

Jane Buchan (Buchan rhymes with truckin' and that other word we sometimes have to say) is a Canadian writer and emotional wellness coach. After spending most of her life as a city girl in Windsor and Toronto, she chose to support her desire to complete *The Buttes*, a novel whose germinating seed first came to her in the aftermath of the Clifford Olson child murders in British Columbia in the early eighties. As Georgia and her farm and family took hold of her imagination, Jane found the novel the perfect place to integrate fears about ongoing violence in the world and to explore how we might create safe and nurturing spaces when we work together in community. After moving to Vermont to finish the novel in the early noughts, she soon found it had a life of its own, including long dormant periods that supported her personal healing process. *The Buttes* revivified during the pandemic following her completion of two other creative writing projects. She's happy to finally share this celebration of her home county with readers longing for safety, peace, community, and wholesome food.

www.ingramcontent.com/pod-product-compliance
Lightning Source LLC
Chambersburg PA
CBHW030252100526
44590CB00012B/381